War and Television

WAR AND TELEVISION

BRUCE CUMINGS

VERSO

London · New York

For My Students

First published by Verso 1992
© Bruce Cumings 1992
All rights reserved

Verso
UK: 6 Meard Street, London W1V 3HR
USA: 29 West 35th Street, New York, NY 10001-2291

Verso is the imprint of New Left Books

ISBN 0-86091-374-0

British Library Cataloguing in Publication Data
A catalogue record for this book is available from the British Library

Library of Congress Cataloging-in-Publication Data
A catalogue record for this book is available from the Library of Congress

Typeset by York House Typographic Ltd, London
Printed in Great Britain by Bookcraft (Bath) Ltd

CONTENTS

ACKNOWLEDGEMENTS

My primary acknowledgement is to the team assembled at Thames Television in London, for the making of the documentary entitled *Korea: The Unknown War*. For their good fellowship and fine skills I would like to thank the executive producer, Phillip Whitehead, producer Max Whitby, the Thames chairman David Elstein, the supremely polite and helpful Jill Service, the outgoing and indefatigable Sue Lockett, cameraman Frank Haysom, sound technician Eric Brazier (good union men both), and above all my friend Jon Halliday, originator and writer of the series. I would also like to thank Mike Dormer, Isobel Hinshelwood, and Tony Lee of Thames Television, and Austin Hoyt and Peter McGhee of WGBH/Boston, for putting up with me (God knows I had to put up with them).

I first joined the Korean War project at Jon Halliday's behest, in 1982. We worked closely thereafter, especially in the period 1986–8 when the film was made. However, because my contractual arrangement with Thames Television was different to Jon's, and because of the legal system in the United Kingdom, I wish to make clear that the facts, views, and opinions expressed in this book are mine and mine alone, and in no way represent Thames Television, Jon Halliday, or any of the people I worked with in making the documentary.

Many others have shared their ideas about the subject of this book with me: among them are Dan Chirot, Chung Kyung Mo, Tom Ferguson, Lloyd Gardner, Michael Geyer, Jim Kurth, Joyce Park, Moss Roberts, Englebert Schucking, Mark Selden, and Sandy Thatcher. I owe particular thanks to Marilyn Young for her extensive comments on an earlier draft of this book, to Ivan R. Dee for his support and helpful criticism of the manuscript, and to Harry Harootunian, who in four years and at the average rate of one good book per week has given me an education in critical theory. Jon Halliday also did me the favor of two close readings of drafts of this book, saving me from many errors. Many thanks also to Michael Sprinker, Anna Del Nevo and Lucy Morton of Verso, for their support and hard work, and to Justin Dyer for painstaking editorial commentary. None of these people, of course, bears any responsibility (or culpability) for this text.

My spouse Jung-en Woo has read this book, like my other work, with her typical mix of good humor, warm support, sharp insight, and scathing commentary. Ian Woo Cumings was born in 1989 and his round-the-clock schedule gave us plenty of hours of 'research time' in front of the family tube; he and my daughter Jackie are a constant reminder that between the simulacrum and the real there is still a vast and wonderful difference.

The author and publishers are grateful to Associated Press for permission to reproduce 'Roundup time in North Korea' and 'Three scenes from Vietnam'; to Sygma for the use of 'TV cameraman in tow'; to US National Archives for 'John Foster Dulles at the 38th Parallel'; and to UPI/Bettmann and the Ngo Vinh Long Collection respectively for 'Reversals'.

INTRODUCTION

The 1990–91 Persian Gulf War was our first 'television war.' Although Americans witnessed the carnage and controversies of the Vietnam War on their home screens, Vietnam was just a way station between Korea and the Gulf: only the latter perfected the full capacities of television for fighting, packaging, and selling warfare. The war in Korea occurred in the early dawn of mass television, but was mostly unseen and therefore unknown. Vietnam occurred after television technology was advanced enough to bring the battlefield to the living room, but before the state understood how the medium could control the message or demolish a Third World enemy. The Vietnamese exploited this technical 'window of opportunity' to win the war, and (several years into the war) television journalism exploited the subversive potentialities of the medium, confronting the state and helping to turn a generation against its leaders. Thus Vietnam was thought to be the first 'television war,' a quality to which some – especially in the Pentagon – attributed the American defeat: won on the battlefield, lost in the living room.

It took the Gulf War, however, to show us the full totalizing potential of war television: the medium as the only message. Our first global network, CNN, kept its round-the-clock eye open during the weeks-long air war and the hours-long ground war – and yet nothing was seen. Now and then the insubordinate cameras, such as CNN's in Baghdad, caught television-guided cruise missiles lumbering slowly over the city skyline, like telephone poles floated up from the ground and set adrift on mysterious currents, disappearing into the bull's eye of some 'military target.' Otherwise the medium was the Pentagon's, and even as we marveled at a nosecone camera feeding pilot's-eye pictures back to the world, we had to accept on faith the Pentagon's claim to perfect accuracy and, more important, its claim to report and interpret the war it was fighting: a kind of auto-television. High technology rendered the weapons smart, and the medium deaf, dumb, and blind. This is one paradox we will explore in this book: how can an open shutter see so little?

The Korean War was also unseen by television. Instead grainy black-and-white photos and films etched its visual memory: gaunt Marines slogging forward along muddy paths, refugees in extended families fleeing the battle, or Chinese soldiers in snow-packed mountains, their padded cotton jackets whipped by the Siberian wind. This war is 'forgotten,' residing in the subterranean mists of American memory.

If the war is forgotten, reviving it through the archival photo (still or moving) ought to be simple. If the camera never lies, the forty-year-old images must be correct – a low-technology equivalent of television's all-seeing objective eye. Yet recuperating the Korean War in the photographic and documentary form proved unaccountably controversial, and the presumed objectivity of the camera spoke back against itself, contradicting the 'text' of the war long after the fact. Here is another paradox this book pursues: how can an unseen, forgotten war, upon retrospective examination, be so unsettling?

The Gulf War was a war fought in the interest of forgetting. It was, for President George Bush, a war to 'put Vietnam behind us.' A new war bursting suddenly upon the world in the dog days of August, its conduct nonetheless interrogated a memory. That memory offered up the following lessons: never again, a war fought 'with one hand tied behind our backs.' Never again, a war blamed on American soldiers, making them unwelcome back home. Never again, a victory on the battlefield lost in the living room. If this judgement was reflexive, the opposition to the Gulf War was reminiscent. Nostalgic for Vietnam, it never transcended that experience. The opposition played out its own 'lessons,' founded in Third World innocence and First World malevolence.

In my view, none of these 'lessons' bear up under scrutiny. The Gulf War was fought for very different reasons by Bush and his advisors, and it was not 'another Vietnam.' But the presumed lessons have weight as representations, pitched for the television. Thus our third paradox: the Gulf War was fought against a remembered war, with the party of forgetting hoping to bury it, the party of remembering hoping to revive it.

So, this is a book about war and the technology for witnessing it. It examines the three American wars of my lifetime through the aperture of the photo, the film, and the culmination of both in mass television. It is also a book about the way we think: especially, why we have been led to think that the camera's eye is better than the mind's eye, and how the archival photo, film, or document interacts with the repository of the mind's eye: memory. It is, then, also a book about history and memory, and about the *point d'honneur* of both the professional historian and the television medium: objectivity.[1]

I am a professional historian, but I also watch TV (something most academics are afraid to admit), and I also have participated in making television. After I examine the camera's eye in its several forms, and its uses in the Gulf and Vietnam, I will turn to a case study of a Thames Television/ Public Broadcasting System series entitled *Korea: The Unknown War*. Making this television film also became a kind of war: a war over interpretation, a war over access to the various 'sides' who fought the war, a war over selection, editing and narration, and finally a war over the screening of the film and its reception in England and America. Obviously I know this case better than the other two, and I use it (along with some personal observations on the making of the film) to illustrate what happens when television, war, and history come together in the present. I will also have some things to say about the 'Other,' the North Korean enemy we fought in that distant war: forty years later and we still do not 'know the enemy.'

Finally this is a book about politics in contemporary America – an ingenious, camouflaged politics known best to those who transgress implicit limits, tread on unvoiced premises, traffic in the heterodox and the exotic . . . or try to make a documentary about the Korean War, four decades after the fact. American politics proceeds, and is studied, with the usual full plate of positivist assumptions: our political process can be known and studied through the objective techniques of the scientist, like opinion polls, voting studies, game theory, and a basic assumption of individual rational action. Television can know it through similarly positivistic, if more intuited, methods; for TV as for political science, the 'public opinion poll' is a central technique. I have come to think that our politics is much more mysterious than that, and that few have plumbed its hidden wellsprings, its encrusted and deeply resistant mythology, its stunning combination of obtuse recalcitrance and rapid, mindspinning change. Only the unplumbed mysteries can explain, I think, the political mastery of Ronald Reagan and George Bush in the recent period, which was founded in television mastery.

It is the elusive, well-nigh inscrutable politics of present-day America that is hardest to get across to students — especially students from the 'television generation.' In the deepest philosophical sense, as Fredric Jameson and others have argued,[2] the challenge is to understand a phenomenon external to oneself, which has also produced oneself: television. This problem I share with students, because I also grew up with a flickering screen in the living room. Thus I dedicate this book to my students, and hope to aid them in probing American and television mysteries.

I will also display for the reader, and the student, some of my 'personal views,' which professors — like television commentators — feign to keep out of their presentations. I do this also to make a serious point of method: in discussing something as human as war, the distinction between fact and value, between objective and subjective judgement, is false. In treating something as baffling as television, what is sometimes called *reflexivity* is essential: not the one-way TV monologue issued forth into the void, but the two-way dialectic of (re)presentation and reception; not the vaunted transparency of TV but the human interaction between those who make it and those who consume it. It strikes me as odd to say it, but television communicates knowledge: and all knowledge is social, interactive, dialogic.[3] Thus 'the personal reflexive' in this account, which is unavoidable by the nature of the material, is unavoidable also as a matter of epistemological principle, unless one wishes to pose and dissemble before the reader.

I completed this book during the latest phase of mystification in the US, the brouhaha over the 'politically correct,' which has bathed students and the university in a national political searchlight unlike any since the days of student protest ended. A book that inaugurated this new debate was Allan Bloom's *The Closing of the American Mind* in 1987, and he and his allies have sustained their claims through the intellectual *causes célèbres* of 1990 and

1991, Frances Fukuyama and Dinesh D'Souza. As a colleague of Professor Bloom I know him to be a dedicated teacher, but he, like many others on the neo-Right, takes a dim view of the contemporary university and its studentdom ('The psychological obtuseness of our students is appalling, because they have only pop psychology to tell them what people are like, and the range of their motives,' and so on). If it is not pop psychology that has undone them, Bloom argues, it is Nietzschean nihilism.[4]

I have a very different view: in spite of all the palaver about the silence, ignorance, miscreance, and greed of the current student generation, I find that, like my own generation of students, they are endlessly folded, spindled, and mutilated by people presuming to speak for them or about them. My students strike me as inquiring, intelligent young people who want to care deeply about something in the world around them, who want to make a difference in their lives and careers, and who have profound doubts about the country they live in.

In other words they seem very much like my generation, which came of age in the sixties. It is for this generation that the neo-Right reserves its supreme contempt. In Bloom's book the entire argument builds toward the penultimate chapter ('The Sixties'), where the world-historical event finally occurs: at Cornell University, in isolated, weatherbeaten Ithaca, when the Hitler Youth marched again ('whether it be Nuremberg or Woodstock, the principle is the same'), when the (black) barbarians stormed the citadel, when only a saving remnant of Platonists went 'into the agora' and did battle with the infidels.[5]

The student 'barbarians' were unlearned enough to protest the Vietnam War, and later became 'tenured radicals' – people who have somehow wormed their way into the professoriate and now dedicate themselves to poisoning the young mind and undermining the American Way with the new opiate of feminism, Afro-Americanism, postmodernism, and popular culture. I suppose I qualify on all counts, except that (through my expertise) I also undermine The West with The East. I have read Nietzsche, too, and hope to demonstrate his relevance to certain aspects of history and television. So, in contemporary stereotype I offer the worst of both worlds, if not all worlds.

It is this sort of wild and irresponsible commentary that creates best-sellers and gets on television and, like the medium itself, becomes another kind of hyperreality. 'In fact' women and blacks are still a miniscule part of the permanent professoriate, radicals of the Left (and the Right) are a tiny minority everywhere in academe, and mine is a lost generation, with thousands of Ph.D.s biting the dust in the job drought of the 1970s. Where radicals exist they do so in the pores of the system, rarely if ever do they gain real influence; instead nearly all of them feel eminently vulnerable, and constantly coaxed to merge with the real majority – the broad if boring middle, which perseveres through every generation with an inexorable, daunting weight. The real significance of the New Right assault on academe, perhaps, is generational: those educated in the fifties strike back at those who bedeviled them in the sixties, a response simultaneously nostalgic and desperate, recuperating the complacency of the Eisenhower era and hoping to erase the non-conformity of the Vietnam era.

The new critics of academe maintain that students are so stupid because they all watch television. They leave out the uncomfortable fact that their parents and grandparents all watch television, too; the whole society watches television (including bookworm academics). It is not students today, but baby-boomers now experiencing middle age, whose early memories call up Dad watching baseball and Mom watching *Queen for a Day*, and the whole family gathering together for *Dragnet* and *I Love Lucy*.

But you don't really get to know television on the receiving end of it – that's the worst place to figure it out. It was only when I spent a few years of my life *making* television that I came to see how right the critics are: not just our students, not just the misguided 'politically correct,' but our whole society has been stupefied by this invention. I was fortunate, however, to work not with the worst of television makers, but the best; learning that the best share in the diabolical qualities of this medium was my fateful lesson.

If I dwell on the mysteries of television and less on those of the other subject of this book – war – it is paradoxically because I both know the latter better, and feel less confident in treating its abstract or general qualities. Television is first of all a technology, with generic features that can be specified with some confidence (even if its effects remain elusive). Although I have no academic training in media studies, I found the literature in that field quite accessible and helpful to my task. The subject of war I have lived with for all of my adult life, first by coming of age during the Vietnam War and then by devoting two decades of my career to explicating the Korean War. There I found the literature much less helpful; indeed at an early point I decided to ignore the secondary mediations and recuperate the Korean War almost exclusively from primary materials.

It is not that we lack experts on war, just as we have experts on the media. It is that war is a setting for the display of our human-all-too-human qualities and our most elemental politics, and is thus a totality that resists partial views. We may take as an example the discipline of military history, which normally excludes both the reconnoitering of origins and the stuff of politics – the former being a question for other types of historian, and the latter being, presumably, the terrain of the politicians. Work like my own on the origins of the Korean War borders on the metaphysical for the military historian, and a book like Michael Herr's *Dispatches* – certainly a central text for Vietnam and maybe the best single account – probably wouldn't be read and would even more rarely be taught.

To single out an expert in both the print and television media who also qualifies as a military historian, we can take the case of Harry Summers. Toiling in the bowels of the Army War College in the early 1980s, he produced a book[6] on the lessons of Vietnam which catapulted him into a prominent position at *US News and World Report* and, later, made him one of the handful of TV experts who guided us through the military aspects of the Gulf War. Briefly put, Mr Summers reads the Vietnam War as another Korea, which ought to have been fought as such: a conventional war, not a guerrilla war, in which the point was to go to the heart of enemy power and destroy it. He predicts the past by arguing that the US should have declared war and invaded North Vietnam. The hands-down champion of the war experts, Clausewitz, is sprinkled through this narrative like the old Chinese scholars used to sprinkle Confucius, in a series of opaque declamations that sound like they ought to be true, but can't pass the first test of logic.

In my view Summers got things exactly backwards: Vietnam was indeed another Korea, both having a common anti-colonial origin, a civil and revolutionary quality, and an inextricable mix of conventional and unconventional forms of warfare. When American forces 'went to the heart of the enemy' by invading North Korea, in came 200,000 Chinese who, with important North Korean help, cleared the area of American forces in a couple of weeks. This then detonated the worst foreign policy crisis in postwar American history, which ultimately destroyed the Truman administration. Lyndon Johnson wished to avoid the same outcome, and thus blocked an invasion of North Vietnam.[7]

We cannot know this unless we know the politics of both wars, as they played out in Washington. Yet this is what Mr Summers chooses to ignore; politics is for the politicians and war is for the generals. Yet his book also has a politics, indeed it is far less important for its arguments than for the way it wafted through the *zeitgeist* of early Reaganism, contributing to the (utterly false) idea that our troops never lost a battle, but were defeated in Congress or the living room. It is thus a deeply political book, in spite of itself.

A view on war that I would recommend, however, is Vincent Scully's recent, remarkable account of the way we memorialize our wars, not in books or television, but in the sacred sculpture to the dead. He begins the account with the controversy over the design of a Korean War monument (which will concern us later), and remarks that such memorials 'are not easy to design, especially today, when Victory . . . shows us an ambiguous face.' Maya Lin's Vietnam Veterans' Memorial in Washington, he says,

> is hopeful, personal . . . but profoundly communal, too. We, the living, commune with the dead, are with them, love them. They have their country still. That is why this monument so broke the hearts of veterans of this war – who felt that their country had cast them out forever.

It is, he thinks, 'America's greatest such monument.' Why? Because it expresses 'the single, incontrovertible truth of war: that it kills a lot of people.'[8]

SOME NOTES ON METHOD

A subtitle like this usually warns the non-expert to flip forward to the next chapter. Method is terribly important, but academic discussion of it often turns into the opposite of communicating meaning; students, in particular, find themselves hopelessly lost. Since without method we cannot understand our subject, and since I also wish to write for my students, I would like to see if I can make some serious points in an unpretentious and – perish the thought – common sense way.

One of my favorite TV shows as a kid was *Dragnet*, and for many years thereafter I followed the Jack Webb method: 'just gimme the facts, ma'am, nothing but the facts.' Jack Webb was what we academics call a 'positivist' or an 'empiricist,' and empiricism tells us not to trust our intuition, nor our viscera, let alone something so grotesque as an holistic world view which seeks order out of the flux, but rather to parse the world, to sever connections, to morsel down knowledge to that which can be observed and verified. Years later I thought of Jack while pondering Friedrich Nietzsche's comment that 'facts is precisely what there is not, only interpretations';[9] I suppose my interest in this aphorism expressed a degree of estrangement from the country of my birth, for Americans as a people follow the Jack Webb principle, they are famous for their pragmatism.

'Americans believe in facts,' Jean Baudrillard tells us, 'in the total credibility of what is done or seen.' And so, he says dramatically, Americans possess an eternal ignorance 'of the evil genius of things.'[10] I'm not sure if Nietzsche is right that there are *no* facts, but I have a deep suspicion that facts are not the currency of television. And what does naiveté toward the real world of facts have to do with the evil genius of things? Let me give you an example.

Empiricism, and the morseling of experience that goes with it, was carried to its logical conclusion, it seems to me, in an editorial by our paper of record on a defining moment of my generation, and of television history: John Kennedy's assassination. All of us mediated that event through the TV eye, and this was perhaps the inaugural event in what is now commonplace: television at the center of every catastrophe. Years later a Congressional committee concluded from acoustical evidence that Lee Harvey Oswald could not have been the only gunman at Dealey Plaza in 1963, and therefore a conspiracy to kill Kennedy had existed. Why, the *Times* editorialized, leap to that 'conspiracy theory' conclusion? Why not admit the possibility of *two* lone gunmen, who just happened to be in Dealey Plaza at the same time? (And who just happened to fire within split-seconds of each other . . . .)

An errant fact (four rifle shots, not three) questions the official story that a lone gunman killed Kennedy. We have moved from Jack Webb to Columbo, from an empiricist to a detective following the I.F. Stone method of investigation: search out the overlooked item that demolishes the official logic. You are left with two alternatives: challenge the fact (the experts disagreed on the acoustic evidence), or challenge the deduction (there was more than one gunman firing away). The *Times*, I believe, was the only paper to challenge the deduction.

Our problems in interpreting our world are much more at the second level than at the first: facts we have in abundance, but interpretations that put them together are rare, especially with regard to a medium priding itself on unmediated access to the facts, leaving the interpretation to the viewer, or to a panel of experts, or to an announced (subtitled and labeled) editorial. Most of the time TV appears to leave the facts uninterpreted.

This question of facts versus some larger reality, or totality – what Baudrillard signals by 'the evil genius of things' – will have general relevance for our discussion, and specific relevance for a people which has not had a major war fought on its soil for well over a century. I would like the reader to keep it in mind.

Now let me add another note on method. As the reader has already guessed, I think I know what I am talking about, and I think some others do not. I thought the same thing during the making of our documentary. That is, I have 'a point of view,' I think it's correct (why else would I hold to it?), and I feel no need to define that point of view for the reader, beyond what I am saying here. To say what I have just said violates basic rules of television discourse. But, interestingly, it also violates basic rules of my profession, history. Somehow television and history join together here, however separate they may be otherwise. The principle: we are not supposed to have a point of view, correct or not, but if we do, we are supposed to say what it is.

This, too, expresses my estrangement from present-day America, if not from the sixties when students did guerrilla theater in the agoras of our great universities, pointing their fingers and thundering 'value free, value free' at bewildered professors. If I didn't understand this particular notion then, however, I learned it as a graduate student when I applied to teach an evening course on Chinese politics. The woman who interviewed me asked if I had a point of view: 'Last year it was just terrible, we had David Wurfel and Allen Whiting and they both had points of view, and they just shouted at each other all the time.' 'No,' I responded, 'I don't have a point of view.' (That still didn't get me the job.) But who is it that does not have a point of view? Is there a species-being like a transparent weathervane, always registering its environment objectively? If we say no, all humans have a point of view, then the question again arises, why have one if you don't think it's correct?

Perhaps a Presidential example will help deepen this dilemma. George Bush, faced early on in his Presidency with an entire nation of raving Iranians calling his country 'The Great Satan,' told us that this was okay. Even *this* is okay. It must be okay, because in the *New York Times* on June 27, 1989, Bush stated: 'They can call us "The Great Satan" and that's fine. That's their view.' This particular Satanic verse communicates the following: 'Yeah, let them call us what they want, even the Great Satan thing, it's just their point of view and who can quarrel with that? (And perhaps – *sotto voce* – who listens outside of Iran anyway?)' But does this mean that the Iranian point of view is correct? That can't be the case. It must be that there's no way to choose between points of view. I have mine, you have yours, and the best we can do is agree to disagree.

This phenomenon has been called *emotivism*, the label Alasdair MacIntyre and others use for the fix we have got ourselves into, with the moral thing: in present-day America there is simply no way to assert the priority of some moral principle, some 'point of view'; every viewpoint must be treated as just as good as any other, no matter how ill-formed, badly understood, poorly put, recently arrived at, or temporarily held it might be. Emotivism, as MacIntyre demonstrates, lies at the heart of Anglo-American positivist philosophy. But television takes emotivism to heart. If child molesters or rapists think themselves badly misunderstood, their feelings hurt, their motives maligned, their needs unmet, they can go on *Oprah Winfrey* and say so.[11] Jane Fonda has a right to her views, whether she is Barbarella, Hanoi Jane, Academy Award-winning actress, Tom Hayden's wife/not-wife, a millionaire workout queen, or TV-mogul Ted Turner's sidekick. Jerry Rubin cannot be taken to task for parodying the excesses of his generation in every decade. Emotivism derives from feelings, feelings are separate from reason, and therefore reason is silent before the claims of 'my feelings.'

MacIntyre puts the point with a bit more rigor than I, and it is worth quoting: 'What emotivism asserts is in central part that there are and can be *no* valid rational justifications for any claims that objective and impersonal moral standards exist and hence that there are no such standards.' And a bit later, 'evaluative utterance can in the end have no point or use but the expression of my own feelings or attitudes . . . . I cannot genuinely appeal to impersonal criteria, for there are no impersonal criteria.' His examples are also a bit more highbrow than mine:

> Bertrand Russell has described how one day in 1902 while riding a bicycle he suddenly realized that he was no longer in love with his first wife – and from this realization there followed in time the break-up of that marriage. Kierkegaard would have said, and surely rightly, that any attitude whose absence can be discovered in a sudden flash while riding a bicycle is only an aesthetic reaction and that such an experience has to be irrelevant to the commitment which genuine marriage involves. . . .[12]

MacIntyre might have added that this rendering, sculpted by Russell in retrospect, camouflaged his self-interest, just as our national emotivism elides fundamental choices illumining the 'thousand points of light' of our myriad, copious 'feelings.'

Unfortunately, MacIntyre tells us, we all now believe in emotivism, and it is daily drilled into our heads by television. If somebody actually has something to say, it goes on PBS under their program *Point of View*, a title which functions as a sign saying 'watch out.' Otherwise it is this random utterance against that random utterance, and who's to choose? No matter how considered your judgement, how deeply you may believe, your view is just one among many: thus television tends to annihilate all significant difference. (When confronted with a strongly put preference, television interviewers will typically respond, 'I hear what you're saying' – which connotes, I hear it but I don't care about it.)

My position is that it is possible to have a 'point of view,' to have arrived at certain fairly unshakeable conclusions, and at the same time to be objective; indeed more objective than the pseudo-scientific rationalism of the empiricists. When one settles on a judgement through a mix of rational inquiry and visceral response, one can grasp how others have arrived at their (perhaps very different) viewpoint, one can in fact retrace it for them and illumine the terrain they have trod. This form of knowing is perhaps what Freud connoted by his 'oceanic feeling,' but it has its highest expression in Nietzsche's philosophy. You know it as that unexpected moment when knowledge touches your core: let's call it wisdom.

Television's role is to tell us our viscera ought not twitch on such a cool medium, our feelings are just feelings, no better or worse than any others, and our brain ought to be unconnected to the rest of our body (a 'talking head,' to use TV jargon). If we come forth with 'a point of view,' it ought to be stated objectively in a short soundbite, with equal time for the presumed opposing view – it being thought that there are but two positions, usually somehow identified with 'conservative' and 'liberal' – and if the shouting then gets too heated for this cool medium, time for Linda Ellerbee to come on and say something ironic. (So it goes . . . .)

Now another problem: I will also occasionally use the term 'liberal' in a way perhaps unfamiliar to some readers, and I will use another term – 'postmodernism' – that is the butt of many jokes. The media wishes to convince us that the whole world is going liberal in the 1990s, but I think we are in a post-liberal period, more properly a postmodern period. Television, which also presents itself as liberal (it champions the market and parliamentary democracy), is the quintessential postmodern medium.

Postmodernity is the completion of the modern project and the supersession of social formations that coexisted with or were created by modernity, such as a traditional agrarian elite or an organized working class or the socialist states which occupied the market and pursued centrally planned industrialization. It is deeply hostile to another formation, the nation-state; its preferred arena is the global market, or world system. Postmodernity's characteristic product is the image, really a simultaneity of images gathered together from disparate places and temporalities in the form of the collage or the pastiche, or simply the flow of global commercial television. History is one victim of postmodernism (it lives continuously in the present), and another is liberalism.[13]

Some years ago to be liberal was to be synonymous with objective, evenhanded judgement: in television history, one thinks of the Sunday afternoon show *Omnibus*, or Walter Cronkite, or Alastair Cooke. In recent years the term has become synonymous with bias: 'the liberal media' as an epithet, the 'L' word, as something for politicians to avoid, because it connotes people who let crazed drug addicts and murderers out on bail, or who have wives who drink their aftershave lotion – 1988 candidate Michael Dukakis was synonymous with The L Word.

The first sort of liberalism – an authentic, principled 'left' wing of American politics – flourished in the 1930s and 1940s and died around 1968, and nothing in the next quarter-century has been able to resuscitate it. In Europe, however, this term refers to the Enlightenment and the bourgeois revolution. Because of that (much richer) heritage, and its death as an active politics in the USA, the hardest thing to get across in America today is the real meaning of this term.

So let me explain what I do *not* mean by this word: I do not mean Dan Rather, Michael Dukakis, Linda Ellerbee, Jimmy Carter, Phil Donahue, George McGovern, Tom Braden, or Tom Harkin, although they are all liberals. I do not mean Zhao Ziyang or Lech Walesa or the Dalai Lama or Uighur firebrand Wu'er Kaixi or Boris Yeltsin or the Emir of Kuwait. (Often termed liberals on TV, these are in fact a communist, a Catholic, a Buddhist, a protesting student, a Russian nationalist, and a feudal remnant, respectively.) I do not mean people who, by virtue of being born in Europe, or through some hard struggle, some dark night of the soul, have come to possess a liberal world view: let's say Hannah Arendt or Martin Luther King, or many of those who have resisted terrorist systems around the world.

I mean instead to include in that term just about every American, born and raised in a 'new world' fragment of the European liberal tradition, people who do not have a world view so much as a set of unexamined assumptions that they think they were born with – thus to connote a narrow, circumscribed politics claiming universality: our politics.

It is a paradox: free and yet constrained, an open politics that cannot comprehend a non-liberal politics, whether a feudal past, an East Asian communist present, or a non-capitalist future; a 'born-free' country with few people who grasp the bloody victories won to make it that way. This argument is of course vintage Louis Hartz, who drew heavily on Toqueville;[14] this liberalism rests on miles of submerged convictions, on icebergs of the unstated, on hidden premises which have a liberating propensity for the bourgeoisie in this most bourgeois of nations, but totalitarian propensities for non-liberal systems: whether feudal, communist, Catholic, orthodox Jewish, Confucian, Platonic, or Islamic, organic systems exist to be dissolved. Why anyone would willingly live within non-liberal systems, in fact, is a question that can barely be posed in this best of all possible worlds.

Why every American? Because the capitalist revolution has gone farthest here, far enough to include almost everybody (in their heads if not their livelihoods, where few are really capitalists) and liberalism presents itself as the modal politics of capitalism. That means our 'conservatives,' 'fundamentalists,' 'neo-conservatives,' 'rightwingers,' 'Reaganites,' 'monetarists,' and even the members of the Heritage Foundation are liberals. Ronald Reagan, Pat Buchanan, Jerry Falwell, Morton Downy, Jeane Kirkpatrick, Milton Friedman, Pat Robertson, Reed Irvine, and Dan Quayle are thus liberals. There are, of course, exceptional individuals who are American but not liberal: Malcolm X, Louis Farrakhan, Allan Bloom. But you don't see them on prime time, since to be on prime time you ought to be a liberal.

Why narrow? Because hardly anyone else in the world truly partakes of our politics, however much they may think they like the Statue of Liberty and *Miami Vice*, until they get their non-liberalism bleached out in a second or third generation, born and reared here (and then it really doesn't matter if you are Azerbaijani or Zambian). A France still fractured by its revolution is schizophrenic, and thus only partially liberal. The haute-bourgeoisie of Vienna is not liberal, among other things because it dislikes egalitarianism as much as it likes Kurt Waldheim. Italians can't be liberal if they let communists run their cities, we would never do that. The aged, taciturn, and licentious elite of the Liberal Democratic Party in Japan is neither liberal nor democratic. Nepalese urchins who tug at the sleeves of American tourists yelling 'Michael Jackson, Michael Jackson' are not liberals. Taking a world spectrum of politics, in other words, America gives you everything from A to B. This makes Americans provincials in a world very different than their imaginings, and yet television throws back their imaginings to them on a daily basis as truth.

Why universal? Because most Americans think – or are taught to think – that their determinate provincialism is what everyone else in the world really wants, to be *just like us*, even if they are Iraqis groaning under Saddam Hussein, Kuwaiti refugees frequenting discos in Cairo, Iranians swaying around the Fountain of Blood, ex-slaveholders in Tibet, Somalians starving in the Sahel, Hmongs or Kurds used and abused by the CIA, refugees from Pol Pot, steelworkers in Gdansk, or the one-thousandth of 1 percent of the world's Uighur population who gained entry to prestigious Beijing University, and then Harvard University. And why not? Aren't we the ones with the 'self-evident' truths? Don't some 150 countries screen *Dallas*? Didn't the Hmongs and Kurds want to come here? And are we watching Kim Il Sung's revolutionary operas?

Television requires talk, indeed oceans of talk (silence frightens producers, since viewers might think the sound isn't working and switch channels), and in talking we cannot but *name* things. In Nietzsche's formulation, 'what things are called is incomparably more important than what they are.'[15] When we 'call' or name things we establish identities. It is not simply that Boris Yeltsin or Saddam Hussein or Deng Xiao-ping need to be labeled and thus familiarized: it is that the television picture always requisitions its own connotations, and these connotations are cultural and political, and cannot be escaped. Directly or indirectly, they indicate television's conception of American politics and the American view of the world, a connotation said to derive from a democratic polity and to be given back to the citizenry through the medium. In other words, a point of view.

More fundamentally, television contributes to the death of a principled liberalism in the real world by simulating its promise and telling us this promise is being realized, before our very eyes;[16] but then, by its nature as the preeminent postmodern medium, television also empties this same liberalism of content:

> The postmodern is . . . the fulfillment and abolition of liberalism as well, which, no longer tenable as an ideology and a value any more than traditional conservatism, can function more effectively after its own death as an ideology, realizing itself in its most traditional form as a commitment to the market system that has become sheer common sense and no longer a political program.[17]

If we turn from television to our other subject, how might we 'name' the three wars under consideration here? I can indicate my 'point of view' preliminarily by saying that they all had an objective quality in which the greatest power on earth pulverized a small Third World country that dared to challenge it, and therefore, ideological pleading to the contrary, all had an incommensurability of the enemy that allows no human being, on reflection, to exult in American victory.[18] If David took different forms, from the unknown Kim Il Sung to the avuncular Ho Chi Minh to the central-casting villainy of Saddam Hussein, Goliath was ever present.

Then again, there was only one American victory. Wars 1 and 3 appear to begin with naked aggression, and the 'lesson' of Munich and the imprimatur of the United Nations are invoked. The United States runs the show, however, and over time the unambiguous beginning unravels in questions about whether some Americans saw the enemy attack coming, and chose not to do anything about it (or even seemed to encourage it – Dean Acheson's 1950 Press Club speech, and April Glaspie's last-minute meeting with Saddam). In both cases a containment victory is won (the aggressor is expelled) and in both a 'rollback' victory is lost (Kim Il Sung and Saddam Hussein still reign). War 1 returns Korea to the status quo ante, restores a dubious regime in Seoul, resolves nothing, and festers to this day; War 3 returns the Middle East to the status quo ante, restores a dubious regime in Kuwait, and, at this writing, resolves nothing in regard to Middle East peace.

War 3 found its qualitative difference with Wars 1 and 2 in the absence of any social question, and the clearcut, well-nigh Bismarckian aggression of Saddam Hussein across well-recognized international borders. The American response lost its initial high moral ground, however, by forgoing a patient isolation and sanctioning of Iraq in favor of a punishing assault – one designed (as in Korea and Vietnam) to deter both the designated enemy and any Third World party who might follow in his path.

War 1 occurred simultaneous with and was the partial cause of a radical shift in American history, in which the US came to maintain a huge and expensive peacetime armed force at home and abroad in the interests of global hegemony, which in turn stimulated the rapid growth of a military-industrial complex and a national security state at home. War 3 occurred simultaneous with the apparent obsolescence of this same far-flung complex (its primary enemy – the USSR – having given up the fight), providing it a new breath of life.

War 2 happened between the alpha and the still-pending omega. It had an indeterminate beginning but a determinate end: American defeat. Much about that defeat can be attributed to the 'Korean lesson,' that 'going to the heart of enemy power' will bring on the Chinese. Thus the definition of victory as a stable southern regime and a divided Vietnam. In the aftermath of defeat, its long-predicted consequences are stood on their head: soon Vietnam and China are at war. Unlike the other two wars, this one rent the fabric of domestic consensus and lodged a premonition of national calamity in the American heart.

Meanwhile, to paraphrase Professor Scully, a lot of people were killed.

CHAPTER ONE

WHAT IS TELEVISION?

Till the eyes tire, millions of us watch the shadows of shadows and
find them substance; watch scenes, situations, actions, exchanges,
crises. The slice of life, once a project of naturalist drama, is now a
voluntary, habitual, internal rhythm; the flow of action and acting,
of representation and performance, raised to a new convention,
that of a basic need.

RAYMOND WILLIAMS

What is television? Is this a question for a professor to ask? We all know
that academics neither watch nor think about television: or so they say.
Somehow the next day my colleagues all seem to have seen the same things
I did the night before, however, so this is our first lesson in television: it
even subverts the highminded professors. Raymond Williams (one of the
few intellectuals to take television seriously) liked to write that academics
practiced *surreptitious* TV watching, but I wish to be honest: I watch it
every day (if not 50 hours a week), as part of my red-blooded American
duty. But what makes the medium subversive – even of the professoriate?
Let me begin with a mundane example.

I was watching the annual Grammy Awards, hoping I could get a
glimpse of Little Richard or Chuck Berry (early heroes of mine[19]). It was
even more silly and boring than the Academy Awards, but I did get to see
Little Richard. At one point a masterful commercial appeared: it was for
batteries, the kind you put in a 'walkman.' The scene was a college
classroom. An ancient, burned-out, thousand-year-old-egg of a professor
waddled from behind his lectern, swayed toward the ceiling his balding
head circled by unruly, wispy white hair, and spit out slowly but with

19

surprising force, 'being . . . and . . . nothingness.' Cut to an adolescent in the class with walkman wires jammed in his ears, whose head clunks to the table upon hearing these three words. The remedy? Get better batteries for your walkman, so they don't run down at critical moments. The next shot shows him bopping up and down in his seat as the professor drones on.

The next day I told my class of some sixty students about this commercial, imitating the thousand-year-old egg, to show them what subversion meant. Why subversion? First, because a student who sits in class with a walkman in his or her ears cannot, by definition, be taught. Second, because the problem of 'being and nothingness' is an important problem (as I say this, I hear a student imitate a loud snore – this at the University of Chicago, where I would take even money that some under-graduate, sometime, actually got from the beginning to the end of Sartre's *Being and Nothingness*. Among other things, this particular problem in philosophy is also one of the problems of television – I-appear-on-TV-therefore-I-am, and the reverse). Third, it is subversive because this commercial shows the effective use of disconnected images to make a point, in contrast to the usual narco-narrative; juxtaposing the prof and the student makes the viewer think, requires him to supply some meaning external to the actual scene, which completes it. And, of course, the commercial subverts education itself: an old fogey blabbing about Sartre has to be tiresome compared to the wonders of the walkman.

The subversive qualities of the medium go far beyond this, however, to the point that television is the postmodern medium, and the postmodern, as many have argued, is the solvent of all that went before. Its conception of time is not historical but synchronic and simultaneous, its product is the image, and the image packages reality as reproducible facsimile, as simulacrum.[20] These assertions can only be defended and explained, however, after we have dealt with some of the essentials of the medium.

Let us ask the experts, what is television? Robert Allen gives a concise and apt definition: television is 'an institution that exists primarily to translate the phenomenon of simultaneous mass viewing into a commodity that can be sold to advertisers.' Thus we grasp how the Orange Bowl got to be 'The Federal Express Orange Bowl,' not to mention 'The Mobil Cotton Bowl,' 'The USF&G Sugar Bowl,' and 'The Sunkist Fiesta Bowl.'[21] So, first, it is a business. What else is it?

Television is part of society, said Raymond Williams, or maybe it is the essence of our 'dramatised society' where all things become docudrama:

> Till the eyes tire, millions of us watch the shadows of shadows and find them substance; watch scenes, situations, actions, exchanges, crises. The slice of life, once a project of naturalist drama, is now a voluntary, habitual, internal rhythm; the flow of action and acting, of representation and performance, raised to a new convention, that of a basic need.[22]

A basic need, to watch shadows of shadows; a new convention, this electronic slice of life. The shadows of life flicker through a box that we take to be a transparent window to the world, a mirror reflecting ourselves back to ourselves; and in its finished form, the television program appears to be 'the result of natural rather than unnatural processes.'[23]

Television has its intricate production processes and its well-honed conventions, Robert Allen tells us, but they are ingeniously 'hidden by their transparency.' Television is a *flow* (Williams's insight) in which multiple texts are linked together and merge 'almost unnoticed one into the other.' The texts have no real author, only a group that submerges authorship: a number of directors function like a committee to produce a 'work,' and their 'directorial styles' ought to be in principle 'indistinguishable from each other.' In spite of the hard work and considerable expense behind even a 10-second soundbite advertisement, television gives 'the illusion of immediate access to reality and truth,' and thus traffics in notions of 'bias' vs 'objectivity'[24] (just like scholars). That is, television partakes of the same empiricism I spoke of earlier, yet raises it to new heights.

TV expert John Fiske writes: '[TV] realism's desire to "get the details right" is an ideological practice, for the believability of its fidelity to "the real" is transferred to the ideology it embodies.'[25] The technology impresses the viewer as unmediated reality, TV people cultivate this notion by presenting themselves as objective bearers of facts, and this practice legitimates the ideology television itself peddles. What is that ideology?

Television is a middle-class medium, operating in the interests of the-class-which-does-not-want-to-be-named (Roland Barthes' insight), *the bourgeoisie*. I know from experience that the mere use of that French word waves a red flag under the American nose. I remember when my daughter was a finalist in the junior high spelling bee (which she lost to two Korean twins whose pronunciation was execrable but whose memorized English was letter perfect) and I sat among the hushed, anxious parents watching the kids tremble and listening to the announcer: 'Word number nineteen: bourgeoisie.' Outrage rippled through the crowd of parents – why give them a word like that? Can't spell it, don't know what it means, wouldn't want to know, *shouldn't* know! But it's the truth, our boob tube is a bourgeois boob tube.

'Economic power is open and obvious; discursive power is hidden,' John Fiske writes; 'only that which is not named appears to have no alternative.' This is a key point. It is precisely television which does not name itself and the class it represents, and which therefore convinces us of its universality – what else is there besides the world according to Dan Rather? But just like the historical role of the bourgeoisie, television 'establishes *its* sense of the real as the *common* sense.' According to Fiske, this does not mean that television's power is uncontested, or that TV's victories are final. We are not mere creatures of moguls who shape our minds, he thinks.[26] But it does mean that the text of indeterminate authorship flitting by on the screen has a history, a locus of manufacture, and a world view – the liberal world view.

In a few short paragraphs we have gotten to important points: TV is a middle-class business that presents to us a flow of deftly manufactured images of ourselves that we take to be transparently true; objectivity indicates a submerged authorship (appearing to be unauthored), whereas bias insinuates a point of view (appearing to be authored). The inauthentic and hidden script becomes the authentic; the authentic and honest script becomes the inauthentic. Television is conformist, sells things, and has hidden authors, but knows what is objective and what is biased: salesmen and yet authors, purveyors of junk and yet scholars, this is no mean feat, this medium.

America is the epicenter of world television culture, and therefore French intellectuals predictably call it 'the world center of the inauthentic.'[27] If so, we cannot blame this on TV alone. In the magnificent foyer of Louis Sullivan's Auditorium Building on Michigan Avenue in Chicago there is a poster on the wall, from the last century's celebration of Columbus's 400th, saying:

400 Years of Retrospection
Imre Kiralfy's
Brilliant Historical Spectacle
AMERICA
The Most
Magnificent Production
of Modern Times

America as production, spectacle, mirage, simulation: no wonder B-movie heartthrob Ronald Reagan did so well. But remember how he did it: long experience in peddling General Electric's 'Better Living Through Electricity' over the airwaves made selling America mere child's play; he wrapped himself in the flag not so much because he was a superpatriot (although he was that), but because, as Baudrillard put it, the American flag is 'the trademark of a good brand'; in some sense it has become a logo. Here television, advertising, and politics flow together, toward the mysterious charisma that Ronald Reagan deployed and that no empiricist inquiry can explain.

We can appreciate the phenomenon, perhaps, by reflecting on Adorno's judgement that through the culture industry, through the confluence of programming and advertising,

> The most intimate reactions of human beings have been so thoroughly reified that the idea of anything specific to themselves now persists only as an utterly abstract notion . . . . The triumph of advertising in the culture industry is that consumers feel compelled to buy and use its products even though they see through them.[28]

Without belaboring this point, I think this begins to explain Reagan's popularity and his 'Teflon' persona, in which nothing thrown his way really stuck, at the same time that most people 'saw through him.'

But to return to the medium: TV gives you 'a flow of consumable reports and products, in which the elements of speed, variety and miscellaneity can be seen as organising: [they are] the real bearers of value.'[29] And how speedy it is: the smallest unit of meaning (and therefore of value) in television is the *frame*, defined as 'a complete scanning cycle of the electron beam, which occurs every $\frac{1}{30}$ second.'[30] So television is a mystifying technology, too: we have no idea we're watching thirty electron-beam scanning cycles per second when we look at Dan Rather's earnest face. The frame produces the image, and the latter is the 'signifier' if you like to talk 'semiotically' (and it seems most academic TV experts do). The word *image* derives from the root *imitari*, as 'an anological representation (the "copy").'[31] Television's thousands of little dots produce an image, an electronic two-dimensional simulation: that is, a copy, Walter Cronkite as facsimile of the newsman-as-wise-man.

Producer Max Whitby had a high-tech editing setup at Thames Television, something like a laboratory, and I enjoyed watching him slice up our filmic efforts. Everything seemed governed by *time*: frames, cuts, freezes, ellipses, pauses, fast forward and fast back, scenes morseled to symbols, interviews to soundbites, this juxtaposed to that – all of this Max did on his machine. The technique had a wondrous quality, the combination of his considerable skills and the beauty of an electronics that slices everything up unseen yet keeps the 'seen' film going, burying the fleeting interruptions in the overpowering flow. But: fragmented flow without an author, shards from the archaeology of an old war without the archaeologist, myself and all the other 'respondents' reduced from a two-hour interview to a handful of thirty-second soundbites.

It is not just the respondents who get chewed up and spit out. The medium possesses vast advantages over its consumers: it emanates from a single powerful center, out to an atomized, powerless private audience which is theoretically universal. Viewers do not know the obsessive attention to detail that goes into a soundbite, let alone a big program. According to public opinion studies, people watch television passively, with their defenses down, although with considerable and, to TV moguls, disturbing inattention: a flipped-on TV is no guarantee that anyone is watching. As anchorperson Tom Brokaw put it, the TV audience is a 'large mass, looking at us in a distracted way.'[32] (He's a bit angry with his fickle public.)

One expert, Todd Gitlin, uses Susan Sontag's idea (itself derived from Walter Benjamin) about the way in which 'imitation and recombination make up a cultural set that pervades the West,' in judging TV to be 'the ultimate recombinatory form,' with infinitely varied (but typically taste-less) juxtapositions[33] – a show on child abuse interrupted by a perfect bourgeois living room where the homemaker gyrates on the couch to the tune of her hemorrhoids, walkman tunes drowning out Sartre's *Being and Nothingness*. For Gitlin the fascination of television is 'the fascination of meaninglessness raised to a universal principle,' and meaninglessness every day of the week leads to 'a sense of cultural exhaustion.'[34]

How can this stuff about cultural exhaustion be squared with the magnetism of TV, an aura that mesmerizes everything from Tibetans to infants to goldfish? Are we just listening to a bunch of intellectuals whose real lament is that we don't read their books? Even in remote Tibet people seek couch-potato heaven: take 'Darchi,' a middle-aged peasant who, as he harvested barley near his mud-brick village, told an American reporter that he didn't really care about independence from China: 'I want to buy a television, and then sit back and drink barley beer and watch TV.'[35]

Or let's take infants: I watch my son toddle into the TV room complaining about an empty stomach or a full diaper, only to be caught up short by a television image: whereupon his eyes grow wide, the complain-ing ceases, and he scopes the tube oblivious to all else. He will sit for a full half-hour watching his grandmother's favorite show, *Jeopardy*. Mr Rogers is his tutor in life's dilemmas (and not a bad one, even if one with 'a point of view'). He holds still while MTV frazzles his pristine synapses.

Or let's take goldfish: in one experiment, some academics observed family goldfish kibbitzing on their keeper's TV viewing by consistently 'swimming on the side of the tank nearest to the television set.'[36] If not just the whole world but even the goldfish are watching, if even they can't resist it, what hope do my TV-deprived colleagues' children have – who rush to our TV room like Bedouins to an oasis when we have their parents over for dinner? What is the overwhelming attraction, that nonetheless sucks our culture dry?

The argument of the critics is that TV not only sells, but consumes: itself, and us. By its incessant replication of images, television destroys individual identity: 'the return of sameness over and over again, in all its psychological desolation and tedium . . . it never meets anything but what it knows already.'[37] Thus the weariness of a culture in which everything has been consumed, or is about to be. In other words television's simultaneity of images and gathering together of disparate temporalities (another name for histories) serves the same purpose as Nietzsche's 'eternal recurrence,' because it allows you sooner or later to satiate yourself in 'seeing it all,' like 'having it all' — and what's left after that?

The electron scanning cycles of television copy the reality they witness, something like a hand-held xerox machine. The result is a facsimile, not a person. Postmodern theorists take this insight to its logical conclusion, viewing television as symptomatic of 'the postmodern psycho-cultural condition — a world of simulations detached from reference to the real, which circulate and exchange in ceaseless, centreless flow.'[38]

The 'arch-theorist' here is Jean Baudrillard, who uses television as 'a metaphor for the regime of simulation in contemporary Western cultures.' TV enters our homes as a relentless pillager of private life, bringing to our living rooms facsimiles of what we think of as 'the real world'; daily life in the home, which *is* real, gives way to a simulated world in which the men radiate Clint Eastwood-style masculinity and the women combine Hollywood glamor with the conceits of independent journalism. The result of this paradoxical inversion accomplished by television, according to Baudrillard, is the merging of public and private, real and unreal, into a postmodern bedlam: 'the absolute proximity, the total instantaneity of things, the feeling of no defense, no retreat.'[39]

Now perhaps I understand why television strikes me at times as an enemy, against which there are few defenses save self-isolation (and that is merely a different sort of isolation than TV produces). If we might disagree about postmodernism and TV's relationship to it, at least the experts have given us the physics behind television's incessant jerks, starts, stops, beginnings, endings, collapsed middles, and synapse-rending juxtapositions. All that is solid fragments into a Tower of Babel (witness the local news people: they absolutely cannot let a split-second go by without babbling; the appearance of a moment of talk-vacuum creates an embarrassed silence that is the television equivalent of a heart attack).

All of the characteristics I have thus far given you combine to make television the first and thus far the ultimate postmodern medium. Perhaps this is best witnessed precisely in the literature of the television scholars themselves, nearly all of whom deploy postmodern theory to understand their subject. This quality in the medium is so powerful that it also subverts the discourse of the experts: a recent and representative compendium[40] includes several essays where scholars range back and forth between abstract theory, scholarly form, and reminiscences of watching *I Love Lucy* as a child; between formal academic presentation and intimate personal asides; between disgust for the effects of the medium and obvious attraction to its mesmerizing power. Above all, like television itself, the authors rely on the invocation of authoritative expertise: only in this case it is Jean Baudrillard, Jacques Derrida, Jürgen Habermas, and Fredric Jameson, cheek-by-jowl with Tony Bennett and Baby Jessica.[41]

TELEVISION NIHILISM

Professor Bloom has an unintentionally amusing chapter in his book where he tries to analyze the music young people listen to. Rock is for him a 'gutter phenomenon,' whose androgynous genius is Mick Jagger, s/he of a type that 'Nietzsche called Nihiline.' Bloom concludes that adolescents know, if nobody else does, what is really at the bottom of it all: 'rock has the beat of sexual intercourse.' The steady bass thumping is all about screwing.[42]

This blatant misreading of young people suggests (1) that Allan Bloom does not like rock, and (2) that he does not watch television.[43] Thus he would not know that it is the television that annihilates, with its morseling juxtapositions, but also by its essence as a camera that claims its victims through overexposure: here is the psychology of its consumption and exhaustion. Some people appear on the screen and one wishes instantly that they would go away and never come back, because they arouse nausea, or make the viewer nervous. (Let us say Nixon during the 1960 Presidential debates, Carter during most of his Presidency. Of course, this is a matter for 'viewer discretion'; I don't ask that you agree with my tastes.) Others appear and create a magnificent moment of attention, after which they plummet because somehow they immediately exhaust what they have just created, by demonstrating that there is nothing beyond or beneath their 'image.' (Arnold Schwarzenegger and his wife Maria Shriver both have this quality.) Some will appear as creations of a riveting moment, but as the moment dies, so do they, suddenly appearing as self-parodies (almost any media 'radical' of the 1960s would qualify, although some, like Jerry Rubin and Eldridge Cleaver, took self-parody to new heights.) Then there are those who have a relatively long run, to the point where one cannot imagine the screen without them, whereupon they die and nothing will resurrect them (comedians are especially susceptible, like Red Buttons or George Gobel or Mort Sahl, or the *Laugh-in* crowd).

Benjamin intuited this aspect of our postmodern world by grasping how the mass replication of images destroys the 'aura' of a work of art (or in this case a personality), through techniques of reproduction that substitute 'a plurality of copies for a unique existence,' which leads to 'a tremendous shattering of experience.'[44] The more reproducibility, the more transitory our experience – and nothing constitutes itself as reproduction more than TV's electronic image. The survivors of television nihilism master the medium, by combining the familiarity of an old friend with a hint of mystery or unintelligibility, or that there truly is no there there (Johnny Carson, Ronald Reagan): thus, like an old shoe, they 'wear well.' The mystery inheres in such people being so adept in the medium that they become the medium, Rorschach inkblots upon which we project what we wish to see.

The apotheosis of television nihilism is Music Television (MTV), or perhaps MTV when a 'rap' group is on (my views on rap are about like Bloom's on rock music, but at least I admit to having no idea why it grips young people). I deeply sympathized with CIA-friendly General Manuel Noriega, when he was sequestered in the Papal Nunciature in Panama City – routinely pronounced as 'Nunciaterra' by American command TV spokespeople, since they had never heard of such a thing – and grinning American GIs put rap 'music' on their ghettoblasters to drive the priests and nuns crazy, and flush Noriega into the open: even jail in Miami was preferable to that, for the opera-loving dictator.

'Rap' perfectly recapitulates the staccato soundbites and inapposite juxtapositions of television, taking the thirty electron-beam scanning cycles per second to another logical conclusion. Nothing escapes the searching eyes of MTV, anything sacred is instantly profaned, anything profane is somehow sacred, and any attempt to derive intelligent meaning from the flashing images can be undercut at the next instant by its polar opposite. Phil Collins can win a Grammy and pass himself off as socially concerned by singing 'Another Day in Paradise' amid the homeless who litter our sidewalks, just as Batman broke boxoffice records in the summer of 1989 by depicting New York City in a terminal state of decay and degradation.[45] But then it's onto an ad for Reeboks, or a video where Madonna does her best simulation of a seductive Marilyn Monroe. The image of the homeless passes as fast as a shake of Madonna's breasts, and one is left exhausted.

MTV exhausts even one's capacity for parody: never could I have imagined that as the Gulf War drum roll intensified, Madonna would get into her red panties, filmy bra, and heavy/SM combat boots for a patriotic lesson in democracy.[46] Draping the flag over her flaming lingerie and bulging boobs, she bends over while two males flail away at her buttocks: 'If you don't vote, you're going to get a spankie!' And then she 'raps' the message:

> Abe Lincoln, Jefferson Tom,
> They didn't need the atomic bomb,
> We need beauty, we need art,
> We need government with a heart.
> Don't give up your freedom of speech,
> Power to the people is in our reach.

Whatever opprobrium one wants to fling in Madonna's direction – how cynical, how opportunist, how many grand ideas you disgrace just by mouthing them – it won't stick; she is beyond parody into what Jameson calls 'pastiche';[47] her recombinatory shamelessness is just par for this course. And above all, it sells – just as rap defeats Beethoven in the war for public opinion. (In the middle of Bush's war, the networks took time out for The Grammies. In the category 'long form video,' the late Leonard Bernstein's Berlin performance of Beethoven's Ninth lost out to acrobatic rapper M.C. Hammer's ' "Please Hammer Don't Hurt 'Em" The Movie.')

As the 1990s dawned, MTV presented the decade of the 1980s in two hours of retrospective staccato images – which I found both fascinating and disorienting. The fascination came from the remnant sixties protest and cynicism mingled with the 'music,' the disorientation from the vertigo of cascading images that gave us 'history' in the metaphor of a dying man watching his life pass before his eyes. MTV is the ultimate medium for a television devoted to turning simultaneous mass viewing into a commodity. MTV makes no distinction between programming and advertising; its videos are both programs and sales pitches for albums, broken up by more obviously commercial advertisements. In its wake, corporations increasingly turn to hard rock to sell anything from Diet Coke to deodorant: even James Brown ('the Godfather of Soul') is not too funky for prime time huckstering now, thanks to MTV.

Once the *New York Times* opened its Op-Ed page to a self-described booster of the virtues of MTV, indeed one of its 'creators': Robert W. Pittman. His medium, Mr Pittman wished to argue, is a force for Good. You just have to understand that baby-boomers are couch potatoes who think differently, indeed who seem to have brains of a new type, knowing only the flitting image and the split-second attention span. They can't sit still to read a book, but not to worry – you can reach them through this new medium called MTV, and make them 'socially concerned' by bombarding them with images and soundbites so that 'information from each source finds its way to a different cluster of thoughts'; don't worry about fractured synapses, because 'at the end of the evening it all makes sense.'[48] (It was a typically disinterested editorial; Mr Pittman just happens to be a senior executive at Time-Warner, Inc.) So, MTV fans, who needs Martin Luther King when you've got Phil Collins?

MTV mogul Robert Pittman's detractors are many, however, and they got a full page in the *Times* to vent their spleen.[49] Read a bit of it; I couldn't have said it better myself. First, Robert Gorham Davis of Cambridge, Mass.:

> Most of the US population spends 50 or so hours a week caught up in a wildly disjunctive fictional world made even more chaotic by interspersed advertisements, equally fictional, and by brief selected flashes of the more sensational events of the real world, usually those that most resemble fiction.
>
> There has been no adequate study of the total effect of television on American society, beginning with its effect on the minds and behavior of those who watch it so much. This is crucial in a democracy, where the

people are supposed to rule, but where, manipulated by images, they are no longer encouraged to think.

Or take Michael A. Baechle of Boonton, NJ:

> Until human beings face the fact that television creates an image of what we would like to be and does not show us who we really are, we will continue to believe that someday it will help us reach our intellectual and social potential as an intelligent life form.

But Professor-emeritus Richard Hyse of Florida gave us the bottom line to Pittman's fantasies:

> The average member of the TV babies generation now in college cannot, for instance, find the Persian Gulf on a world map, calculate 6 percent of some sum without a machine, or give an organized account of a simple theorem.

So, we are left with a dilemma: this medium turns brains to mush, yet its importance is so great that these days the first thing revolutionaries think of is to occupy the television stations. 'All revolutions are [now] tele-revolutions,' says Timothy Garton Ash, as we saw in Bucharest: 'Romanian television has been telling the world what is going on,' an exultant ABC correspondent said. We saw it in Moscow, too, when in the wake of the failed coup in 1991 Diane Sawyer had her microphone thrust into Boris Yeltsin's face, and he later appeared with Gorbachev on a special 'town meeting' of *Nightline*.

Of course, you can always get back at TV by do-it-yourself nihilism, or what Fiske calls 'zapping,' which allows the viewer 'to construct a viewing experience of fragments, a postmodern collage of images whose pleasures lie in their discontinuity, their juxtapositions, their contradictions.'[50] So, be of good cheer: you are zapped, but you get to zap back. But is he right? What is it that we actually 'see' in our zapping? What is our 'viewing experience'?

If I were to describe what I see in a scholarly fashion, something would be lost. I would have to point out that some channels are good, like the Discovery network, Public Broadcasting (usually but not always), and of course Cable News Network. So let me be 'reflexive' and tell you what I really think I see, most of the time, as I whip through the potpourri of television offerings on my thirty-nine channels: five religious fanatics (at least three of whom seem to need institutionalization); five types of sports (including one where monstrous trucks with airplane wheels burrow ten yards into the dirt); five old movies (one is colorized, making Humphrey Bogart look like a popsicle); five sitcoms offensive to the sense of humor of a ten-year-old; three varieties of mayhem played to rock music; three channels telling what's on the other channels; two workout queens; two channels that merely show a disembodied hand fingering a gold necklace; two talk shows with the host mercilessly badgering the guest; two professional wrestling dramas where a red-blooded American takes on an evil black-caped Russian (or, lately, evil ill-shaven Arab); a weather channel with catatonic metereologists; C-Span, which finds interest in stupefying Congressional testimony or academic conferences on foreign policy; a World War II or a holocaust documentary; and, finally, CNN — window to the world of what's-happening-now. If there isn't anything big happening in that world, we usually settle for the documentary.

In short, it seems to me no more satisfying to flip through the thirty-nine channels than it is to zap a program you don't like (or just turn the set off, perish the thought). The only satisfaction is in obliterating some face from the screen; constructing my 'viewing experience' is small comfort in trying to overcome a medium which makes all the selections in advance, and then gives us but a superficially broad range of them. The feeling provoked is something like the ultimate boredom of the proverbial 100 flavors of ice cream: when all is said and done, it's still ice cream. But TV is also more than that: the illusion of choice is greater, and perhaps the reality of choice is too, in a peculiar and inexplicable way.

The thirty-nine channels have the maddening quality of purveying a deadening sameness day in and day out, mocking our claims to pluralism and individuality. At the same time one can sum them up in the phrase 'What's my provincialism?' Within a narrow range (the parameters of which are somehow intuited but rarely mentioned) there appears to be something for everybody, including World War II addicts like myself. Geraldo Rivera, a pioneer of tabloid television, answered critics of his Rupert Murdoch approach to programming by saying the viewer has thirty or forty channels to choose from, and that's what makes our democracy

great. But the superficial diversity emanates from a concealed and conformist grabbag. 'Something is provided for all so that none may escape'
was Adorno's prescient observation.[51] We get novelty without connection,
the imagined national audience begets no democratic polity, no
community.

COMMUNITY AND POLITICS IN TELEVISION

It is obvious that my account is different than television's account of itself.
In a world now become a global village, television purports to connect it
all, and us all, together: to create community. Witness the broadcasters
when some big disaster hits, like the San Francisco earthquake: 'I think
we're drawing together as a country now, perhaps we can even say as a
common community of suffering, with those unfortunate people who are
now homeless,' and so on. Or, an anonymous ambulance driver retrieves
Baby Jessica from the bottom of a well, gets on *Nightline* and greets Koppel
as he would a friend – 'Well, Ted . . . .' He's playing the media game that
we're really not a bunch of aimless atoms bouncing off each other in a place
called America, where the public sphere in the proper sense of that term has
shrunk nearly to oblivion, but we instead embody a community with a
common purpose.

One remaining element of community (if not democracy) in America is
surely the family. Television goes out to families, as the modal viewers, and
knows it: thus it quakes at the thought that 'family values' will be upset by
its programs, yet it finds profit in titillating heterodoxy. Here is one large
source of the insoluble squabbles that periodically erupt, ranging between
the fraudulent moralism of a Jimmie Swaggart and the exhibitionism[52] of a
Geraldo Rivera. But the family is also a model and a microcosm for
television: it loves stories 'that allow it to celebrate the unity of the
National Family.'[53] In the past *éminences grises* like Cronkite or Eric Sevareid
were television's *pater familias*; nowadays the boyish looks of a Peter
Jennings or Tom Brokaw make them more the sons and brothers of the
national family. It then follows that when the nation goes to war, television
has a bias toward treating the calamity as the family does: no messy

arguments ought to disrupt the solemn fact that a child or sibling might die, and the family (or the nation) ought to draw together.

This fictive community was not television's invention, however, but Hollywood's. The American dream of upward mobility, middle-class solidity, the single-family home, and the perfect husband/wife/children was an invention of European immigrants. Many of them were from Eastern Europe, where they lived in the interstices of peasant societies and suffered appalling discrimination. Within single lifetimes they went from itinerant peddling to vast wealth and influence, and the films they made expressed both their incredible individual trajectories, their gratitude to an America that made their rise possible, and their continued striving toward bourgeois respectability.[54]

Theirs was an acquired liberalism, in other words, in a society the world view of which they did not fully understand, and about which they were deeply ambivalent – in part because no matter how wealthy they became, they were never accepted by the Yankee elite. Thus America became in their manufactured images both Horatio Alger simulation, and far more open to talent from below than they implicitly knew it to be. Indeed, their incredible lives probably remained deeply mysterious, attributed far more to happenstance than to liberal openness. Propertied WASPs, of course, did not need to be tutored by immigrants about American virtue. But for the mass of Americans in mid-century, so many of whom came from ethnicities and races that were anathema to the ruling ethnic group, Hollywood reflected back to them their hopes and dreams.

The television and film industries were intimately connected in the 1950s, when television first entered most homes, with many of its early stars manufactured in Hollywood. Because it went into the hearth and home, however, it has had to be a much more middle-class industry, eschewing the bohemianism, flamboyant lifestyles and frequent scandals of Hollywood stars in favor of stolid, often tutelary propriety. With shows like *Ozzie and Harriet*, *Lassie*, *Leave it to Beaver*, and *All in the Family*, TV deployed and deeply reinforced a simulated middle-class perfection (or the warts and small pleasures of lower-middle-class imperfection, in the last case) that rarely accorded with the reality of daily life in American families.

Translated into politics this simulation assumed that American politics was the norm. Just as televised family life in a comfortable suburb was unavailable to the mass of Americans, so liberal politics, in spite of its proclaimed universality, was unavailing to Americans from the wrong gender, race, or ethnic group. Nonetheless this television simulation was deeply attractive and seductive, and played back to its viewers an image of what life ought to be like. To the extent that one's own life fell short, as it almost always had to, the tendency was to blame oneself. Today that middle-class image radiates outward to the entire world, two-thirds of which has no hope of recapitulating its simulated bourgeois lifestyle.

I think the postmodernists are far closer to the truth about television than its self-definition as an instrument of community. Television is an instant series of discrete snapshots that disconnect us, that make imposs-ible (if not absurd) a life lived as purposeful narrative: I had this purpose, I did that from early adulthood onward in fulfilling my goals. Imagine Jane Fonda describing her fifty-year-old purpose, whatever that might be, and instantly the videotape shows her Barbarella phase, or her Hanoi-Jane phase, and her present-day telos is revealed to be . . . just another media event. In this sense the morseling empiricism of television is subversive of everything: every pretension, every stuttered 'my life is (or was) . . . ,' every attempt at achieving the Good, everything that went before the television age.

Well, not everything. A self-aware TV could cut from Jane Fonda to the life of, say, Averrel Harriman; here he is a little boy, at play with fellow 'wise man' Robert Lovett on his father's sumptuous estate, there is his father's railroad empire that paid for it, then a move to Averrel's Groton and Yale education, his own sumptuous estate (now belonging to Colum-bia University), his early rise in Washington, Ambassador to Moscow, advisor to seven or eight Presidents, the millions of dollars given to Columbia University when he died . . . a ruling class life, well lived into the nineties. Television could cut to his myriad affairs, his half-century junior wife, his time of troubles when CIA Counter-Intelligence chief James Angleton launched Operation DINOSAUR to smoke an aged Averrel out as the hidden Soviet mole. Given Averrel's status, however, these are mere peccadilloes.

Here would be the narrative life of an American kingpin, a life lived toward the fulfillment of aristocratic system-maintenance. Or you could do David Rockefeller, or John J. McCloy, or one of the celebrated 'wise men.'

Or just take Henry Kissinger. Challenged by Tim Lehrer to say whether his business dealings with China had anything to do with his advocacy of warm relations with the post-Tiananmen China leadership, he turned Lehrer into a bowl of jelly with just a hard look and a remark about how outrageous such an insinuation was. TV is good for those rare moments: it revealed the fear in Lehrer's eyes. But it is not good for explaining why such trepidation should afflict one of broadcast journalism's best practitioners when confronted with raw, discomfited power.

Television can also, however, make mincemeat out of our elected leaders. They are items for consumption, we tire of them as rapidly as our cars, unless they are as skilled as Reagan in becoming the television they project, or unless TV becomes an adjunct of their policies, like George Bush in the Gulf. Like everyone else who watches TV, I can't look at Gerald Ford without thinking of a golf ball caroming off his pate. Just a glimpse of Jimmy Carter reminds me of his 'not for prime time' aura. This President died, for television purposes, when he allowed himself to be interviewed about beating off a rabbit swimming menacingly toward his fishing canoe, a spot featured that night as the first story on 'all three networks.' No matter what he did, he was finished after that. Richard Nixon was the anomaly. Television made his flawed character all too apparent, and television people disliked him (often passionately). Nonetheless he won the Presidency twice. Perhaps we were still 'pre-TV' then.

Presidents who understand the medium can quickly triumph over it and turn it to their own ends. Kennedy's television mastery first gave him an eye-whisker victory over Nixon, and then became an adjunct to his administration. His televised news conferences showed how a witty, quick mind can disarm and overwhelm television journalism; today the master practitioner of that art is Mikhail Gorbachev. Reagan was the model, however, but not because of his news conferences (which were appalling if he had no script), and certainly not because of his quick wit. His mastery embodied the same quality Gertrude Stein found in Oakland: no there there. He was an empty man, a 'television' in the sense conveyed by the character Chance in the film *Being There*. By becoming the medium, he projected what we wanted him to project. With his boyish handsomeness (even in his late seventies), his broad shoulders and good carriage, his no-flies-on-me smile, he spoke to the Jungian *persona* of what a leader should look like – even if he slept through much of his Presidency. And it was precisely this mysterious connection with our subconscious that Jimmy Carter lacked: stooped, harried, worried, he played back to us an image we shunned.

These Presidents are representations of the media-created reality: undoubtedly, Carter was the better President, and the better man. But Reagan dominated his era. The expertise of our television pundits is also a representation. It is the essential quality of the contemporary foreign-interpreting technocrat: have expertise, will travel. We will look at the multitude of experts called forth by the Gulf War below. Let's look at an earlier case here, one which I know well because for once television bathed the obscure area of the world that I study in its shining light.

The time was the spring of 1989, when 'China' entered the window of our television, and stayed there for weeks. Since our infant kept us on call at all hours during this period, we kept round-the-clock tabs on what all thirty-nine channels were saying about China (twenty-eight said nothing). Without question CNN got high marks for opening a window on these events, as it did later on one East European revolution after another: I am the first to admit that I cannot do without this channel, and I admire the no-nonsense style of its reporters. The seeming transparency of the medium rewards a transparent, deadpan style in reporting the news.

Still, even CNN's China experts were all drawn unerringly from a pool of people known (but how known?) to be responsible and trustworthy – not to say something trustworthy about China, but trusted not to say something upsetting to Americans' view of themselves, something outside the putative consensus. Somehow a handful of people are stamped 'okay for *Nightline*,' and they perform accordingly. China experts materialized who rendered for us 'China,' so that the events were exhilarating or upsetting in the proper, American liberalism-legitimating way, but not such as to upset our relationship with Bei'zh'ing.[55] Amid the many experts trotted out on various channels, not once did I see the China scholars I know to have independently formed, critically aware views that could have told the viewer something about China, and something about ourselves.[56]

Such people could have told the viewing audience, for example, that any Chinese group using the Statue of Liberty as its symbol is bound to fail because it's our statue, not theirs. Instead, experts who knew better chimed in with former Ambassador Winston Lord in agreeing that what the Chinese wanted was 'our kind of democracy.' The viewer was really given no way to understand the situation except through the morality tale of evil communist malefactors demolishing idealistic democratic students. Yet that was also a problem for American policy: the experts pussyfooted around the simple fact that the rape of Beijing revealed kindly old reformer and putative America-lover Mr Deng to be a player of hardball; the word Bei'zh'ing kept ricocheting in their brains, like the bullets on Changan Boulevard.

The daunting events from China were simultaneously left shot through with interpretation, and ill-understood. It is not that there are no explanations. Instead there are too many explanations,[57] all inevitably in the soundbite language of television; the wretched excess can be imagined if Morton Downey had a show on China (maybe he did), but the common fare was to affix assumedly well-understood labels to Chinese figures (none of whose names could be pronounced, except by the experts). Thus Deng became a 'hardliner,' 'conservative,' 'reactionary,' or 'fascist.' Zhao materialized as 'softliner,' 'moderate,' and 'liberal.' The labels then became a text that simultaneously interpreted, transcended and submerged the events appearing in television's window, while rendering them acceptable (i.e. Zhao's just like us). Chinese students wanted 'freedom,' which included an undifferentiated list running from basic political rights to rock-and-roll music to the 'right' to sport green hair. (Some brilliant student caught this atmosphere, marching in the Beijing spring with this banner held aloft: 'I want a ticket in the Pennsylvania lottery.')

It was just 'news,' interpreted by experts who mock I. F. Stone's method: he once said he wanted to apply the tools of scholarship to investigative journalism; they apply the tools of journalistic mediocrity and an undigested one-thing-after-another to the task of scholarship: and thus the events remain unplumbed, uninterpreted. Meanwhile from the murky depths bubble words and names governed by the American consensus, from a hidden but predictable text. We had no discussion of how we define democracy (apart from the unexamined American-style democracy), what the long history of scholar-elites had been in China, whether one could be a democrat and still not love the market (a central conundrum in Eastern Europe and Russia that gets little TV attention), or what the possibilities were in 1989 for democracy in a China that still was about three-quarters peasant.

What if someone had piped up in the middle of the fleeting chinoiserie that preceded the June massacre and said to the television audience,

> The democratized self which has no necessary social content and no necessary social identity can then be anything, can assume any role or take any point of view, because it is in and for itself nothing.

That is, once you get your rights, the main one will be the right to believe in nothing, and be nothing. A true pluralism of diverse views is mocked by a simulated pluralism in the midst of hyper-conformity. This is from Catholic thinker MacIntyre,[58] an elaboration of the idea that emotivism leads to an inability to agree on moral principle. The market elevates this insight to a reigning, if unarticulated, master principle: let them all believe in nothing.

Of even greater moment than China was the succeeding 'Revolution of '89' in Eastern Europe, where I again applauded CNN for its blanket coverage, and again shouted myself hoarse at the commentary. Here was a moment like no other since Hitler was tracked to his bunker lair by the Red Army, truly history created before one's eyes . . . or at least CNN's eyes. But the American couch potato would have none of it; ratings plunged whenever Dan Rather emoted at the Berlin Wall or Tom Brokaw weighed in from the Kremlin.

I watched every last thing I could. Witness the demonstrators: whether they were disciplined East Germans marching in Leipzig every Monday night, courageous (communists) in the Romanian Army tracking down evil (communists) in the 'Securitate,' or Lithuanians giving Gorbachev what-for – they all wanted freedom, they all wanted to be just like us. (Except for the Azerbaijani and Tadzhik demonstrators: they got no press, but Gorbie got a pat on the back when he gave them a whiff of the grape.) One had to read the fine print in our paper of record to discover an alternative interpretation:

> As [Hans] Modrow explained to Mr Baker, the push for unification from East Germans is being driven . . . not by visions of a grand Germany, but visions of videocassette recorders.[59]

Or this interpretation, at the tag end of a long article:

> In [businessman] Mr Summers's view an independent Lithuania (or Estonia, or Latvia for that matter) would be able to attract capital – and modern factories – from nearby Scandinavia. 'Where else,' he asks, 'can you hire high-quality labor for one-eighth the wage of a South Korean?'[60]

Television's immense late twentieth-century power was manifest in the failed Soviet coup of 1991, where the plotters seized the state broadcasting headquarters, but chose not to expel CNN: which then became a critical window on the quick unraveling of the coup – a participant and not just an observer, operating by ingenious feedback loop (short-wave radios, Voice of America) upon the events themselves. But TV's political force was evident throughout the 1980s, for anyone with a memory. Let's flip back to 1982, when Ronald Reagan got his good friend, Charles Wick (then Director of the Voice of America), to broadcast 'Let Poland Be Poland.'

This was to be 'the greatest show since the creation of the world,' as TV stars and heads of state (in that order) would read messages of solidarity with Lech Walesa and the Polish people: Frank Sinatra, Bob Hope, Charlton Heston, were all there. TASS branded it 'telesubversion,' and Paul Virilio likened the program to 'a new kind of frontier violation,' noting that an entertainer like Frank Sinatra actually deploys 'a political power really capable of founding the American state and its cultural hold on the world.'[61] He is right, and although the couch potatoes didn't like that program either and tuned out in droves, it was television's sustained bombardment, not Reagan's missiles, that made it impossible to sustain the walls of Stalinism in Europe.

Since I criticize the TV experts, perhaps I should describe my own experience as 'expert.' I appeared on *MacNeil/Lehrer* in June 1987, during the mass mobilization that ended Chun Doo Hwan's tenure. I said some perfectly reasonable things about Korea, it seemed to me, while trying to fend off Karen Elliot House, a reporter from the *Wall Street Journal* who had just returned from Seoul, and who spoke with utter confidence of things Korean about which she manifestly knew nothing; virtually every comment adumbrated the line taken by the American Embassy. I found out later that the staffers thought I had been 'too radical,' and I haven't heard from them again (so it goes . . .).

Ms House, however, has recently been dubbed America's 'Media Queen,' wife to the 'Media King,' Peter Kann (CEO of the Dow Jones Corporation, of which she's a vice-president). In a piece redolent of the tony sleaze now passing for 'high cool' commentary, a cover article on this 'new media power couple' reported on their 'unabashedly right-wing' views and said that while some 'ethicists' might question such 'corporate incest,' 'when all the handwringing is over, one fact remains: if you're the boss you can do whatever you want.'[62] During the Gulf War I saw Ms House holding forth on 'the mind of the Arab.'

In the tumultuous summer of 1989 I got a call from *NBC Nightly News* asking for an interview on North Korea. They had a crew in P'yŏngyang during Kim Il Sung's summer youth festival, and wanted to ask me some questions. A friendly reporter from Chicago's NBC affiliate showed up, acknowledged off the bat that he knew nothing about North Korea or the NBC visit there or what they were planning to say in their program. He conducted a forty-five minute interview with me.

I appeared in a ten-second soundbite, where they extracted what they wanted me to say from the forty-five minutes I had given them. The same process occurred once again in September 1990, when a young woman from CNN, also professing utter ignorance of the topic, took a thirty-minute interview, from which CNN used about six seconds. It is an odd feeling, to know that a long, interactive interview will be cut without the slightest concern for whether it renders your views accurately: a quoting-out-of-context which would not meet basic principles of print journalism, let alone scholarship. But it is the fate of TV experts to be soundbitten, and so perhaps we should not hold them to account for what we hear them say on the tube: authors of their own thoughts, they are not responsible and not accountable for how television uses them.

Television is a paradox: invader of the hearth and home, bender of minds, frazzler of synapses, pillager of soundbites, yet indispensable and all-powerful. But there is more to tell: by its very nature TV is said to be a transparent, objective mechanism of advanced technology; far from xeroxing our world for us and calling the product reality, it is said to be unbiased just where we humans are so biased, rational where we are emotive. How so?

BIAS AND BALANCE IN TELEVISION

Hard as it is for me to write these words, the fact is that television presents to the average viewer their measure of objectivity. The seeming transparency of the medium and the presumed objectivity of the camera's eye disarms the critical faculties or drowns them in the fascinating flow of images. Television is addictive, particularly when a facility like CNN becomes our 24-hour-a-day companion in opening a window on breaking events that are themselves of high moment: like the fall of the Berlin Wall or the Soviet coup or the execution grounds where Ceausescu was laid low not one week after he and his Lady Macbeth of a wife had seemed omnipotent.

I can no longer imagine living my life without CNN, just as I look forward every morning to reading the *New York Times*. Yet both these mediums-of-record are exasperating in their politics and biased in their reporting, even if they hide it well. Raymond Williams's influential definition of television as a flow assumes a succession of images with no logic or cause and effect – 'a single irresponsible flow of images and feelings.' The word *irresponsible* is the key term, both in the camouflaging of cause and effect and the location of the authorship, and the absence of accountability for the impact on the audience.

The submerged authorship nonetheless exists, and its main goal is authorial distance, the achievement of consensus, television by committee. It fears not just *my* point of view, but *any* obvious point of view. Thus TV employs 'bias checkers,' people paid to ferret out messages that might offend some group or (more often) cause the cancellation of a sponsor.

But what makes a point of view obvious? Only something that causes it to climb out of the soupy mess of consensual programming. Thus TV is, as Williams said, led not by capitalist moguls or bourgeois ideologues so much as a 'mediocracy,'[63] which sniffs the outer limits of middle-class sensitivities with the instincts of a bloodhound. How this acute power of scent is acquired, however, is quite inscrutable.

The outer limits of acceptability today are anchored by Patrick Buchanan and Reed Irvine on the Right (both in my view little more than schoolyard bullies, with brains to match) and assorted liberals 'on the Left,' almost all of them lacking a critical stance toward the state (Tom Braden,

Buchanan's exhausted 'left' foil for many years, was a former CIA employee; the new foil, Michael Kinsley, is less a liberal than a neo-conservative, and comes across as the proverbial 99-lb weakling whom the schoolyard bully victimized). Here television recapitulates the narrowing and rightward movement of the media in general during the 1980s, with *The New Republic* being at the point of the neo-conservative lance, yet still perceived as a liberal anchor in the impoverished, slim pickings on the American Left. Out in left field are those independent critics who rarely get airtime, but who have diverse and, to network television, heretical views.

In America nothing is easier than to be a Buchanan or an Irvine, or a less flamboyant and therefore more acceptable Karen House, paid handsomely by the corporations and supported by the Reagan/Bush White House; nothing is harder than to be a person perceived to be on the Left, lacking funding and hated by the Reagan/Bush White House. Irvine's 'Accuracy in Media' (AIM) pretends to ferret out liberal or leftist bias in the media. A far less prominent organization, 'Fairness and Accuracy in Reporting' (FAIR), has done several surveys showing that programs like *Nightline* and *MacNeil/Lehrer* draw their guests mostly from pools of conservative or centrist elites in government, business and academe.[64] This is obvious to anyone who watches them, and demonstrates how far we have come from the post-1968 Vietnam era when truth did occasionally confront and discomfit power, even on TV.

The consensual and ideological anchoring is mostly unconscious, however; in that sense the Buchanans are rare. Indeed this is what gives the process its formidable strength and its opaque mystery. Todd Gitlin is right, I think, to locate the mobilization of television bias in an 'internal gyroscope' that keeps the directors on the beam . . . or should we say always somewhat off the beam, with some hidden ballast tilting the scope, giving the medium a homing energy that keeps it from spinning out of control, out of the parameters set by the body politic and the corporations that sustain it. Gitlin's position is that 'the networks generate ideology mostly indirectly and unintentionally, by trying to read popular sentiment and tailoring their schedules . . . toward what they think the cardboard people they've conjured up want to see and hear.' Even better is to anticipate the public mood and 'encapsulate it in a show.'[65]

Semiotician Roland Barthes points out that television must anchor the fleeting $\frac{1}{30}$-second image in *connotations*, which attempt to fix and freeze meaning, that is, to tell you what you are seeing. The anchorage is usually ideological. The events in Kuwait or the opening of the Berlin Wall demand interpretation and equally demand confinement; the fleeting news is liberated only to be captured in the web of television conformity. East German Prime Minister Hans Modrow may have told Secretary of State Baker that his young people fled to West Germany for VCRs rather than democracy, but the opening of the Wall must be another moment to celebrate ourselves. When Andrei Sakharov died, I heard a CNN reporter remark that he was a deep believer in human rights and free-market economics. The first was true, and the second a travesty of his democratic socialist views and his frequent condemnations of capitalist nihilism and decadence.

The dominant ideology encompasses television and informs the gyroscope, and yet it itself, as Douglas Kellner puts it, 'is saturated with contradictions.'[66] David Rockefeller and Henry Kissinger may think, in November 1989, that it is time to cozy up to Deng Xiao-ping again, letting the bygones of spring 1989 be bygones, and they may get the Bush administration to do it through Kissinger Associates' (former) employees Brent Skowcroft and Lawrence Eagleburger. But other elites didn't like their surreptitious (the *New York Times* even said 'furtive') visits to the Forbidden City, and said so all over the airwaves.

So still, the question is begged: who ballasts the gyroscope, who gets the 'signals' straight on television, if hegemonic ideology is contradictory? According to Jürgen Habermas, the ideological template derives from what he calls 'paleosymbolism', with 'paleo' meaning 'before symbolism' or 'underneath symbolism.'[67] Pierre Bourdieu makes a similar point in linking the methods through which we take and perceive photographs to a 'process of internalization of objectivity' which creates 'durable dispositions' that correspond to class ethos (or 'habitus,' in his terms):

> the myriad 'small perceptions' of everyday life and the convergent and repeated sanctions of the economic and social universe imperceptibly constitute, from childhood and throughout one's life, by means of constant reminders, this 'unconscious'.[68]

This 'paleo' business gets us closer to the unconscious Grail of television.

Somewhere deep down, I believe, there is a paleosymbol or a template of what's good and true, bred in by 'myriad "small perceptions" of everyday life.' This creates an archetype of the objective television conduit of the Good and True: the Good and True is mined from the mythology of eighteenth-century America (before the factory, the city, the corporation, the central state, and the empire), and the conduit of the Good and True looks and sounds like Walter Cronkite, with a Founding Father's visage and a Council on Foreign Relations wise man's delivery, with an infallible wet willy held to the shifting winds of Washington and Wall Street – thus to produce a perfect facsimile of firm, responsible, sound judgement.

In an earlier time this might have been the recipe for a perfect Supreme Court judge, but our real judges now hold forth on the electronic box. Walter Cronkite – who used to be deemed 'the most trusted man in America' – was a perfected image, and television is a technology for producing an image, thence a moving image. But remember this: every assemblage of television images into a program is a deeply subjective, contrived, manipulated human effort, resting on a template of more or less hidden, more or less self-conscious assumptions that are inescapably biased. That is our unshakeable position, our 'point of view.'

Albert Wasserman, a producer of CBS's *60 Minutes* with many fine documentaries to his credit (*Out of Darkness*, *The Daisy Chain*), takes the opposite view of television, that is, the consensual view: television must be balanced; if it is not, it is biased. But what is 'balance,' and who decides? 'It is not appropriate for a television network to take a partisan position,' Wasserman says predictably,[69] but as he elaborates the nuances get interesting:

> A television documentary cannot seem to be saying to the audience, this is the way I feel and I want you to feel the same way. A television documentary must seem to be much more dispassionate.

At *60 Minutes* there must not be 'one persistent point of view,' but 'each story stands on its own.' If there is a point of view, Wasserman thinks, that must emerge

> from the characters in the story, the facts that are presented, and the objective research that has gone into the story . . . .

The point of view should emerge *from the story* (the counterpart of the historians' injunction to 'let the facts speak for themselves'). A bit later Wasserman remarks, 'the film maker should be behind the scenes, rather than up front.'

Now, read in one way, Wasserman has something profound to say: we humans do know when we are being sold a bill of goods, and it makes our skin crawl. I also agree with Wasserman that the effective filmmaker (or historian) 'should be behind the scenes,' letting 'the thrust of the story . . . emerge from the substance of the film.' But whence comes the substance? Wasserman is talking about techniques of effectiveness, not substance.

We can grasp what Wasserman means by 'substance' if we strip the above quotations to their key words (soundbites): 'point of view must emerge from . . . facts . . . objective research . . . .' In other words substance = Jack Webb's method, the historian's fiction, scientism's crutch: 'the facts.' But Wasserman is a bit more than an empiricist, as we see in this stripping:

> A television documentary cannot seem . . . the way I feel . . . you . . . feel.
> . . . A television documentary must seem . . . dispassionate.

Note the emphasis on *semblance*: the documentary cannot *seem* to be saying something, must *seem* to be dispassionate. This is the emotivism of 'feelings' (about which we must be dispassionate because facts and science are silent) and the simulation of television: it is all about what the documentary 'seems' to say, that is, inadvertently Wasserman leaves substance for the subjective terrain of impressions.

Mr Wasserman has not given us a television producer's sophomoric notion of 'the facts.' He has given us a virtual paraphrase of the established historian's position. Listen to Donald Watt, from an article on 'the problems the historian faces with the media in making of historical films.'[70] The historian's criteria for judging such films include a test of objectivity 'within the acceptable definition of that term as understood by professional historians,' to wit:

> There must be no recognizable and obvious bias. It must seem to understand rather than to condemn . . . the events described, the 'facts' outlined, must

be accurate, that is, in accordance with the present state of historical knowledge.

Stripping Professor Watt, we also find semblance:

> no recognizable and obvious bias . . . seem to understand . . . the 'facts' . . . must be accurate . . . .

The pretense of objectivity demands a semblance of impartiality, which leads television broadcasting 'into the impasse of a false symmetry': every controversy is presumed to have two sides, usually somehow identified as liberal and conservative, and each must be given equal time.[71] Here two things happen: the bipartisan consensual limits of our politics are reproduced as a matter of television principle, and a formal but fictive balance is represented. A consumer advocate is equated to a corporate executive, the heavily self- and state-censored remarks of a Pentagon strategist are balanced with those of an underpaid academic; the television host mediates between them, seeking 'equal time' and a point of compromise – again, as the objective balancer appearing to lack a point of view.

Emile de Antonio suggests virtually the opposite of this principle: that the point is to be self-conscious about one's prejudice. 'I happen to have strong feelings and some dreams and my prejudice is under and in everything I do.'[72] Prejudice – a template of preference – is under and in everything television does, too.

The late and deeply missed de Antonio was for my money the most interesting American maker of documentaries. He made films with no narration because he hated didactic voice-overs, relying instead on (Wasserman's) 'behind the scenes' techniques, which de Antonio used to virtuoso effect:

> I wanted the feature line to be organically contained, unified, without any external noise, without any narration explaining anything. I wanted the thing to be self-explanatory political statement.

Strip out the word 'political' here, and you have Wasserman's point. In short, de Antonio was more honest than Wasserman.

The infuriating genius of our liberal politics is to make de Antonio look like the biased manipulator, and Wasserman seem to be the soul of even-handed judgement. Why infuriating? Because of the pose of objectivity, the conceit which plays to simple empiricist notions of a world that exists somewhere out there, in pristine form, waiting for the equally pristine observer to recount its truths for us.

De Antonio, furthermore, made documentaries: the legitimator and *point d'honneur* of the television profession. We will now examine that particular form, which makes the most powerful claim to be 'the facts' of the 'moving picture' domain.

CHAPTER TWO

DOCUMENTARY AND

DOCUDRAMA

Documentary: Designating or of a motion picture, television
program, etc., that dramatically shows or analyzes news events,
social conditions, etc., with *little or no* fictionalization
[emphasis added].
Webster's New World Dictionary

There was no narration. It was my film.
EMILE DE ANTONIO[73]

Why does my television flipper scan the thirty-nine channels and come to rest on World War II and holocaust documentaries? I don't have an answer. It is a combination of many things: fascination with a global cataclysm in which the enemies were commensurable, and grouped themselves according to clearcut categories of good and evil, and with a shameful and perhaps (for once) *not* human-all-too-human horror.[74] Another reason is a desire for uncovering, for excavation, that has deeply to do with a modernity in which both our selves and our society mask a duality of public and private that is not explained by liberal doctrine, and in which our public face is interrogated by a very different private soul.

Another reason, however, has to do with the camera's eye: this did happen. At any point before the invention of the camera and after the last victim had died off, the memory of the holocaust would have depended on oral tradition, the written word, the historian, and the artist – all unreliable. But the camera and, even more so, the moving picture document this carnage with the indelibility of the evaporated human shadows on the bridges and buildings in Hiroshima. The soul of the victim is engraved on a collective and undying memory. And since this is so, holocaust documentaries provide the occasion for reflection on how truly horrifying and precarious the twentieth century has been. Let's have a look at the old, low-tech forerunner of television, the camera, from which derives the presumption of the unmediated reality of the documentary form.

CYCLOPS, THE UNBIASED

What makes us think the television image is real, and, more than that, a technology of unbiased truth, CNN's window to the world? Television's illusory transparency and objectivity derive from the same roots as the camera – from Allen Funt's *Candid Camera* to the minicams jammed into the nosecone of a Tomahawk missile. The lore of photography offers up this aphorism: 'the camera never lies.' This is a semiotic falsehood, of course. A moment's reflection and you know that cameras can lie.

Let me take my examples from two of the most obscure books published in 1989. Dae-sook Suh, a leading scholar of Korean communism, produced a picture in his biography of Kim Il Sung that shows a bunch of Korean communists marching in Manchuria in the late 1940s, trailing along behind hoisted placards with pictures of Marx, Engels, Lenin, and Stalin (the sort of serial photography communist regimes love, and that led Western reporters to dub the sequence 'the history of shaving'). Left off for some reason was the last placard, bearing the visage of Kim Il Sung. I knew this because I had the same picture, but hardly anyone else has ever seen it.[75] Or take a new book on the Soviet occupation of North Korea in the late 1940s. On its inside cover is a photo of a bunch of unfortunate Korean miscreants, sitting on their haunches, lassoed together with rope, and ready to be shipped to some dungeon. The reader will naturally think these are good democrats on their way to the North Korean version of Siberia. Actually they are rebels against the South Korean system trussed up for shipment to the dungeon or to their death, as photographed by Henry Luce's *Life Magazine* in 1948.[76]

So we have a cropped picture, and a photo ripped from context. In the latter case the cover designers had a habit of not crediting photos, so the reader was not informed that this was a picture from the Luce file on South Korea's past, not North Korea's. The connotation thus can only come from habituated ideology: behold, victims of communism.

Yet these are easy cases. The deeper problem is that every photograph is ripped from its context, just as every photograph is cropped by the author, when peering through the lens. It registers only what the camera can see. Every photograph is a mobilization of bias. It records what the photographer wishes to record, in the ahistorical moment of a flash-frozen 'present.'

This was apparent at the inception of the technology, when the pioneers of photography constituted themselves as 'cameras,' in camera-obscura rooms,[77] lined with black paper and only a hole through which to observe the passing world. De Antonioni underlined the resulting tunnel vision masterfully in the final scene of *The Passenger*: a victim peers through the open door of his hotel room into a courtyard, where his imagined murderers are strangers moving to and fro, into and out of his purview – until the murder itself occurs, the murderer's anonymity prefigured in the camera-obscura of the victim's imagination.

It was Marx, however, who brilliantly remarked that the optic of an entire class may be this way: 'in all ideology men and their circumstances appear upside-down as in a *camera-obscura*.'[78] The bourgeoisie views the rest of the world upside-down, assuming its narrow vision opens out to the universal aspiration of everyman. American television suffers from the same inversion. Just as photography is a 'middle-brow art' with conventions corresponding roughly to social class,[79] so the incessant connotation of TV is anchored in the lifestyle of the middle class, as if everyone on earth aspired to the same things as Sam Donaldson or Diane Sawyer – the latter deemed by a TV producer to be 'as gorgeous and glamorous as a female news anchor can be *and still be credible* [emphasis added].'[80]

The camera lies because human beings lie. It is unreliable in the same measure as General Sir Anthony Farrar-Hockley's epistemology. What is this? Well, Sir Anthony was my main counterpart at Thames Television, 'principal military consultant' by title, and when the going got rough in the Thames seminars he would fix me with his formidable gaze and announce, 'My deah boy, I don't care *what* your documents say, I was *theah*!' Indeed he was, and an authentic war hero to boot – while I was a second-grader putting together plastic models of Sabre jets and Mig-15s, or reading comic books about howling, savage North Koreans.

It is the historian's pedantic duty to point out, however, that Gibbon wasn't in Rome, either, and that a run of declassified documents from the time is far better than Sir Anthony's optic, vetted through the mists of four decades of memory, not to mention the ideology of a confirmed Thatcherite.[81] Like the photographer, our good General was just looking through a peephole of his own, the lens of his eye, which could survey only so much, and even that was surveyed as a belligerent. All cameras are camera-obscura, and the human lens is the most obscure of all. All memory is memory-obscura, and the older the memory, the more precarious the result. Even recollections of traumatic, burned-into-the-brain events turn out to be faulty.[82] Most people, of course, have the tendency to believe the General, not the upstart scholar.

Yet the optic of history only deepens the problem of objectivity, since the 'declassified documents' I beat Sir Anthony over the head with are also mere fragments of a complex scene, and Sir Anthony's problems of memory and ideology are shared by all historians. The historian's conceit is to write about documentaries and films as if only the scholar possesses the truth and the full measure of objectivity, against which the moving picture medium (and, it goes without saying, television) must eternally be damned for inaccuracy or bias.

Thus Bernardo Bertolucci's magnificent film *The Last Emperor* (which somehow found a mass audience in America, to the astonishment of many) has been pilloried in one review after another for getting the facts of Emperor P'u Yi's life wrong. My position is this: give every historian a dose of what Bernardo has been taking, and maybe then they will muster something of his flair for politics in the grand style, the pageantry of history, the panorama of the human condition. Of course, none of the historian-critics understood that, for Bertolucci, P'u Yi was a camera with his eye trained on a half-century of Chinese history. He putters around in the Forbidden City and Roaring-Twenties Tientsin, plays Manchukuo Marionette, gets taken to Russia, comes back to 'thought reform' in a Chinese prison camp, and finally putters around his home garden – and it is only he who has not changed. From his Manchu knickers to his drab Mao suit, he is just a passive register of the world swirling around him.

The photograph may lie, but it is better than the General's misty eye, and often the historian's, because it has the quality of a fossil: subject to interpretation and all that, true, but some fossils exist and others do not. The photo makes undeniable one's presence at a historical moment: you can find Farrar-Hockley 'theah' in Korea in 1951, but you can't find me. Like a good declassified document, it is evidence difficult to impeach.[83] The transformation of our perceptions by the photo was nicely captured by Carlo Rim:

> The advent of modern times dates from the moment the first daguerreotype appeared on the scene. The camera lens, capturing the appearances of fleeting instants, has marked out the past with a succession of presents. The day photography was born humanity won a precious victory over time, its most redoubtable enemy . . . was this not a way of stopping time, a little at least, in its dread course?[84]

But this was also a transformation of history. Why? The great empiricist historian Leopold von Ranke also had a conception of the 'innocent eye,' the eye of the historian, and it is Rankean history that still holds sway as proper method in the doing of academic history. Ranke was misinterpreted by American historians, who did not understand that his empiricism commingled with a German romantic and Nietzschean subjectivity. But the misreading was in consistently and predictably positivist ways, making them 'more Rankean than Ranke.'[85] Rankean disciples assumed that the historian could be trained to the objective standard of a camera lens, achieving results identical to the popular notion of the innocent eye of the camera: the historian's 'eye' is merely there to record 'the facts'; he then somehow performs the linguistic magician's trick of letting them 'speak for themselves.'

Benjamin articulated a much different, indeed a postmodern, conception of photography as metaphor for history, and vice-versa. 'The true picture of the past flits by,' he wrote,

> The past can be seized only as an image which flashes up at the instant when it can be recognized and is never seen again.
> Every image of the past that is not recognized by the present as one of its own concerns threatens to disappear irretrievably. (The good tidings which

the historian of the past brings with throbbing heart may be lost in a void the very moment he opens his mouth.)

Here Benjamin joins the photo and the image with the doing of history – the passage is about history, not about photography or reproduction:

> To articulate the past historically does not mean to recognize it 'the way it really was' (Ranke). It means to seize hold of a memory as it flashes up at a moment of danger.[86]

Or we might put it this way: history is picture is memory is history is picture is memory, but only the picture objectively holds history still – a slice of life, a flitting moment, yes, but *this happened*. Now what happens when we seize hold of this reproduced memory, flashing before our very eyes? What do we do with a photograph? We interpret it, because it cannot 'speak for itself.'

Everyone's first question about the Korean War is 'who started it?' There is no known photo, let alone a film, of the start of the Korean War. Thames Television substituted instead footage of some sort of artillery going off somewhere (without labeling this a simulation). But it is possible to find all kinds of photos of the war, to find them in vast multitude, virtually for free, in the US National Archives. The American empire documents itself in multimedia variety, and our taxes pay to house the records of our empire (not to mention paying for the empire).

American units occupied Korea with film and still cameramen on hand, courtesy of the Signal Corps, so that posterity can appreciate Cardinal Francis Spellman with Gen. John Reed Hodge on the bridge of the command ship *Catoctin* as it deployed off of Inch'ôn harbor before our occupation forces disembarked on 8 September 1945; we can observe the silent streets of Seoul as American troops marched in later that day, silent because Japanese mounted police kept them silent. We can find both documentary footage and photos of the National Police collaring protesters, Korean women guerrillas on the march, Syngman Rhee with his odd Austrian wife Francesca, General William F. Dean giving a medal to some rotund Korean official for bringing in a good rice collection, and so on.

I had studied early postwar Korea for fifteen years before discovering that Cardinal Spellman landed with American troops in 1945. I still don't know what he was doing there, how he got on the ship, what he did when he landed (if he landed), and when he left. But many other pictures I turned up in pristine, unused quality in a wonderful room given over to photographic archaeology in the National Archives, or that Jon Halliday found in his wide searches, were revelatory, and undeniable at some level: Spellman was 'theah,' he was on the *Catoctin*. Women guerrillas did exist. Syngman Rhee's wife did look like Pearl Buck. Kim Il Sung was the only clean-shaven communist leader among the placards (although I had to tell you that). Pursuing our Cartesian-rational standpoint, Halliday and I produced a book of such photographs, to accompany the documentary and interpret in yet another medium 'the unknown war.'[87]

The Signal Corps films and photographs appear to be the perfect representation of the reality of early postwar Korea not just because most had never been used or 'seen,' and existed pristine in the archives when we found them, as if they were developed a few days before. More than that, they are the record of the victors, yet they occupy the same status as Barthes' press photographs, which appear to be a 'mechanical analogue of reality,' 'a message without a code,' sufficient in themselves to reproduce 'the facts.' The essential idea in fulfilling the canons of neutrality and objectivity, Barthes wrote, is when one 'strives to copy reality meticulously,' as if the historian were . . . a camera (Ranke again). Or a hand-held xerox machine (television again). Of course, Barthes hastened to add, all photos are interpreted, connoted; indeed, the fascination of photos is how this neutral, camera-never-lies medium nonetheless finds an anchoring in historically conditioned 'second meanings,' otherwise known as ideology.[88]

The US Signal Corps was both interested in recording the American occupation (or later the Korean War), and doing so in a favorable light. Thus the many films and photos of disorder, rebellion, guerrillas, and the like in the archival files exist *in spite of* the intended connotation, their very unmediated and undeniable 'reality' contradicts the a priori, so that we intuit the photographer's dilemma: I am here to record the American Occupation. Why am I always recording resistance?

And so the photos must be stamped with the Occupation's 'second meaning' imposed on them, on the back-side of the photo. The photographer snapped the picture, and then some bureaucrat back at the office parasitically imposed a ubiquitous category: communists did this, communists did that. Or, if it is unconnoted communist photography or film that we got hold of, the Army enjoyed adding the subtitle 'unverified communist footage.' (In other words resistance to the Occupation is either the 'verified' or the 'unverified' variety of 'communism.')

The back-side connotations themselves have a curious, innocent-bystander quality – as if the photographer recorded not an Occupation or a war in which Americans were dominant, but events captured by someone who just happened to be there. We see an avuncular, smiling Syngman Rhee, whose position in Korea was deeply dependent on American support, indeed he was deposited back in Korea through an American intelligence operation, and on the back he is described as Korea's 'leading rightist politician.' If a journalist were to say the same thing – 'the key American-sponsored politician is also Korea's leading rightwinger' – this would appear not as fact, but as bias.

The photo, as Barthes and others have noted, has a here-and-now reality in itself, representing the 'it was,' the 'this happened'; it resurrects the past for contemporary contemplation. Thus the Signal Corps photos resist their original anchoring, and still possess their own energy. Somehow an unintended reality lies dormant in a photographic archive, ever ready to subvert the official text of the Occupation and the Korean War, just by its public revelation.

The resurrected photograph requisitions its own connotation, and thus elicits a retrospective interpretation. The photos are of the past, yet they challenge the future – as time passes the same photos will experience encoding and recoding: the 'text' of the photograph 'produces (invents) an entirely new signified which is retroactively projected into the image.'[89]

The best example of this phenomenon is the war's most famous snapshot: John Foster Dulles in a bunker at the 38th parallel a week before the war, his chiseled Calvinist visage eyeballing Kim Il Sung through grandmotherly rimless glasses from under his ever-present homburg hat. (See Plate 1.) The North Koreans have never tired of reproducing this photo to prove that the US provoked the war, or of reproducing the line, 'what do you think Dulles was doing at the parallel – wasn't picking daisies, was he?' The picture is theatrical – Dulles's funereal garb, his riveted expression, the simultaneously obsequious and sinister smile on the face of South Korean Foreign Minister Ben Limb, behind Dulles in the porkpie hat; the diminutive, even tiny Defense Minister Shin Sung Mo in the pith helmet, attending to Dulles. It all appears to have been staged. Indeed, it is as if Kim Il Sung were the director and producer.

This Cold War artifact was another Signal Corps snapshot with an innocuous caption/connotation on the back, as if Dulles were one of the many dignitaries who frequented the 38th parallel (which he was). Apparently the North Koreans captured a copy when they occupied Seoul, or got it from a later Associated Press (AP) release. The men in the photo know nothing about what came a week later. Yet the North Koreans' retroactive connotation did stick some doubt in people's minds – for example, diplomatic historian Herbert Feis. After the war he said to Acheson, 'Are you sure his presence didn't provoke the attack Dean? There has been comment about that – I don't think it did. You have no views on the subject?' (Acheson's deadpan response: 'No, I have no views on the subject.') George Kennan then interjected, 'There is a comical aspect to this, because the visits of these people over there, and their peering over outposts with binoculars at the Soviet people, I think must have led the Soviets to think that we were on to their plan and caused them considerable perturbation.' 'Yes,' Acheson then remarked, 'Foster up in a bunker with a homburg on – it was a very amusing picture.'[90]

A snapshot becomes retroactive proof for P'yôngyang, and the butt of yet more jokes about Foster among the 'wise men.' Both are *historical*: the epistemology of Kim Il Sung's allegation or Acheson's humor has the same source.

The immanent connotative energy of the photograph may be appreciated fully if we imagine a captured snapshot from June 19, 1950, of Vlasicheyev Molotov, chiseled Stalinist (or Calvinist, take your pick) visage eyeballing Syngman Rhee through grandmotherly rimless glasses from under his ever-present homburg hat, with North Korean officials flocking around. The United States would then and forevermore have used it as proof of aggressive intent, and Stalin and *his* 'wise men' (secret police chief Lavrenty Beria, others) would have sat in the Kremlin chortling about old sit-him-on-a-block-of-ice-and-he-won't-move-unless-I-tell-him-to Molotov.

Another Signal Corps photograph shows two black American soldiers with their North Korean captive. (See Plate 2.) The subtitle might be 'bird in a cage.' But why not birds in a cage? The drooping eyelid of one of the black soldiers may have been an accident of the shutter, but it remains as a mark of the man's oppression or, to racists, a suggestion that he is feeble-minded. Immediately we are reminded of the social condition of American blacks in the 1950s. And anyone but an American of the 1950s would see in this photo no difference from France's African soldiers in Vietnam, Joseph Savimbi's black guerrillas working with South Africa, or England's ubiquitous imperial gendarmes, the Ghurkas.

One Signal Corps photo shows two somewhat elderly, forlorn, white-raiment-clad 'guerrillas' captured on Cheju Island during the terrible repression there in 1948–49 (10 per cent of the island population died, most at the hands of Syngman Rhee's suppression forces). The men are probably village elders, from one of the many towns that were thoroughly anti-government. They have the static, 'it was' quality of the snapshot; we can ruminate on them, but we sense that 'these people are history,' as the television pundits like to say.

Then, however, in hour one of our documentary, we see film of the same two men, moving into a police station. The Signal Corps had photographers and film cameramen working together; now we can appreciate the apparently unmediated, objective quality of the documentary form, not just the photograph, and the difference between the two. Suddenly the scene springs to life; it is not the 'it was' so much as the 'You Are There' (the title of a 1950s show combining film with manufactured docudrama). The men become kinetic reality, but they do not walk into the station, so much as lurch, shamble, creak into it – as if they had been tortured, or even emasculated (a not uncommon torture in early postwar Korea).

The Signal Corps photo/film teams enable us to grasp the paradox of the still shot within a film, the arrested action which takes us out of the flow of the moving picture and gives us time to think. Barthes was very much intrigued by this paradox, although what he says about it strikes me as wrong.[91] The still, he says, offers us 'the *inside* of the [film] fragment,' not as a sample but as a quotation, 'at once parodic and disseminatory.'

It is true, of course, that the photo of the two elders-cum-guerrillas illustrates and abstracts from the text of the film, much as a quotation. But the more important point, it seems to me, is that the still fragment has all the qualities of the photograph, except that we also know the filmic flow from which it is drawn. The still gives us arrested motion, and thus the same opportunity for aesthetic contemplation of a photo or, for that matter, a painting; yet we know we can return to the very different aesthetics of the flow.

The arrested motion of the still enables an interrogation of the scene apart from an editor, except for the editing of the photographer (who in any case is the cameraman and not the editor). The still freezes a moment in the flow of experience and holds it there for thought, in a kind of rigor mortis with which Heidegger identifies all historical thinking, deeply imbricated with the naming of things, with connotations that freeze our thought in what we call memory.[92]

One of our pictures is an AP shot titled 'It's roundup time in Korea.' (See Plate 3.) Taken in North Korea during MacArthur's march to the Yalu, it has within it a connotative energy resisting the usual notions of what this war was about. The communist, lassoed like an Indian in the old West (thus the AP title) and wearing the tattered peasant raiment which Americans called 'white pajamas,' is extraordinarily handsome and strong, almost 'Western' in his good looks, and very much like the male poster iconography of North Korea (also inadvertently 'Western'). There is fear in his eyes (as well there might be), but a compelling fear like that cultivated by Hollywood heroes, hinting at an imminent reversal. We almost expect him to throw off the lasso and trounce his captors singlehandedly.

The captors, on the other hand, have a movie-heavy quality. Dressed impeccably in American-style uniforms, mounted on horseback, they seem to be enjoying their work a bit too much, gloating at the sudden reversal in Korean fortunes accomplished by the Americans. It is not hard to imagine what they have in store for their captured 'Indian,' who is in fact their native brother. He evokes our sympathy, but they do not evoke our admiration for their just-won victory. Instead, as Proust once put it, such a photo can be 'doubly striking, because it surprises us, takes us out of our cocoon of habit, and at the same time brings us back to ourselves by recalling to us an earlier impression.'[93]

Elsewhere in our book Halliday and I have a photograph of a South Korean spy, dressed up in a North Korean uniform just before being airlifted behind the lines in an attempt to set anti-communist guerrillas in motion. In contrast to the lassoed communist, he looks like the American (or South Korean) image of the communist: diminutive, furtive, scheming, homely, no threat to anyone in his apparent impotence if not ridiculousness – unless lifted from the deviant ranks and set in motion by Soviet masterminds. When the book was published in South Korea we received a letter from this very man, happy to be memorialized and anxious to reestablish contact with his boss, Ellery Anderson – who told us in interviews how useless the South Korean guerrillas had been.

A few of our photographs came from Chris Marker's classic book, *Coréenes*.[94] An avant-garde filmmaker and brilliant photographer, Marker got into North Korea shortly after the war ended and produced a countertext that subverts the Cold War image of this devastated country. Focusing on daily life and frequently on women, he presents to us stoic and uncommonly handsome people, somehow thriving in the midst of an awful destruction. (See Plate 4.) Some are proletarian, like the men and women dancing to accordions in a public park, but some are rakish and arresting, like a man with a porkpie hat (the South Korean foreign minister's?) observing reconstruction work with an insouciant air. The women carry hods, drive trucks, and make steel, but also dote on their babies or cast subtly inquisitive glances toward the camera; one has her baby tied to her back with timeworn blankets and wraps, while peering intently at a poster announcing the success of the Soviet Sputnik, and thus the forward march of the socialist world.

Marker's photos are an indelible tribute to the humanity of the enemy, allowing us to pause and drink in the devastation we wrought and the incredible powers of resilience of ordinary people. Perhaps for that reason his book is unknown in the United States.

The abstraction of the still, then, opens a new window on history, a new interaction with history. The immediacy and flow of the motion picture succeeds when it carries us with it, toward some meaning which is inextricable from the sequence of the flow, but which also distorts the meaning of the individual frame (the basis of the still): the still, however, distorts the meaning of the editor (who is the historian of filmic evidence). Standing by itself, the still provokes thought.

Stanley Kubrick uses a dialectic between film and stills to brilliant effect in *The Shining*, where the demented caretakers of a summer resort appear in the present tense of the moving picture and the past tense of the still, thus mixing up chronology, reversing history, and finally driving the protagonist, a writer played by Jack Nicholson, to distraction when he discovers himself in a resort snapshot from the 1920s. Somewhat like Hitchcock's still shot of Cary Grant holding a knife sticking out of a man's body in *North By Northwest*, Kubrick mixes the flow of film with the indeterminate but importunate connotation of the photo. (Who would believe from the photo that Nicholson was not there? Who would believe that Grant did not stab the dead man?)

The arrested motion of the still elicits our cognition much more directly than the flow of the film. But the daunting aspect of contemporary television is that there can be no stills extruded from it, apart from grainy, indistinct pictures (i.e. using photography to represent television). Indeed, Fredric Jameson finds this to be television's essential difference: the technology of 'fragments in flight' is a physics locking the viewer into television's conception of time. There are no real separable elements or individual units making it up like the frame of a movie still, but just the $\frac{1}{30}$ second electron-scanning beam, and Williams's unending, seemingly authorless flow.[95] I think that paradox will come to an end, however, as high-definition and digital methods overcome the old scanning technology and establish television's affinity with the still and the moving picture; what will remain, of course, is the infernal soundbite, the jarring juxtapositions, and commercial TV's analogous practice of destroying narrative with advertising.

What the photo lacks in mobility and kinetics compared to the film, it gains in time, in the dilating pupil of the mind as it contemplates a photo — whereas for film and television there is 'no time,' no pause allowing the imagination to be engaged as it is by the photographic image, such that thought is provoked. There are about twenty pictures in the book I co-authored with Halliday that no one can contemplate without saying to themself, Well, this war was a nightmare, this war was different from how it has been represented in the West. As Benjamin put it,

The painter maintains in his work a natural distance from reality, the cameraman penetrates deeply into its web. There is a tremendous difference between the pictures they obtain. That of the painter is a total one, that of the cameraman consists of multiple fragments which are assembled under a new law.[96]

Halliday and I assembled our pictures under the law that the Korean War was not forgotten, so much as unknown; when illumined it becomes for the people who experienced it perhaps the most terrible war of the twentieth century.

A photo can give you tricks of perception – for example, throughout the summer of 1989 I thought the 'Batman' logo was four teeth in a laughing mouth rather than a flying bat, until I 'thought about it.' But film can do that without you knowing it, and sustain it from start to finish, and give you no time to 'think about it.'

The still photo allows a dilation, an exercise of the imagination, but it rarely suggests omniscience; its virtue is to capture a slice of time and place that is still only, and obviously, a slice. The 'moving picture' camera, however, creates the illusion of omnipresence and omniscience, bringing life to life, as it were. Theoretically it can be everywhere (like a spy satellite); presumably it also 'never lies'; presumably it directly mediates its environment (and most effectively when it is hidden, as if it were there but not there – the camera as voyeur, the Allen Funt *Candid Camera* method). Here Emerson's all-seeing eye seems to have its technical equivalent.

So, it is not just television, but the moving camera that suspends thought and obscures authorship: as Duhamel put it as early as 1930, 'already I can no longer think what I like. Moving images substitute themselves for my own thoughts.'

The kinetic maneuvers leave no time for thought, we are carried along on someone else's flow. Nor is TV's powerful role in projecting American culture as the standard for everybody anything new: Paul Virilio reports that, for his wife, what was most unbearable about the Nazi occupation of France was 'the feeling of being cut off' from Hollywood movies,[97] and therefore, one assumes, from the world of what's-happening-now. The unnoticed insensitivity of this remark (I suffered: the Nazis wouldn't let me see Hollywood) makes it all the more interesting. Still, the film camera is merely a technologically adept eye, a kinetic aperture, always in a 'war of movement' with its subject.

'Documentary television' is a form summing up much of our preceding discussion. It combines the photo, the moving picture and television, giving us the 'it was' and the 'you are there' in the preferred mode of 'objective programming.' Documentaries are to television what sources are to the historian, what evidence is to the scientist, what revelation is to the theologian. It is the legitimator of the television form, its *point d'honneur*, its exemplary medium. And this explains all the fulminations about the corrupted version of this form, the 'docudrama.'

Documentary television presents the same problems of evidence and objectivity found in writing a book, but it fools the viewer because it seems like 'an open book,' or as a book does to one who has never written and rarely read one: as a miracle, beyond criticism. The artifice behind it is well hidden, and the moving camera seems to record with such fidelity to fact. Yet filmmakers found out within a decade of its invention that film was more subject to manipulation and illusion, even falsification, than to 'never lying.'[98] The possibility of 'docudrama' was there from the beginning.

Still, the subjectivity of this medium is overwhelming. If the photograph records that 'this happened,' the documentary film records that 'this happened and I saw it happen.' Thus it was that I grasped the enormity of the holocaust in the ninth grade, flipping channels one day until suddenly caught up short by scenes of a bulldozer shoveling lifeless human bodies into open pits, the driver's mouth covered with a handkerchief against the stench. The scenes were indelible enough to engrave themselves instantly and forevermore on the screen of the mind's eye . . . and to call forth the shame that holocaust survivors so often speak of, the shame of seeing and knowing that this happened, that human beings (victim and victimizer) had been reduced to this.

Now it so happens that my wife teaches at a fine university which holds within its ivy walls a professor who says the holocaust was all a hoax. True, the cameras recorded a mere few thousand bulldozed corpses, not the millions who were burned. But those few thousand were enough for me never to trust a German more than fifteen years my senior, just as the roped-together living corpses in Bert Hardy's Korean War photography (banned in Britain during the war) are enough to convince anyone of the

Rhee regime's squalor.[99] That is the power of the camera-document, which when combined with the flow of television can be overwhelming.

RADICAL JUXTAPOSITIONS

In *Annie Hall*, Woody Allen plays a character who does little else besides watch Marcel Ophuls's documentary *The Sorrow and the Pity*. The attraction of this film goes beyond its tonic effect on holocaust masochists (although Ophuls has plenty for them). It illustrates in a liberal film the radical potential of thoughtful juxtapositions, and in so doing provides a terrific lesson in history.

Courtroom or public dramas often take the form of eyewitness testimony or remembered event, balanced against a document from the earlier time. We saw this throughout the televised hearings of Watergate and Irangate: recall versus 'the facts,' and when the facts prove uncomfortable, sudden lapses in memory. Richard Nixon's inexplicable failure to burn his Presidential tapes occasioned a long-running soap opera, in which the President's vast dissembling skills were tested against his own memory, John Dean's formidable recall, and finally the tapes. The tapes won, and sent King Richard winging off to nurse his neuroses in San Clemente rather than the Oval Office.

Ronald Reagan posed a different problem in Irangate: was he a master dissembler, or (unlike Nixon) did he actually believe his untruths? Was he trying to hide what welled up in his memory, or was there no memory?

> 'Try as I might, I cannot recall anything whatsoever about whether I approved an Israeli sale [of arms to Iran] . . . . My answer, therefore, and the simple truth is, I don't remember. Period.'[100]

Nixon succumbed before irrefutable evidence, the 'smoking gun' tape which documented his leading role in a coverup. But Reagan did not go under when nearly everyone grasped that Oliver North and John Poindexter would not put pen to a document, let alone shred one, without explicit Presidential authority. The irrefutable evidence of Reagan's involvement in illegally shipping weaponry to the Nicaraguan 'Contras' dissolved not because it was untrue, but because it called to account a man who slept through much of his Presidency. We might call this 'the narcoleptic defense,' and place it with other high moments in American law, like the 'Twinkie defense.'[101]

The historian contemplates the juxtaposition of remembered event against documentary evidence in every aspect of his work, and rightly comes to prefer the document from the past to contemporary memory. Rarely, however, is the historian able to confront a participant with the record of his actions. The documentary form has the potential to bring this confrontation to life by pitting past against present, memory against reality, all with the immediacy and impact of moving pictures. This is what Ophuls does in *The Sorrow and the Pity*, and it is what Thames Television should have done and failed to do with the more recent experience of the Korean War.

The film offers a radical perspective not in its implicit politics (although of course we know that Ophuls doesn't like collaborators with the Nazis – and who does, by the way?), but in the confrontation between events that 'did happen' (not necessarily 'the facts' or 'the truth,' but events that archival film documents to have happened) and the participant's historical construction: first, an elision (the interviewee fails to mention participation in carting away Jews, for example), then the old film, next the chagrined retraction, and finally the explanation – with Ophuls's camera lens mercilessly closed up to catch the emotion of the sequence. The camera's 'eye' is not transparent. It cold-bloodedly skewers the liars, and bathes the person of integrity in a warm aura, like a halo.

A hairdresser named Madame Solange, her face severe, her mouth pinched, recalls her ordeal of punishment in 1944 as a collaborator – immediately distinguishing herself, to be sure, from the worst such people, who 'went out with German men' and after Liberation had their heads shaved, or were paraded naked through the streets. Someone unfairly denounced her, that was all, and she spent a month in jail; shortly she was called out and tortured to make her confess to crimes of which she was not guilty. She was a backer of Pétain, of course, but then not really: 'I wasn't political.'

Then comes the document: it develops that she denounced a friend to the

Gestapo, according to a letter in her own handwriting that was introduced in court. The camera closes in on her face, whereupon she claims that an enemy copied her handwriting. (That is, the document doesn't count.) Later she admits to getting a fifteen-year sentence, and that her 'enemy' was a resistance fighter: 'I was for the Marshall [Pétain] and they were on the other side. That's all, I think.'[102] That's all: just the collaborators against the resistance, nothing more.

The camera is the facilitator for Pierre Mendès-France, by contrast, in coaxing out the story of his heroism, not without humor and affection. The beautiful Maurice Chevalier prided himself in making the camera his accomplice, but Ophuls refuses him this artifice, instead cutting back and forth from his days of service to Vichy to his pathetic, bubbly attempt to cover it up, set to song for his fans:

> Why don't you try to
> Take life the way I do....
> Let it rain, let it snow
> I'll be up on a rainbow,
> Sweeping the clouds away.

This film is a case study in camera bias.

Only one character clearly defeats the method, and he is the most riveting in the film: Christian de la Mazière, a French aristocrat who enlisted in the 'Charlemagne' unit of the *Waffen SS*. Most people find his presence revelatory of the hidden passion which some (many?) French felt for the fascist cause; his very existence undermines layer upon layer of postwar French mythology. Like other interviewees and like Nazis we will meet shortly, he wishes to be objective: 'we really ought to get the facts straight,' he argues, there weren't nearly as many resisters as claimed, and so on. [103]

What was truly interesting, however, was the unrepentant, even insouciant air with which de la Mazière responded to the interviewer's questions. He recalls with aplomb a Parisian cafe society hardly quaking under the German knout: '*Maxim's* was full. *Le Boeuf sur le Toit* was full. The movie industry was in full swing.' And the films were better, too, 'because "a certain kind of producer" had gone into exile in the U.S.'

Would it bother you to say you were then a fascist, the interviewer asks, and we expect a tortured denial. 'No, it wouldn't bother me at all.'[104] Here the present does not reveal a buried 'it was,' so much as bring forth the insistent 'it is'; de la Mazière gives us the past in the present, as if decades had not intervened, and thus places into question the entire French reckoning with Vichy.

Our Thames producers liked the time-lapse method, without the radical juxtaposition or the close-up pressure on the interviewee. Thus they were happy to find in some film from 1950 a cameraman whom we had interviewed, to show him then and now and allow the viewer to measure the passage of time through his face. But their interviewing technique put the interviewer out of the sight and sound later to be projected, and immediately discouraged probing questions that put pressure on the interviewee.

I discovered this when I conducted my first interview for Thames, with Dean Rusk. He would seem to have perfect recall for where he was when he got news that the Korean War had broken out: at Joseph Alsop's house, having dinner. But when I asked him what he was doing at the Plaza Hotel in New York the night before (where according to the Chinese Ambassador's diary entry he was trying to find a civilian regime to replace Chiang Kai-shek, against whom Rusk and others were mounting a coup), his memory went completely blank.

I was encouraged not to pressure Rusk, however. Later Austin Hoyt of WGBH showed up to see that I did not pressure or insult Henry Kissinger; of course Kissinger can take care of himself, and when I cited critical passages about him in work by Seymour Hersh or Roger Morris, his face clouded over as if someone had just called him a war criminal, and he responded with curled-lip contempt. Here the problem was the untoward consequences of discomfiting the powerful, who after all might just walk out and deny us use of the interview.

Peter Davis confronted power effectively in *Hearts and Minds*, when he caught a squirming Walt Rostow on film and had the guts to use the clip. The interviewer asked why we were in Vietnam, and got back this: 'Are you really asking me this goddamn silly question?' – Rostow steamed from ears and nostrils, and demanded that the clip be dropped from the film . . . while on film.

The deeper problems of radical juxtaposition occur with this question: from what point of view do we challenge the interviewee? Ophuls could stand on the correct consensus that French who collaborated with the Nazis and have since hidden their past deserve to be flushed out in the open. What do we do with Korean interviewees parroting a memorized script? How should we handle a discomfited Henry Kissinger? From what standpoint do we challenge Dean Rusk's rendering of the Korean War? The answer, of course, is from an independent position and full knowledge of the issues of the war, neither of which Thames had, and neither of which it really wanted to have, as the producers discovered this 'forgotten' war to be unaccountably controversial.

SHOAH: 'YOU WANT HISTORY – I'M GIVING YOU HISTORY'

Claude Lanzmann's ten-hour film about the holocaust instantly undermines the possibility of doing docudrama about anything truly important. Lanzmann's technique of interviews juxtaposed against the overgrown weeds and sometimes pleasant vistas of contemporary Auschwitz or Birkenau brought history, memory, and morality to life in a completely original way. In so doing, he forced the viewer to imagine what had happened: an imagined history becomes more powerful than history itself, as rendered in books or documentaries. *Shoah* is not photographic fact and it is not a documentary; it is not fiction and it is a documentary. It is both and neither, somehow rising above the usual concerns of fealty to fact and objectivity to give us the experience of history, and truth.

Shoah's epistemology takes a page from postmodern theory, and from the intuitions of good historians: History means the conveying of meaning. It means memory. It means seizing hold of meaning and memory 'as it flashes up at a moment of danger.' It means History has no capital 'h' except at the beginning of a sentence. History is just words and texts, vetted through the imagination of the historian, which is in turn shaped by experience, by 'durable dispositions,' by convention, by the interaction of brain and viscera, by sources, by the language used to convey meaning, and by time.

Time is very important to *Shoah*. By demanding of the viewer ten hours, Lanzmann mocks the soundbites and snatched moments that activate our lives; it is also daunting to realize that a script which takes ten hours to watch can be read in two hours, but with far less impact. More importantly, Lanzmann demonstrates in the first few minutes how time dims not just the fields of Auschwitz and the memories of victims, but the interpretation of the holocaust itself. He does not believe that there was a past that can be retrieved 'just as it was.' There is only that past rendered in the present (for better or worse) by frail human beings, most of them unmindful, indeed blithely unaware, of how their ideas about the past were formed, and how their utterances about the past partake of the same processes by which historians write their books – the interplay of conscious voice and unconscious impulse.

So how then can meaning be conveyed? What is the text and who is the historian in *Shoah*? *The text* is the interview done in the present, often at the present place of past crimes, memory flashing up in a moment, at the point of past danger. The historian is the imagination of the viewer, mediated by an artful Lanzmann, conjuring pictures flashing up in the mind's eye in place of those usually supplied by the documentary form.

Lanzmann also gives the viewer the stuff of history: no empiricist, he still uses empirical detail to its best effect, getting his interlocutors to recapitulate step-by-step how people were transported to the camps, exactly what happened when they arrived, how they were gassed, what was done with the corpses. Here the facts are like photos: they make you say, this happened. It is a kind of arithmetic, which sums to an indelible truth in the imagination. [105]

Lanzmann makes effective use of the typical method of the historian: a primary document from the past, used to recuperate reality. Walter Steir, ex-Nazi, former head of Reich Railways Department 33, tells Lanzmann he was 'strictly a bureaucrat!' and that he did not know about the murder of Jews: 'The extermination. Everyone condemns it. Every decent person. But as for knowing about it, we didn't.' Cut to historian Raul Hilberg, who displays 'Fahrplananordnung 587,' which demonstrates that the Reich Railways people knew all about it. He then says:

When I hold a document in my hand, particularly if it's an original document, then I hold something which is actually something that the original bureaucrat held in his hand. It's an artifact. It's a leftover. It's the only leftover there is. The dead are not around. [106]

In its simplest form, that is the way to make a documentary.

Minus a couple of lapses here and there this is also a Nietzschean film, bereft of intrusive morality. Unlike Ophuls, Lanzmann rarely inserts his views (or himself) between the viewer and the text. The exception would be, perhaps, his delight in showing the anti-Semitism of present-day Polish peasants. Otherwise he recapitulates in fine detail what happened, and leaves the judgement to the viewer's imagination. Lanzmann also lies to get his material, as in the surreptitious taping of the German, Franz Suchomel; it was well worth the breach of conventional morality.

Suchomel is an empiricist, of the loathsome variety. Whereas Lanzmann uses details to peel away the morality that gets in the way of knowing (the horror, the insanity of the holocaust), Suchomel plumbs the details at the expense of the enormity of what the Nazis did, quibbling over numbers rather than summing up a daunting arithmetic. Thus he is concerned to point out that whereas 'the Jews' say there were five ovens on each side at Auschwitz, 'I say there were four' (*Shoah*, p. 61). Oh.

Suchomel, of course, recapitulates in his person the banality that Hannah Arendt found in the good-bureaucrat, accountant-like way that Adolf Eichmann went about his business, and in the standard operating procedures for the holocaust. Thus we find a memorandum from 1942 on the 'processing' of people in carbon-monoxide-driven death vans: 'the vans' normal load is usually nine per square yard . . . loading to full capacity would affect the vehicle's stability,' and so on (*Shoah*, p. 103).

But then Suchomel is also human, all-too-human, and, some would say, German-all-too-German. At one point he apologizes for mispronouncing a name: 'I have false teeth.' With gusto he breaks into a marching song for those forced to work at Treblinka: then he takes a look at Lanzmann's presumably disapproving face and exclaims, 'Don't be sore at me. You want history – I'm giving you history' (*Shoah*, p. 106).

Often those things most important to our lives have *no names*. The bourgeoisie, as we saw, is the class that does not wish to be named. The Japanese bacteriological warfare practitioners referred to the prisoners they performed gruesome experiments on as 'logs.' The enemy in Korea and Vietnam had no name, but sloughed together as gooks or dinks. Jewish laborers at Sobibor remembered that the Germans 'forbade the use of the words "corpse" or "victim." The dead were blocks of wood, shit . . . the bodies [were] *Figuren*,' like puppets or dolls (*Shoah*, p. 13).

The Nazis at the camps specialized in a spurious but reassuring cause-and-effect. When Jews built the ovens at Auschwitz, they wondered what they were for; 'an SS man told me: 'To make charcoal. For laundry irons.' That's what he told me. I didn't know' (*Shoah*, p. 102). Victims believed these and the more well-known Nazi explanations (the showers are for 'delousing') because the alternative was too terrible to contemplate. This is merely a more horrifying lesson in all manner of patriotic and soul-soothing history. ('America tells one story: the unbroken, ineluctable progress of freedom and equality,' wrote Professor Bloom,[107] and never mind that we were among the last nations in the world to give up chattel slavery.)

History also is a Freudian discipline, where attention to the missing or to the badly remembered or to the revealing slip may be more important than the facts themselves. Thus the riveting wife of a Nazi schoolteacher in Poland, Mrs Michelsohn of the curled lip and meticulous presentation, gets Poles mixed up with Jews; when asked what's the difference, she makes it simple: 'The Poles weren't exterminated and the Jews were. That's the difference' (*Shoah*, p. 83). Dr Frank Grassler, deputy to the Nazi commissioner of the Warsaw ghetto, mistakenly substitutes the name of the commissioner (Auerswald) for that of Adam Czerniakow, a courageous resister in the Warsaw ghetto:

> LANZMANN: When was the first deportation to Treblinka?
> GRASSLER: Before Auerswald's suicide, I think.
> LANZMANN: Auerswald's?
> GRASSLER: I mean Czerniakow's. Sorry.
>
> (*Shoah*, p. 187)

Czerniakow had also written that Germans always associated Jews with typhus, Lanzmann told Grassler, eliciting from him this response: 'Maybe. I'm not sure if there were grounds for it' (*Shoah*, p. 180).

We expect: 'of course there were no grounds for it.' Instead in the 1980s we get one or two little things from Grassler to suggest an unreflective if not necessarily unrepentant Nazi, 'concerned about the evidence.' It is a masterful touch.

AMERICAN DIFFERENCE

The documentary form in America has nothing to compare to this; I cannot call up a filmmaker with the historical consciousness of an Ophuls or a Lanzmann. But there is a pragmatic muckraking form that is capable of rendering history through critical distance and inapposite juxtaposition, and which is typically American. In 1990 one such documentary played to surprisingly large audiences (to my amazement). Even more amazing, it was a throwback to the humor, bravado, and populism of the 1960s: this was *Roger and Me* by Michael Moore and his 'Dog Eat Dog Productions.'

Mr Moore, a mildly overweight, usually disheveled, apparently unpromising man in his mid-thirties, with a deadpan delivery as the vehicle for his hilarious script, spent a couple of years chasing after the CEO of General Motors, Roger Smith, and chasing around Moore's hometown (Flint, Michigan), a perfect example of the many small American cities devastated by the multinational march outward of one corporation after another. Mr Moore offers himself and his film as a snug, homey 1990s version of the uncompromising irreverence, populism, and hilarity of 1960s politics, at a time when conditions for the average working stiff are far worse today than they were then.

General Motors so dominated Flint that for decades it had more GM workers per capita than any other city. Smith closed eleven GM plants there in 1986, however, and moved a lot of production to Mexico, where wages were about seventy cents an hour. Flint collapsed with this remove south of the Rio Grande, and now suffers the typical post-industrial symptoms of low wages from fast food joint jobs or no wages at all, eviction from one's home or no home at all, depression, crime, industrial detritus, and degradation.

The reception of this film by one of our best critics, in one of our best magazines, illustrates the pathetic conformism of our contemporary politics. Pauline Kael did not like this documentary. I divide New Yorkers into two categories: those who like Vincent Canby (the *New York Times*) and those who like Pauline Kael (then of *The New Yorker*). Canby's sensibility is utterly reliable and has saved me the price of a movie ticket many times; just his columns alone are worth the price of our paper of record. Kael is florid, catty, self-important, and often unreliable (while still being one of the handful of serious film critics in a field overrun with morons).

The film was 'shallow and facetious, a piece of gonzo demagoguery that made me feel cheap for laughing.'[108] Moore is 'a big, shambling joker in windbreaker and baseball cap' (true); his interview style is designed to make people look like 'phonies or stupes' (false). Phonies there are in this film, beginning with Roger Smith, and stupes as well: indeed it is hard to find a person in the film who appears to have a three-digit IQ, except for a black autoworker who remarks that no one in Flint seems to know how to tell time, that is, they have no idea what has hit them. And there are phonies and stupes in one person – like Bob Ewbanks, the emcee of television's *The Newlywed Game* (a bit of a joker he is, too, although without baseball cap: he makes a pathetic anti-Semitic 'joke' on camera).

Moore puts his mike in front of GM publicity people, who make 'squirmy, evasive statements,' according to Kael. He makes 'brutal fun' of an Amway 'color consultant' who charges people for telling them what colors go best with their skin, and takes his 'final jab'

> at a woman with a Jewish name, whose job promoting the attractions of the city has been eliminated. He asks her what she's going to do next. When she says she's going to Tel Aviv, Moore seems to be drawing the conclusion that the rats are deserting the ship . . . .

Is Mr Moore to be held culpable for this depiction? Perhaps Pauline Kael is above 'watching TV,' but two minutes of *The Newlywed Game* is enough to certify Mr Ewbanks as a phony and an idiot (his show has been on prime time for two decades). Miss Michigan (soon to become Miss America) seems phony, stupid and gutless all at once, as she strives to say something pleasant and acceptable to Mr Moore's camera about deprived and depraved Flint. The rabbit lady may be a bit overdone ('pets or meat' is her slogan, and she dutifully hammers a cuddly 'pet' bunny to death on camera, to get 'meat' for the family dinner), but Moore is due some license, I think, in a film that places humor in service to politics (the two being such a rare combination in America).

Corporate public relations people appear on television all the time, paid handsomely to parrot corporate positions and to ridicule some underpaid or volunteer citizen as misinformed and off base in suggesting that Exxon hasn't cleaned up its oil mess or that Philip Morris cigarettes give you and everyone near you cancer; and in my experience the publicity people are almost always 'squirmy and evasive.' The Amway color consultant may have been reduced to her ridiculous occupation by Flint's disaster, and Mr Moore does have sport with her by getting his pasty face color-coded, but that is what Flint (and America) offer to a proud class of industrial workers: door-to-door sales, slinging hamburgers at McDonald's (which now employs more labor than the steel industry, at one-fourth the hourly wage), or turning up one's roots for the storied opportunities of the Sunbelt.

Moore does have sport with the woman 'with a Jewish name.' The scene where she's about to depart for Tel Aviv is followed immediately by a clip of the Intifada, as masked Palestinian youths fling stones at the Israeli police on the West Bank. This juxtaposition, presumably, is okay for a documentary about Romania or Azerbaijan or South Korea or South Africa, but not if it invokes Israel's hamhanded repression of the rebellion.

Kael hammers Moore at the level of 'the facts': Moore was 'too glib' for Kael, and so she 'stopped believing what Moore was saying very early.' Some scenes were out of sequence, others were distorted; President Reagan didn't come to Flint and tell unemployed autoworkers to go to Texas, 'in fact' Reagan came to Flint when he was but a candidate in 1980. (And? And he wouldn't have said it after the inauguration?)

She concludes by declaring Moore 'almost perverse' to suggest that Roger Smith might be at fault for Flint's plight, the film little more than 'the work of a slick ad exec,' and herself 'humanly' very offended that *Roger and Me* 'uses its leftism as a superior attitude.'

We historians get this style whenever we open a journal of the field. Kael borrowed the complacent historian's recipe for savaging the uncomplacent, in perfect form: use a label ('gonzo'), a genre ('demagoguery'), an *ad hominem* attack ('shambling joker'), trot out the tried-and-true 'not objective!' and follow it with 'contrary to the facts!', and end by declaring yourself deeply offended at such leftist hypocrisy.

I have seen this in action for my entire adult life, and have never seen it directed (in this sequence, measure, and vitriol) at the Right, let alone the pudgy middle which throughout the 1980s was led by a shambling joker of a demagogue who wouldn't know a fact if it slapped him in the face.

For the first time in God knows how long someone comes along who uses the documentary form to hold one of our biggest corporations responsible for its devastating effects on a community, one of any number of similar communities that dot the old industrial heartland; he does it with humor, intelligence, and courage; he gets an audience (which dumbfounded me) – and Pauline Kael is 'humanly' offended. (Next to her article is an ad for 'personalized information about quality products,' which tells you to call a telephone number to hear about the 'test drive program' for Chrysler automobiles.)

For years I have been reading *New York Times* articles by reporters who venture to Gary, Indiana, or Clairton, West Virginia, or Youngstown, Ohio, and find (1) an industrial wasteland of boarded-up businesses, houses for sale, soon-to-be-homeless people, and (2) how the people are all so befuddled – 'they just don't know what happened.' Some blame the Japanese, some blame their old employer, most blame themselves. Far be it from the reporter to supply the missing connections that would help them grasp their plight. These same reporters (and Pauline Kael) have to step over the homeless, avoid the panhandlers, watch out for the prostitutes and muggers, just to get inside their offices near Times Square. But Michael Moore is to blame for the dark crime of 'leftism as a superior attitude.'

The *cause célèbre* of American documentaries in recent years was PBS's lengthy *Civil War* series, done by Ken Burns. It first screened in the fall of 1990, and achieved a much wider audience than anyone expected. Its strengths and weaknesses say much about documentary programming today.

Burns's finest achievement was in making a virtue out of the absence of film footage from this war: instead he hung portraits on the TV screen – soldiers, generals, wives, sisters, slaves – which enabled the eye and the mind to pause and think about a lost past, thus to recuperate it in the imagination. The photograph became the text of this 'film,' often with a letter home or a heartfelt poem running on the soundtrack. Like Lanzmann, Burns demanded a commitment of time (eleven hours in this case) and refused to be swept into the inherent speed of the medium. Thus the photographs became real people who stepped to life and held the viewer in their grip, narrating the film and recreating the drama of an America in which, for once, the middle did not hold.

The drawn-out, stately pace of the film is punctuated time and again by the destructiveness of battle, bringing home to viewers the stark horror of the last war fought on American soil. The contemplative mood with which we view the passing array of people-photos, or listen to the time-honored music of the war, is shaken by the visual and written record of mass slaughter, and we recognize ourselves in the tragic presence of young life gone to death.

Somehow the stills and the horror get enveloped in a warm cocoon, however, in which the viewer is urged to reflect on what a wonderful country this is, in all its complexity, humanity, and violence. The film has a museum quality, a bucolic and distantly perceived grainy texture, that places its subject comfortably in and of the past. Burns's film carries the inert 'it was' quality of antiquarian history,[109] which we observe much as we would a family album or a stamp collection.

Above all, there are no radical juxtapositions, no new or unsettling interpretations, to discomfit the viewer and make them think. Burns's *Civil War* is a deeply conservative film, pitching a syrupy (if often eloquent) 'meaning' to an audience satiated on the banality of network television but too complacent and fearful of being disturbed to want controversy. Burns's history is the settled interpretation of the authorities, deftly conveyed by the wise, avuncular Shelby Foote, a master of the anecdote. It has little to do with the debates, arguments, contested texts, and ongoing tensions through which the real history of the Civil War retains its life and vitality. Instead Burns appeals to the popular notion of history spelled with a capital H, the settled wisdom of the ages, the 'it was' that we all ought to know and reflect upon, and forget at our peril. And so Walter Goodman, a television critic deeply imbued with this notion of history, pronounced the film brilliant in its evocation of 'our war the way it was.'[110]

DOCUDRAMA

What is a docudrama, how do you know it when you see it, and what relation does it have to the documentary form? Well, Joseph Campbell was an ace at docudrama. This is the much-celebrated author of *Transformations of Myth Through Times*, lecturer on nationwide PBS-TV, and mesmerizer of talk show host Bill Moyers. Campbell could stand up in front of the camera and tell the most absurd tales from the past, utter fictions, while pretending to disabuse us of our myths, and thereby convince his highbrow audience that they had heard the true history of 'individualism.'[111] This was pure docudrama.

The television quiz shows of the 1950s were also docudramas, as I learned at a young age. I was in the eighth grade when an experience with television, professors, and my own father turned me into an inveterate skeptic. It happened the same dreadful year the Brooklyn Dodgers moved to Los Angeles (from which some mark the beginning of the end for New York, if not for America). The occasion was Professor Charles Van Doren's amazing run on the highbrow television quiz show *Twenty-One* (notice they didn't call it Blackjack). Van Doren was wiping the floor with the competition, week after week. So one week my father took him on. Professor Van Doren was known to go for the high-rolling questions, a ten and an eleven. Dad worked out a conservative strategy: a couple of sevens or eights, and then Charlie flubs a ten or an eleven, and Dad wins.

The night approached, making me famous among my eighth-grade peers. Dad walked out on the stage, cool as a cucumber, chatted about being a former college president (educators were favorite contestants), entered the containment booth, and answered his two questions perfectly. Unfortunately so did Charlie. I basked in the glory of this media event until Charles Van Doren, Ph.D., was found to have gotten all the answers in advance from the producers (sometimes I had the uncanny sense that that was happening on our documentary, too). Like rock-and-roll disc jockey Alan Freed (whose wonderful radio show introduced me, also at fourteen, to a funky and often very black genre of rock music) sacked for payola, Van Doren was just another cashiered jerk who ran afoul of the sanctimonious hypocrisy of the 1950s.

It was years later before the thought crept into my mind that Dad had never evinced much interest in obscure generals of the Revolutionary War, or second-rate French impressionists, the subjects of his two successful answers. I never had the heart to put this one to him, though.[112] Anyway, I am in complete sympathy with Philip Roth's remark, as rendered through

Zuckerman's interlocutor, Alvin Pepler (who had three weeks of success on *Twenty-One*): 'In my opinion the beginning of the end of what's good in this country were those quiz shows and the crooks that ran them and the public that swallowed it like so many dopes.'[113] Yes, either that docudrama or the defection of the Dodgers.

According to Walter Goodman, 'The usual failure of the docudrama is that in trying to deliver an emotional punch, it hypes the facts . . . all docudrama tends to permit the facts to wane as the melodrama waxes.'[114] I don't disagree with this comment, unless it is meant to suggest that history is never melodramatic. Was not the shooting down of KAL 007 in 1983 (the subject of the docudrama Mr Goodman here criticizes) full of melodramatic hyperreality – including a rumored warning to Richard Nixon not to take that flight? Is there no melodrama in 'real life'? Furthermore, how do we know which facts are 'hyped' and which are not?

The television medium *is* at its best with the documentary form, with 'little or no' fictionalization, as our introductory definition put it. And it *is* often at its worst with the 'docudrama' – but why? Perhaps because in a docudrama we see the uncertain hand of the television 'historian.' Instead of unmediated transparency, you get mediated inanity. Documentaries appear to be based in 'primary sources,' like a historian's text. Docudramas rely on secondary sources, some sort of reconstruction of the event. Thus the first appears as fact, the second as fiction; *cinéma vérité* is the epitome of transparent documentary form, just as reenacted television docudrama – an increasingly common form – sometimes appears as the epitome of television bad form, and bad taste.

How would we define the docudrama? First, as Mr Goodman says, it is exaggerated experience. The genre takes a pool of 'known facts,' and roils the waters with dramatic license. Soul of probity Walter Cronkite inaugurated the postwar docudrama with *Victory at Sea*, a series that mangled the facts but that made the American heart go pitty-patter, just as Frank Capra did with his state-sponsored war films. *You Are There* was an even better example. What else is docudrama, besides exaggeration?

Mr Goodman, like Pauline Kael, uses the historian's test: 'the basic crookedness of the docudrama is that it encourages people to believe that they are getting the real thing . . . the cosmetic of reality is applied to conceal the underlying make-believe.' Showing an unaccustomed illiberal streak, he hints at censorship: 'the only good docudrama is an unproduced docudrama.'[115]

Let's have a look at this implied definition: docudrama is crooked because it deceives people into thinking they are getting 'the real thing.' This might be a good definition of television itself, with its $\frac{1}{30}$-second scanning beams creating human forms out of a bunch of dots. As for 'the cosmetic of reality is applied to conceal the underlying make-believe,' that seems to me a perfect definition of Arthur Schlesinger Jr's court history of Robert F. Kennedy, or Cronkite's *Victory at Sea*, or Pauline Kael's review of *Roger and Me*.

We can imagine the presentation of history in effective dramatic form: it's called theater. Charles Laughton as Henry VIII, Robert De Niro as Jake LaMotta, John Huston as Noah Cross (Oriental despot of Los Angeles), Jack Nicholson as Jake Gittes (detective/historian of Los Angeles), Rip Torn as Richard Nixon in an early ABC docudrama on Watergate – here is fine history, and magnificent art. Even the most ridiculous docudrama ever made about the Korean War, the Moonies' fantasy called *Inchon* (which the South Korean Government backed to the hilt), the film that for its time set the world record for costing more and bringing in less – this has the funniest depiction of Douglas MacArthur that I have ever seen. Sir Laurence Olivier sends up the film by playing Doug as a five-star drag queen, hair died to the blackest black, 1950s-red lips, cadaverous white skin, blowing kisses to the Joint Chiefs of Staff over his shoulder as he points his pointer toward Inch'ôn on the map.

If *Inchon* was the worst film of the 1970s, the best was Roman Polanski's *Chinatown* – a fine specimen of docudrama/history. Anyone who knows a thing about Southern California in the early part of this century knows that its history was deeply shaped by private and public schemes involving the delivery of water. Polanski's hegemonic despot, Noah Cross, manipulates water supplies and LA politicians toward the goal of great wealth and power. Having owned the 'public' water system outright in the past, he gave it up to 'public' control: he put his son-in-law (who thinks 'life begins in the sloughs and tidepools') in as water commissioner. The despot also manipulates his daughter (Faye Dunaway) and his other daughter (sister/daughter to Dunaway) toward the end of male dominance and the preservation of incestuous secrets. Despotism, water control, nepotism, incest: it is the Asiatic Mode of Production in our own backyard.

This film reversed East and West and turned American politics on its head. For Adam Smith, Montesquieu, Hegel, Marx, and many others, Asia had a peculiar social system characterized by huge water-control projects and a lack of private property, leaving no space for a middle class (*bourgeoisie*, that awful word again), just a stupefied mass at the mercy of successive despots. The Asian satrap found in the delivery of water the source of ultimate power. Our Chinatowns, successive generations of Americans believed, were populated by inscrutable deviants given to Tong wars, nefarious conspiracies, sleazy double-dealing, mayhem, and general depravity.

In the climactic final scene, set in LA's Chinese community, Jake Gittes, the detective (read 'investigative reporter' or 'historian') who has uncovered all these truths, is led away from the bloody site of filicide by his colleagues: 'Forget it, Jake, *it's Chinatown.*'

The real problem is with Goodman's 'the real thing.' What *is* 'the real thing'? There *is* no such thing. Every reality is mediated through the subjective mind of a historian, the fragment of a snapshot, the cyclops bias of the moving camera, or television's bending of time to the demands of the program, the clip, or the soundbite. Some docudramas are more accurate than others, some are more skillful than others: the more accurate and the more skillful, the more they resemble the historian's craft, a sometimes magnificent sleight-of-hand whereby bias parades forth as 'Mr Objectivity' or 'Mr Facts.' Arthur Schlesinger Jr's Franklin Roosevelt or Bobby Kennedy is a skillful but mythic resurrection. Daniel Boorstin's vision of America is an effective celebration of a fictive American dream. Allan Bloom's Nietzsche-driven student nihilists are the figment of an imagination stuck back at Cornell in the late 1960s. But if you sit students down and let them watch *Chinatown*, they'll have a better grasp of California's movers and shakers, and the minorities who have done America's work, than all the textbooks in US History 101 (which routinely elide the water and power controversies of 1905–28 in LA).

So, docudrama is exaggeration, is fantasy, is documentary, is fiction, is non-fiction, is life itself. Docudrama is another form of doing history. So is its seeming opposite, *cinéma vérité*. They differ in how they carry off their respective illusions, how they manage the 'little or no fictionalization' inherent in pointing a camera at anything. The obverse of disgust with 'docudrama' is the ease with which *vérité* initially won favor, and this is inseparable from the inherent empiricism and positivism lying at the basis of Anglo-Saxon philosophy; *vérité* is the magician of *camera-lucida* illusion. And, as we have seen, television claims for itself the transparency and immediacy of *cinéma vérité*.

Read what Emile de Antonio has to say about its claims:

> *Cinéma vérité* is first of all a lie, and secondly a childish assumption about the nature of film. *Cinema vérité* is a joke . . . . It is the empty-headed pretentiousness that gets me. *The belief of lack of prejudice.* There is no film made without pointing a camera and the pointing of that camera is already, in a sense, *a definitive gesture of prejudice, of feeling.* You cannot cut a piece of film, you cannot edit film without indicating prejudice [emphasis added].[116]

Television specializes in presenting itself as an unmediated, objective eye on the world: a pernicious doctrine, for the reasons Jay Ruby adduces:

> If we perpetuate the lie that pictures always tell the truth, that they are objective witnesses to reality, we are supporting an industry that has the potential to symbolically recreate the world in its own image. Technology grows out of a particular ideology. The Western world created image-producing technologies out of a profound need to have an irrefutable witness – to control reality by capturing it on film.[117]

Thus de Antonio and Ruby both equate the mirror-like qualities of *vérité* and television with lying, and thereby recuperate the 'unscrupulous benevolence' Nietzsche found in positivism itself: 'the objective man is indeed a mirror,' Nietzsche wrote;

> he is accustomed to submitting before whatever wants to be known, without any other pleasure than that found in knowing and 'mirroring'; he waits until something comes, and then spreads himself out tenderly lest light footsteps and the quick passage of spiritlike beings should be lost on his plane and skin. Whatever still remains in him of a 'person' strikes him as accidental, often arbitrary, still more often disturbing: to such an extent has

he become a passageway and reflection of strange forms and events even to himself.[118]

Here the 'objective man' meets the stalking candid-camera of *vérité* and the typical television weathervane, with 'the habit of meeting every thing and experience halfway,' and accepting everything that comes his way with 'sunny and impartial hospitality.'[119] Here the 'cool' medium meets and merges with a 'cool' positivism: the objective man-become-mirror looks at life and is interested – 'but, as it were, merely epidermically interested; a coolness on principle, a balance, a fixed low temperature.'[120]

It was on the continent that the presumption of mirrored camerawork was undone, by people like Jean-Luc Godard and Chris Marker, who insisted that verisimilitude required not the apparent absence of the author/director, but their palpable presence[121] – whether in documentary or fiction film – thus to connote that truth is dialectical (between the observer and the observed, in a war of movement with each other) and that truth is constructed by human beings (even in pointing a camera). Here is the analogue of de Antonio's demand to know the identity – and thus the 'prejudice,' the point of view – of the documentary maker.

Here the educators also need education; de Antonio, 'mere' filmmaker, intuited the position of 'metahistorians' like Michel de Certeau and Dominick LaCapra (themselves very much the minority in the history profession), that the historian needs to know himself or herself as a 'constructed' subject-historian observing the 'constructed' historian's subject, the 'real world,' 'the facts.' The historian's monograph, Hayden White says, 'is no less "shaped" or constructed than the historical film.'[122]

In the end we all need education: there is no reality apart from the meaning which you, and if not you someone else, attach to the event, to the experience. Either you learn how to 'do it yourself,' or you will remain an appendage to this television pundit or that Professor of the History of the World.

Unsettling, isn't it?

CHAPTER THREE

VIETNAM:

A 'TELEVISION WAR'?

'I have done that,' says my memory. 'I cannot have done that,' says
my pride, and remains inexorable. Eventually – memory yields.
FRIEDRICH NIETZSCHE[123]

A generation that had seen America stalemated in Korea,
humiliated in Vietnam, cocky in Grenada, puzzled by Panama and
struggling to keep up with the new economic wunderkids on the
block has a sense of moral self-righteousness. It felt good to win.
ANN MCFEATTERS, White House correspondent
for the Scripps Howard News Service[124]

Imagine a war in which the daily horror of modern warfare is kept from the
screen, in which the television anchorpeople function as patriots and
guardians of military secrets, cheerlead for Presidential and Pentagon
policy, and focus on the courage and professionalism of our boys in action
or the infallible accuracy of our high-tech weapons, in which the enemy is
demonized as cruel and fanatical, in which dissent from the war is
represented as miniscule or unpatriotic or both, and in which the war seems
mysteriously to be part of some widely shared community feeling, deeply
colored by images of good and evil: which war was that?

It was the recent Gulf War, to be sure. But it was also the Vietnam War
from 1961 through the Tet Offensive in 1968.[125] And it was the Korean
War, even if it occurred before the era of mass television. How then to
account for the many conservative verdicts that the Vietnam War was 'lost
in the living room'; or the position of many journalists that a courageous
and independent press told the truth about a dirty war?

Listen to Richard Nixon:

> In each night's TV news and each morning's paper the war was reported
> battle by battle, but little or no sense of the underlying purpose of the
> fighting was conveyed . . . . More than ever before, television showed the
> terrible human suffering and sacrifice of war . . . the result was a serious
> demoralization of the home front, raising the question whether America
> would ever again be able to fight an enemy abroad with unity and strength of
> purpose at home.[126]

How can conservative icon George F. Will think that television is somehow
inherently pacifist? 'Had there been television at Antietam on America's
bloodiest day,' Will opined, Americans 'might have preferred disunion to
the price of union, had they seen the price, in color in their homes in the
evening.'[127]

Nixon and Will assume first that television is a transparent window to
reality. Second they recuperate the one anomalous period in our three wars,
that from 1968 to 1973, when television brought into the home not the
carnage of war, but the yawning fissure in the American consensus that
underpinned this war in the previous period. Even then television never
did this most of the time, just part of the time; it never did this out of its
own conceits of crusading independent journalism, but because ruling
elites fell out over the war (also precisely in 1968); nonetheless television
infiltrated amid the soundbites and juxtapositions an alternative and
critical view of the war, and thus hinted at the immense subversive
potential of the medium. That alternative view came from the streets of
America and the jungles of Vietnam, and was covered because it had to be
covered: it was massive, it was news.

Television's own, very new prominence as chronicler of history – which,
as we said, most people first noticed when Kennedy was assassinated –
deeply shaped the idea that Vietnam was a first, something entirely new
and different, precisely because of television itself. As the media scholar/
star of that early period, Marshall McLuhan, put it in 1968,

> We are now in the midst of our first television war . . . the television
> environment [is] total and therefore invisible. Along with the computer, it
> has altered every phase of the American vision and identity. The television

war has meant the end of the dichotomy between civilian and military. The public is now participant in every phase of the war, and the main actions of the war are now being fought in the American home itself.[128]

It took the Gulf War to make clear how wrong this television guru could be.

To most observers who lived through Vietnam, the wars in Korea and the Gulf differed from it by the nature of their beginning. Kim Il Sung, like Saddam Hussein, launched an unprovoked invasion in the early morning hours. The United Nations courageously resisted both acts of aggression. The first act of both wars then functioned as original sin, coloring all previous and subsequent history with its hue. Vietnam is a war which only ended climactically; its beginnings seem remote and no one asks 'who started the Vietnam War?'

This is a politically constructured discourse. As I suggested in the introduction, Kim Il Sung crossed the five-year-old 38th parallel, not an international boundary like that between Iraq and Kuwait; the counter-logic implied by saying 'Koreans invade Korea' disrupts the received wisdom or renders a logical reconstruction impossible, even for a political theorist with the rhetorical skills of Michael Walzer.[129]

More important, until the rupture of Tet, original sin also marked North Vietnam – the 1964 attack on American ships in the Tonkin Gulf, or the 'indirect invasion' which it sponsored via the Vietcong insurgency in the South. The US had committed no sins, but with its allies was engaged in a collective-security response, 'pacification' in South Vietnam (the 'police action' of the 1960s).

Thus in November 1961 the White House spoke of strengthening South Vietnam against 'attack by the Communists,' as if they were outsiders to Vietnam, and television reports never questioned the legitimacy of the Cold War premiss that American policy sought only to preserve an anti-Communist South.[130] Vietnam was fought not as 'a new kind of war' but as *another Korea*, with success defined as a permanently divided Vietnam – as the Pentagon's propaganda film *Why Vietnam?* stated in 1965.[131]

Nor was Vietnam the first war brought into the home. World War II was also a 'living room war,' with film and radio the medium of conveyance. The American high command closely monitored Hollywood films, when it wasn't making them itself.[132] Edward R. Murrow's voice brought home the London blitz, his words enabling an imagined reconstruction of the violence, verified by photos in the newspapers the next day.[133] If by the 1960s television made it possible to bring war violence home dramatically, it rarely did so – both because the cameras were not in the midst of the fight and therefore could not 'see' the war,[134] and because of basic truths about the limits of programming.

Daniel Hallin's valuable reconstruction of TV coverage of Vietnam shows that television's presentation of the war was structured by a set of assumptions about which television itself seemed barely aware (in other words, they came from the subconscious realm of the paleotemplate): War is a national endeavor. War is an American tradition. War is manly. War is rational (and therefore can be grasped empirically in terms of body counts, percentages of enemy matériel destroyed, and the scientific application of strategy and technology). Winning is what counts.[135] Written before the Gulf War, Hallin's book might be a script for television in that latter conflict.

Hallin illustrates the paleosymbolic assumptions with detailed accounts of television coverage. Here is Dean Brelis reporting the ground war for ABC, February 9, 1966:

> Brave men need leaders. This is a leader of brave men. His name is Hal Moore. He comes from Bardstown, Kentucky. He is married and the father of five children. [And now Moore on camera:] They are the greatest soldiers in the world. In fact, they're the greatest men in the world. They're well trained, they're well disciplined . . . their motivation is tremendous. They came over here to win.

Then ABC cuts to Dan Rather, who describes Col. Moore as 'hero of the Ia Drang Valley in November, and itching for another head-on clash.'

Journalists had no direct access to the air war over Vietnam and had to take reports at face value; they were gaga over the 'electronic gadgetry,' precision direct-hits, and Pentagon-touted professionalism of our soldiers and pilots – 'the hottest jet pilots around,' according to TV reports.[136] Neither TV nor print journalism was willing to report hard facts that everyone knew to be true. Reporters instead engaged in self-censorship. As in Korea, few of them reported on 'the hostility that many American soldiers felt' toward all the natives, whichever side they were on, and yet veterans of both wars frequently remark on this ubiquitous hostility.[137]

In the Gulf War, Pentagon brass-speak coined the term 'collateral damage' to account for civilians who happened to be in the way of our warfare. Here is Jack Perkins of NBC, observing the burning of a Vietnamese village: 'This is not callousness; this is not wanton destruction. Everything in this area for years was Vietcong.... The whole village had turned on the Americans, so the whole village was being destroyed.'[138] (Including the women and children who lived there.)

It was the enemy that was callous and cruel, using terrorist methods to corral and cow the cringing peasantry of Vietnam. Here is a CBS report of November 1, 1967, about a Vietcong assault on a Montagnard village in the central highlands: 'This is how South Vietnamese independence is marked by the Vietcong . . . by burning hamlets, by kidnapping civilian officials, and by terrorizing people.' At about the same time, Walter Cronkite hawked the Johnson administration's view that the Vietcong ruled through terrorism, in introducing a report about a bus full of refugees that hit a land mine: 'Well, today the war provided a bloody example of that terrorism.'[139] Hallin finds that in early coverage of Vietnam, those who complained or dissented were often asked if they had 'been over there' (I would spell it theah) – this being equivalent to seeing Vietnam 'the way it really was.'[140]

My television memory parallels the progression that Hallin describes. The war first entered my consciousness in 1964, around the time of the Tonkin Gulf incident, when I watched our Ambassador to Vietnam, Henry Cabot Lodge, hold forth on television about the character of the war. He described how the Vietcong cut off the heads of village leaders and paraded them around on the ends of sticks, thus to terrorize the peasants into supporting them. I believed him, but thought this was a war I wanted no part of. I watched Howard K. Smith of ABC, who berated people who raised questions about the war by asking if they had 'been over there.' Yes, I thought, to know the war you must 'see' it for yourself.[141]

A year later I saw the famous Morley Safer report where Marines took Zippo lighters to peasant huts, finding this odd and again determining not to be a part of this war. By 1966 I was in graduate school and exposed to the growing debate about the war, which I followed intensely. In March 1967 I got the first hint of a television text which was beginning to crack over the lies and obfuscations of Washington's policy: I turned on the *CBS Evening News* just as Walter Cronkite came on to say that the Pentagon had requested 200,000 more troops for the war effort; suddenly (and for the only time in my experience) CBS's picture dissolved and the screen went blank, then the news started up again, without any explanation, and with no mention of 200,000 troops. I searched the newspapers the next day for news of this major escalation of the war, and found nothing. But declassified documents later showed that General Westmoreland asked for 200,000 more troops on March 18, 1967, over and above the existing ceiling of nearly half a million troops in or on the way to Vietnam.

That my government lies occurred to me around the same time, courtesy of television coverage of Vietnam-related testimony in Congress by Dean Rusk. I rediscovered this in browsing through the diary I kept then: 'I was appalled by [Rusk's] evasion, mendacity, double-talk and distortion. Can he think people are really so foolish [as] to not see through him?'[142] Television had detonated a war of movement in my mind, like so many other minds of my generation.

The Tet Offensive in early 1968 opened a major and lasting breach in American judgements about the Vietnam War. Ever since, people like General Westmoreland have claimed that television coverage of events like the temporary occupation of the US Embassy in Saigon by the Vietcong grossly distorted the simple fact that Tet was a terrible defeat for the Vietcong. Walter Cronkite returned from a trip to Vietnam and broke with the administration, causing Lyndon Johnson (a President who watched three television newscasts simultaneously every night in the White House) to exclaim that 'Cronkite was it,' i.e. his editorial destroyed support for the war.[143] Shortly Johnson retired to the Pedernales. Was this television's fault?

In fact Tet opened a breach among the American elite, with Lyndon Johnson calling in 'the wise men' for advice (including Dean Acheson of Korean War fame), some of whom came to think the war was unwinnable no matter what the US did and urged a winding down of the conflict, others of whom worried about central problems in the global economy like the run on the dollar, and thought that Vietnam was a peripheral drain on

American attentions and resources. [144] Tet also inaugurated a televised war of movement at home, between a growing opposition now spilling into the mainstream, and an increasingly palsied establishment trying to retain its grip on the levers of influence. Only when that breach became clear – when by the force of the mass it became 'news' – did television open itself to critics of the war, and these were almost always tepid, mainstream critics from 'inside the beltway.' As Max Frankel of the *New York Times* put it,

> As protest moved from the left groups, the anti-war groups, into the pulpits, into the Senate . . . it naturally picked up coverage . . . . Because we're an establishment institution, and whenever your natural constituency changes, then naturally you will too. [145]

The major studies of TV coverage 'all reject the idea that the living-room war meant graphic portrayals of violence on a daily basis, or that television was consistently negative toward US policy'; before Tet, only about 22 percent of all film reports showed actual combat, and what they showed was minimal. If Vietnam coverage was different than Korea, it was because this was the first war in which reporters were not routinely subject to censorship. [146]

Hallin is quite right to say that 'television's very power . . . has the ironic consequence of making the medium particularly sensitive about the boundaries of legitimate controversy.' [147] Hallin attributes this in part to the brevity and simplicity of TV's presentation, the personal interlocution of that presentation (or, better, representation), and to worries about aiding and abetting the enemy. In any case, this is the subtext of TV self-censorship.

Vietnam was not lost in the living room, but in the jungle, in the minds of elites, in the streets of America – and in Korea. The courage of the Vietnamese and the memory of Chinese action in Korea placed limits on what US strategy could achieve, and the lesson of a Democratic administration blasted to smithereens by the 'China' issue stayed the hand of Lyndon Johnson, creating Daniel Ellsberg's 'stalemate machine'; thus Washington pursued incremental escalation and pussyfooted around domestic divisions, ultimately losing the war and the home front at the same time. After Tet it became our first (and, so far, last) 'television war' in the usual understanding of that term. Making a 'television war,' in other words, is an editorial decision.

VIETNAM IN TELEVISION HISTORY

Television came to Vietnam in the 1960s, and television history came to Vietnam in the 1980s. In between, the whiphand of history was held by the party of forgetting. 'Consensual amnesia was the American reaction, an almost instant reaction, to the Vietnam War,' wrote Martha Gellhorn; television reinforced the forgetting by maintaining 'a respectful silence' after 1973, even though this new 'forgotten war' was not over.[148] Galloping along in amnesia's wake was the party of revision. The first was prerequisite to the second, and by 1980 Ronald Reagan campaigned on the position that Vietnam had been a 'just war.' But that war had been, to use Alexander Solzhenitsyn's metaphor, an iron crowbar of history that descended upon and branded an entire generation. Thus the parties of forgetting and revision have had to contend with the party of memory.

The preeminent film of documentary memory was, of course, PBS's thirteen-part *Vietnam: A Television History*. It was because of my respect for this film that I looked forward to working on the Korea film with Austin Hoyt and Peter McGhee of WGBH/Boston: Hoyt had done two of the thirteen programs, and McGhee had been instrumental in producing and screening a film of this length and sensitivity. Unlike the usual soundbite and sitcom fare on prime time TV, the length of the series required a commitment from the viewer, not to mention a huge committal of time, money and effort from the many people who helped make it. If the film's comprehensiveness remained unsatisfying to a historian's taste, it was still unprecedented for television to go so deeply into Vietnamese history and culture, the colonial background of the conflict, the missed opportunities of the late 1940s, the contradictory outcomes of the 1950s, and the like, all before arriving at America's 'Vietnam War.' Although the film was not without problems, it met the best expectations one can have of prime time public television in America: it was well researched, replete with fascinating footage and memorable interviews, reasonably balanced, and narrated with an understatement that left viewers to their own conclusions.[149]

The understated narrative masked a refusal to 'name' this war and its protagonists with any degree of accuracy or fealty to history, however, and a desire to operate within consensual boundaries of American interpretation. Thus the film had nothing important to say about the sources of American hegemony in Southeast Asia, or the deep-running commitment to self-determination and social revolution that animated the Vietnamese through three decades of warfare. By focusing on a 'central question [that] never changed: what is the *evidence* that supports showing or saying this,'[150] the filmmakers adopted a naive epistemology that would inevitably limit their inquiry – just as it legitimized the inquiry in their own eyes. (The terms American hegemony and Vietnamese revolution cannot be understood without a conception and a logic of hegemony or revolution, which then illumines evidence 'showing or saying' that it does or does not exist.)

This naiveté was further compounded by an early decision to 'show only observers giving first-hand accounts,' actual participants in events 'rather than journalists or academic experts.'[151] Who is the observer with the first-hand account? An eyewitness who was uninvolved? In which case they render the actions of those involved, and how do we know they're right? Perhaps this was an eyewitness participant? In which case the rendering partakes in the subjectivity of all participant accounts, well known to any courtroom lawyer. And when is the account taken? In 1965, when it happened, or in 1980, when vetted through the cobwebs of memory and the exigencies of current interpretation?

The list of questions could continue on, but what is the point? The participant-observer was 'there,' and presumably has greater purchase on the truth; by interviewing those who were 'there,' the documentary will rely on 'primary' rather than 'secondary' sources, and, like the good historian, will be more objective. We already probed the problems in being 'theah,' as Farrar-Hockley was. The point is that history ought to be done by measuring the accounts of those who were 'theah' against other such accounts, against written documents from the time, and against varying interpretations about the meaning of the event, illuminated by broader conceptions and by logic: which is inevitably the responsibility of the television historian/author (who ends up being the editor).

The PBS method had good effect when ordinary people, American and Vietnamese, recounted their experiences. It had bad effect when high-level people were allowed to be the historians of their own failed policies, which was all too often. The bland PBS narrative was matched in the book that accompanied the series, but unlike that book (about which more below) the documentary film and the television image incessantly undercut the tame desires of the producers, bringing the war into the living room again in all its terrible passion – the facts and evidence inseparable from 'the evil genius of things.'

Part of that passion was supplied by our Vietnamese enemy, which had a commanding presence in certain segments of this film – a valid but highly unusual 'balance' to the American perspective, the source of which was unquestionably the Vietnamese victory itself. Had the outcome been quick and decisive like the Gulf, or a prolonged, indecisive stalemate like Korea, the enemy 'other' would have had no such standing. I particularly liked Ho Chi Minh's old comrade Pham Van Dong, who met interviewers' questions with varying degrees of insight and candor, but with an unvarying broad, insouciant grin that said one unmistakable, unpalatable, resonant thing: we won, you lost. (I'm sure his ear-to-ear smile connoted outrageous insolence to many viewers: evil genius personified.)

The film unpacked and examined several of Vietnam's indelible television images: especially Morley Safer's 1965 Zippo lighter episode, which hour six recuperated through American and Vietnamese eyewitnesses, and reconnoitered in the village of Cam Ne itself. If Vietnam was not really a 'television war' before 1968, the occasional presence of TV cameras made it a war which we could step back into both retroactively and in the present, reconnoitering not just Cam Ne village but the fascinating difference between the event 'it was' in (televised) reality and the event 'it is' as (televised) history. The original people are in repose, they are older, less compelling; the unique, shattering event of 1965 (American soldiers burn villages?!) merges with the commonplace verdict on the war (American soldiers burned villages); the old memory 'flits by' as the new perception 'leaps up,' each converging at a point of inevitable loss (in Benjamin's words).

Stanley Karnow wrote the book of the series, *Vietnam: A History*, subtitled 'The First Complete Account of Vietnam at War.'[152] The book was suggested to Karnow by PBS president Lawrence Grossman, and carries a WGBH/Boston copyright. It has the strengths and weaknesses of the journalist-as-historian. Karnow reported from Southeast Asia off and on since 1950, and sprinkles his chronological narrative with personal observations and anecdotes – including a priceless vignette from S.J. Perelman, on a 1946 evening spent in Hong Kong with 'His Highness,' Emperor Bao Dai[153] (an unapologetic Francophile who also lit up the PBS series). Karnow wrote the book for the lay reader, and it satisfies the common notion of comprehensive historical narrative, year-one-to-the-present.

Otherwise the book is unsatisfying. It is by no means a complete account of Vietnam at war; the Vietnamese are mostly silent, and its comprehensiveness applies at best to American involvement in Vietnam. It instantly betrays the tell-tale signs of history with a capital 'H' that butt many jokes among professional historians. On the first page we read, 'history is a seamless series of causes and effects, the past, present, and future inexorable.' Or, further on, 'history is an organic process, a continuity of related events, inexorable and yet not inevitable.' As for debates among historians (which are nowhere evident in this book), 'no single theory tells the entire story, yet each contains a grain of truth.'[154] It is hard to disagree, because the statements say everything and nothing. Not a single footnote intrudes on Karnow's story.

Like television pundits during the Gulf War, Karnow reincarnates Vietnam as 'a laboratory for technology so sophisticated it made James Bond's dazzling gadgets seem obsolete' – ultrasensitive devices to detect 'heat, light and sound refraction' from the enemy, chemical defoliants, phosphorous and napalm, and the 'Walleye,' an air-to-surface missile with a television camera in its nose. Unlike most TV journalists, Karnow notes the aimless destructiveness of these 'smart' weapons, dependent on frail humans to point them toward presumed targets: the result was a blunderbuss – 'like a steamroller,' according to one witness.[155]

The tone of the book is melancholy, imparting a tragic and futile note to everything about Vietnam. Like a television narrator, Karnow tries to avoid commentary. Ultimately he must say something indicating his 'point of view,' however, and he says this: 'the war in Vietnam was a war that nobody won – a struggle between victims . . . whether a valid venture or a misguided endeavor, it was a tragedy of epic dimensions.' This is his conclusion, even if it comes early in the book (at the end, the narrative simply tails off with the Vietnamese reclaiming Saigon in 1975).[156]

It would be difficult to invent such a peculiarly American perspective on Vietnam. That nobody won the war will come as a surprise to Pham Van Dong, the Vietnamese people, and American veterans. That the US was a victim just like Vietnam could only occur to someone who has never stepped back from this war and looked at it without American blinders, and who wished to absolve American planners of the consequences of their own actions. Karnow's evaluation of American responsibility ranges between 'valid venture' and 'misguided endeavor.' Is the transposition of nouns (valid endeavor and misguided venture) subconscious? Or does it connote a complacent, mixed verdict that Vietnam was a valid, but misguided endeavor – or perhaps venture? In any case we are back to the 'soupy mess of conformity' that informs American television; Karnow has not interpreted the war so much as connoted that he remains within the goal posts of bipartisan Washington politics.

When read next to a recent general account of the Vietnam war by historian Marilyn Young, we become aware of the losses inherent in Karnow's method. Young uncovers a war with aggressors and victims, located by a thorough and wrenching inquiry which does not privilege Americans at the expense of the Vietnamese. It recuperates an indigenous anti-colonial and anti-feudal revolution, Vietnamese men and women (especially women) who fought for their ideals with unmatched determination and resourcefulness, and Americans who found their own resolution and courage in rising up against the war machine. (See Plate 5.) All these emphases are barely whispers in Karnow's account. Dr Young 'lets the chips fall where they may,' and they drop on liberal internationalists who systematically deepened American involvement (like Dean Rusk, Walt Rostow, McGeorge Bundy, Henry Kissinger). Her view of the war is not muted and conformist, but direct and strong:

> [T]he United States invaded Vietnam against our stated values and ideals and . . . did so secretly and deceptively, fighting a war of immense violence in order to impose its will on another sovereign nation.[157]

Although mainstream critics lauded the PBS film and the Karnow book, rightwing pressure group 'Accuracy in Media' launched vitriolic attacks on both. It produced its own film (*Television's Vietnam: The Real Story*). It is sloppy, hapless, and utterly ideological – as well as testimony to the difficulty of drawing a line between documentary and docudrama. Rather than dismiss it for the rot that it was, however, WGBH/Boston yielded to AIM's demand that it be screened, 'creating a situation almost without precedent in US broadcasting history. PBS seemed to be yielding to political pressures of the worst kind.'[158]

PBS apparently did so in deference to 'balanced' programming. This is an odd, interior, auto-induced damage, because implicitly PBS equated itself and its own laboriously produced film with AIM and its ludicrous conception of 'the real story.' But what this remarkable departure from independent, self-assured programming really did was certify the prison-house of our politics: it stretches from a WGBH which can give us Vietnam in wonderful footage, a commendable range of interviews and liberal pablum by way of interpretation, to an AIM interested above all in polemics and censorship, giving us a 'Vietnam' that no honest person can countenance.

Now let's see what a self-consciously political documentary filmmaker does with Vietnam. Chris Marker, whose picture book on Korea we discussed above, made *Far From Vietnam* (1967) as a series of juxtaposed representations of the war.[159] We hear General Westmoreland on television, but also the family of a Quaker who immolated himself in protest at the war; we see footage from North Vietnam, demonstrations in Europe, Americans fighting in the South. The dramatic moment comes, however, when Jean-Luc Godard intrudes in a section called 'Camera's Eye,' and asks whether it is possible to make a film about Vietnam at all. He cannot go there (having been refused a visa), Marker can get little more than Western newsreels, better just to focus attention on his high-tech American studio camera, in all its mechanical perfection and impotence. Or, the film suggests, why not ask the Vietnamese to invade us, to see what the war is 'really like'?

Emile de Antonio made a film purely from juxtaposed images, without narration, and, 'like all my films,' the theme was history. What history?

The first thing I did was read about two hundred books in French and English on Vietnam, because I figured that was one way I could find the images. Many who do compilation documentaries today come from an anti-intellectual generation, or have no historical sense, and they're motivated primarily by flashy images or simple prejudices, when what they should be looking for are historical resonances which are filmic.[160]

He found the ironic flow of images and footage for his classic Vietnam film *In the Year of the Pig* right where others had also looked – or, rather, overlooked. In one stretch of footage, for example, Vietnamese rickshaw pullers drop their French guests, attired in pith helmets and white suits, at a fancy Saigon cafe where a tall Moroccan wearing a fez contemptuously waves the pullers away: 'It's the equivalent of a couple of chapters of dense writing about the meaning of colonialism,' de Antonio said.[161] The archival researcher has the same experience, time and again, of mining gold nuggets from documents pawed over but not used by previous historian-prospecters; the 'primary sources' remain inert without a mind to give them energy – or in this case, a mind with a point of view about colonialism.

So this is history – but history done according to what epistemology? A skeptical, querulous epistemology of juxtaposed image, with no narration, no 'moral,' thus requiring the viewer to supply meaning to images that could not all be 'true' (and could never lull us into thinking that 'none tells the entire story, yet each contains a grain of truth'): in short, to make the viewer the historian of the filmic images, interpreting them. De Antonio subverts the phony objectivity of network television at both ends. He refuses to pretend that as a filmmaker he is or can be unbiased; he is a man of 'prejudice,' which underlies all his work. And he demands that the viewer refuse to be spoonfed 'the facts.' The juxtaposed images assault the viewer, making us uncomfortable, pushing us off balance, necessitating a new, parallax view of the history under scrutiny.

De Antonio's own parallax view extended to acute self-consciousness about his *oeuvre* and its reception by an audience – signifier and signified, two very different things. He remembered being thrilled when people laughed at the right time in his first film, *Point of Order*, and being discomfited when college students applauded at SAM 3 missiles downing American planes in *Pig*. I had the same feeling, sitting in the audience that May Day in 1969 at Columbia University, watching this film:[162] the applause came too easily, without thought, without thinking through the consequences, without staying power in the mind. The SAM 3s were ephemeral images, like television; there was no empathy with others in our generation, on the receiving end of the missiles (a fraternity brother of mine was a bomber pilot over Vietnam, and I remember looking for his face in the film). The SAM missiles and the American pilots were put there for perspective, for us to ruminate on the meaning of innocence and responsibility in this war, for us to be the historians giving meaning to it – and not to gloat over American flyers shot down in 1968, only to gloat over Iraqi SCUDs missing their targets in 1991.

Hearts and Minds (1975), by contrast, played to this distanced sense of moral superiority to the 'bad guys' of the war. They seemed to be any Middle American wrapping himself in the flag, from high school football coaches to low-ranking veterans like Lt George Coker, who is mercilessly lampooned as he repeats Pentagon explanations of the conflict for the home front. American pilots speak excitedly about their technical mastery, intercut with scenes of the carnage in peasant villages below. It is all too easy and predictable; viewed today, it is a pretentious and timebound work. The film has some excellent scenes (particularly W.W. Rostow's fulminations), but it is testimony to the wide swath cut by radical chic in elite opposition to the war, symbolized by Susan Sontag in Hanoi, or Leonard Bernstein hosting the Black Panthers.

Some years later I helped to arrange another showing of *In the Year of the Pig* at Swarthmore College, with de Antonio present; my great pleasure in meeting him was only matched by my distress at a new generation of students who were, with some exceptions, hearkening to the parties of forgetting and revision. Soon thereafter I saw *The Deer Hunter* (1978), Michael Cimino's film which reversed black and white and stood history on its head, as if the print negatives came out backwards: it was the Vietcong terrorists who burned villages, who delighted in fiendish tortures, who seduced and destroyed the minds of our soldiers. It was America where the loyal and decent patriots lived, blue-collar working folk in Appalachian steel mills with a simple, abiding faith in family and the flag. Cimino's rank cynicism in screening history in reverse both in Vietnam and America (the region was then dying because of shuttered steel mills) was the point at which amnesia ended, and the political war of movement for memory began. Through film and television, political reconstructions sought to fill the newly emptied vessel that was 'Vietnam' in the American mind.

Television history was ever present in the eye of the filmmakers. If Cimino wished to erase Morley Safer's Zippo lighters, or place them in enemy hands, he nonetheless reacted to a television image. Francis Ford Coppola did the same by infiltrating a television crew (with Coppola as cameraman) into battle scenes in *Apocalypse Now*.[163] Both insinuated a reviving Orientalism that sought to 'make strange' Vietnamese who were all too familiar to the American viewer; paradoxically they regurgitated a Hollywood and TV Orientalia that was also familiar, through decades of Fu Manchu and Charlie Chan imagery. Coppola's thin, portentous 'heart of darkness' theme returned Vietnam and Cambodia to a paint-it-primitive savage state, where the (pure) American both met his match, and was corrupted. Oliver Stone's *Platoon* (1986) returned the Zippos to American hands, but also revived the classic war film genre of soldier-buddies confronting a dark, shadowy enemy. Vietnamese whom at least some Americans had come to know as people were returned to the blank, opaque realm of the 'other.' Through all three films, the drumbeat was 'the horror, the horror': it was another way of saying, 'Forget it Jake, it's Chinatown.'[164]

Lee Iacocca, Chrysler chairman and icon of Japan-bashing, played the theme in a commercial timed for the TV release of *Platoon*. Sitting in an army jeep, he intoned that the film

> is a memorial not to war but to all the men and women who fought in a time and *in a place nobody really understood*, who knew only one thing: they were called and they went. It was the same from the first musket fired at Concord to the rice paddies of the Mekong Delta: they were called and they went. [emphasis added].[165]

The narrative carries an unintended irony: does the 'they' refer to Americans in the rice paddies, or the Vietcong, fighting a war of independence?

If *The Deer Hunter* did more violence to Vietnam War history than the other two, it was the most prescient in anticipating and reinforcing a developing American mood. As Michael Klein put it,

> The film is permeated with a bewildered sense of nativist pride, bruised innocence and loss, a structure of feeling that is resolved in a vision of a

beleagured but unified America – standing together, standing tall – in a hostile, evil, and incomprehensible world of Asian and Communist demons.[166]

That world included not just the Vietnamese enemy, but a world political economy in which Japanese and Korean industry were devastating the rustbelt archipelago where much of the film took place, an experience which is also represented (especially in the press and on TV) as a bewildering, unexpected, strange denouement to the American dream for the people concerned.

Films like *Casualties of War* (which attracted no audience in 1989) and Oliver Stone's *Born on the Fourth of July* (which hit big in 1990) illustrated that anti-Vietnam War sentiment was still alive in Hollywood. The continued war of movement owed little to television, however; these were personal statements by the party of memory, embodied in the walking wounded (or paraplegic, in Ron Kovic's case) from Vietnam and the haunted veterans (like Stone). Although neither film had a political analysis of the Vietnam War, both inscribed the continuing obsession with its meaning (if only for Americans).

The one stunning exception to these rules of Vietnam War film and television discourse was Stanley Kubrick's *Full Metal Jacket* (1987). Unwilling to do for Vietnam what he did for World War I (in his brilliant antiwar statement, *Paths of Glory*), Kubrick instead savagely parodied the wounded pride and supercharged chauvinism of America in the 1980s – by taking on the Marines: first in boot camp, where the inventively foul-mouthed drill instructor 'turns boys into men,' then in the war, where the Marines try to turn Vietnamese into Americans ('We are here to help the Vietnamese because inside every gook there's an American,' says one Marine officer), finally to the symbolic defeat of Marine Corporal Joker at the hands of a tiny, scrawny, even skeletal Vietcong child/woman, blasting away with an AK-47. She dies a stoic and courageous death in the end, but only because she is vastly outnumbered by the big brawny Marines.

All three films are signs that the Vietnam crisis has not ended, and will not end, for the generation that suffered it. That is, however, only one American generation. The broader tendency, put simply, has been for the parents of the Vietnam generation to reach down, around and through the aging but active memories of their sons and daughters, to the *tabulae rasae* of youth. The 'Rambo' films of the 1980s were truly frightening examples of how far revisionism and the reconstruction of myth could go; although Sylvester Stallone was barely above the level of John Wayne in *The Green Berets* (a film which so clashed with television's Vietnam in the 1960s that it flopped), his films played to large and predominantly young audiences[167] which television had prepared through its complicity with Reaganism, just as Reaganism parlayed Rambo-style victories like Grenada into a new cult of TV-simulated patriotism.

All were to celebrate through television the quick-in, quick-out 1983 invasion of an island the size of Martha's Vineyard: witness the American students rescued from Grenada's 'leftist thugs,' who kissed the ground upon their return to the homeland. Meanwhile the Grenada invasion itself was unseen, because the state excluded television reporters. It was a formula Margaret Thatcher pioneered during the 1982 Falklands War, where television film was dramatically censored or delayed, and where state-friendly journalists s(t)imulated 'a surge of patriotism' (Max Hastings, later the maker of the BBC's Korean War documentary, led the flagwaving charge).[168] Both the Falklands and Grenada were brought to you by people who thought Vietnam had been lost in the living room.

There is perhaps more to be said about Vietnam, but I would prefer to keep this chapter the shortest in the book: the reason being that the sometimes obsessive attention to this war has consumed or eclipsed other wars in other times which similarly marked a generation – World War I, for example, which haunted those who experienced it and spawned an entire literary movement; or wars that actually had more lasting and fundamental impact on American history, if not on the generation that suffered them – Korea, for example, which is as unknown to my generation (which lived through it) as it is to the nation as a whole.

Second, the indelible knowledge gained during intense struggle on the home front and on the battlefield – of right and wrong, of courage and weakness, of corrupt state power and righteous citizenry – has tended to slip away, or to be consumed in a different sense: consumed as private nostalgia, consumed as Hollywood entertainment, consumed by a cynical

New Right intent only upon erasing that estimable moment in American history. This is a disgraceful stain on that same proud moment, but I fear that now is not the time to say more; the words would also be, simply . . . consumed.

CHAPTER FOUR

'NO MORE VIETNAMS':

THE GULF WAR

> The history of battle is primarily the history of radically
> changing fields of perception.
> PAUL VIRILIO[169]

Remember the Gulf War? Or was that last season's hit show? The Gulf War was a war fought to demolish a memory, but it was also a war that produced no memory. It was our first 'television war': not blood and guts spilled in living color on the living room rug, not the transparent, objective immediacy of the all-seeing eye, not George Will's instrument of pacifism, but a radically distanced, technically controlled, eminently 'cool' postmodern optic which, in the doing, became an instrument of the war itself.

Iraq was the perfect surrogate for the party of forgetting bent on wiping out a 'Vietnam syndrome' that had hampered America's global policeman role for twenty years, and that (or so the Pentagon thought) had its origin in the living room. An ironic reversal took place, in which the antiwar cry of the 1960s, 'no more Vietnams,' became the battle cry of the 1990s. The 'lessons' of Vietnam had a television or celluloid tinge to them. When George Bush said we won't fight this one with one hand tied behind our backs, he implicitly harked back to Rambo: 'Are they going to let us win it this time?', Rambo says in *First Blood*, the prelude to his 'return to Vietnam.' When Bush said the Gulf War would 'put Vietnam behind us,' he echoed Coppola's justification for making *Apocalypse Now*. Thus stubborn memory propels an unnecessary war to necessity.

If Saddam Hussein's Iraq served Bush's amnesiac purposes, it was a poor surrogate for Ho Chi Minh's Vietnam – as antiwar protesters understood immediately, because they tend to be sincere people. Hardly a thing could be said on Saddam's behalf, he had no constituency in the US, Iraq was far more threatening than Grenada or Noriega's Panama, something truly important was at stake (hegemony in the Persian Gulf), and so the war became a surrogate for the wars the US could not win in Vietnam and Korea – a victory without cost, interrogating the past and preparing the future.

Neither the air war nor the ground war needed to be fought.[170] Whether United Nations sanctions would have worked to get Iraq out of Kuwait, given sufficient time, is not the issue (although I think they would have). We never had a chance to find out; peace was not given a chance, and Bush forfeited what could have been a dramatic, just, hopeful, collective-security beginning for his 'New World Order' (or what he calls 'the vision thing'). But then if our 'kids' (as the President liked to call them) didn't get a chance to show their stuff, how would we put Vietnam behind us? How would we deter the next Third World aggressor? If Iraq's military machine were not crushed, how would we avoid 'another Korea,' where we would have to hold a line decades after the war ended? In one hundred hours the ground war was over, and Bush gave his blessing: 'By God, we've kicked the Vietnam syndrome once and for all.' All it cost was a needless few hundred American and a needless few tens of thousands of Iraqi deaths.[171]

Our paper of record saved its investigative account of how the war came about until it was safely over,[172] but it made clear that Bush determined on making war very early after the Iraqi invasion, that his administration decided to move from Desert Shield to Desert Storm before the October 1990 Congressional elections (but held back the enabling orders until two days after the votes were cast), that the extraordinary size of the buildup (to half a million American troops, the level of the expeditionary force in Vietnam at its height) was dictated by a Pentagon determined that it would have everything it could possibly need this time, and that Bush's order to launch a ground war was communicated in advance of the diplomatic flurry that led to Iraq's last-minute decision to evacuate Kuwait – thus providing the spectacle of troops withdrawing and surrendering while under massive attack.[173]

It was possible to find such things out before the war ended, but not on television, and only if one had the indefatigable sleuth-like instincts of an

I.F. Stone. In the last paragraph of a very long *New York Times* article, for example, one learned that in his first months in office, Bush was told by Pentagon and CIA officials to 'deal with third-world threats unambiguously':

> In cases where the US confronts much weaker enemies, our challenge will be not simply to defeat them, but to defeat them decisively and rapidly . . . . For small countries hostile to us, bleeding our forces in protracted or indecisive conflict . . . may be victory enough.[174]

Michael Klare was almost alone in pointing out how the Bush administration's reaction to the Iraqi invasion dovetailed with extant plans (like the above) to win big in the Third World.[175]

The New Yorker ran a piece by Milton Viorst in January 1991 which was one of the few to highlight the Iraqi notion that it had been victimized by a joint US–Kuwait effort to dump oil on world markets, drive the price down, and thus pressure OPEC hardliners like Iraq, while helping the American economy.[176] Hardly anyone pointed out that Kuwait was the historic territory of the British Empire which we and our big oil firms inherited in the late 1940s, or that control of Persian Gulf oil gives the US tremendous leverage over economic competitors like Japan and Germany. Hardly anyone drew connections between the war and the $591 thousand million that Saudi Prince al-Waleed bin Talal poured into Citicorp, becoming the largest shareholder in America's largest bank (but one rumored to be in deep trouble).[177] Television journalism rarely got into this background, preferring emotivist, tit-for-tat 'debates' between experts who tended to cancel each other out, leaving the viewer ignorant and the moderator in the position of even-handed balance.

The long period before the war commenced, however, gave hints of what an aware and independent television might contribute to democratic debate: from time to time we saw serious opposition to Bush's policies. The Gulf War sequence reversed Vietnam: whereas television served state policy in the first phase of the war and questioned it in the second (after Tet), Gulf coverage interrogated the war in the months before Desert Storm, and served the state once the storm broke. If the sequence was reversed, the explanation is the same: American power elites were sharply divided over whether to go to war or not. If Henry Kissinger and Jeane Kirkpatrick were sure the war was just and winnable, others gave conflicting signals.

Carter administration officials were prominent in urging that United Nations sanctions be given a chance to work, but they were hardly the 'McGovernites' of rightwing mythology. Zbigniew Brzezinski and James Schlesinger, both of whom were instrumental in bringing Reagan's 'New Cold War' policies to Washington before Reagan arrived,[178] argued consistently against launching a war in the desert. George Ball, a prescient Vietnam 'dove,' gave full voice to his typical investment banker's distaste for messy warmaking. Rightwing bully Patrick Buchanan didn't want war, either, because he couldn't find any communists in Iraq or Kuwait; thus his Old Right isolationist roots pushed up ground. All-round bully Edward Luttwak was vociferous and obnoxious in opposing both the air war and the ground war. Oliver Stone conflated the reminiscent quality of much antiwar protest with his own celluloid *recherche du temps perdu*, on the eve of the ground war: 'I see a parallel reality. There is a major time-warp going on here. The quickening of the American pulse. We all feel the '60s are coming back.'[179]

I particularly liked Luttwak. On the *MacNeill/Lehrer News Hour* in August 1990, he was well into a rendition of why Saudi Arabia was the most disgusting place on earth, when he paused to remember North Korea: sorry, that's the worst place on earth. After the war ended, he referred to 'the kind of governments you have in the Middle East, people running around with towels on their heads, thinking the earth is flat, running Mach 2 aircraft.'[180] All one has to do to see which gutter that belongs in, of course, is just substitute yarmulkas for 'towels' (otherwise known as khafias).

In this early period elite television went so far as to interview pariah dissidents, like Noam Chomsky and Edward Said, both of whom appeared on *MacNeill/Lehrer* shortly after the invasion of Kuwait; both were quite moderate and supported UN sanctions, demonstrating my point about the differences between a Saddam and a Ho, and the sincerity of the American antiwar constituency. They rarely got on the major networks, however, and were nowhere to be seen once the air war began in January.[181]

This highbrow and conflicted punditry, however, was a television service, and vastly preferable to the 'experts' paraded by on major network news night after night.[182] The daily flux of television coverage is remarkably isolationist, as David Halberstam has pointed out; TV moguls think ordinary foreign news doesn't sell because ordinary folks aren't interested in it. The eight-year Iran–Iraq War, for example, was a 'non-event' for American TV.[183] Then along comes the Iraq–US War, and out of the woodwork come hundreds of instant experts, even entire new fields of expertise (desert warfare, war psychology for children). Most were from inside-the-beltway universities and thinktanks; they fulfilled television's need for representation (the subtitle read 'expert') and for 'balance' between two symmetrical opposites. Whether they knew anything or not was less important than their facility for sparing the American psyche untoward cognitive dissonance.

Take Judith Kipper, for example, a Middle East consultant to ABC so reliable and serviceable that she also appeared on *Nightline*, *MacNeill Lehrer*, C-Span, CNN, Discovery – touring the thirty-nine channels all by herself, as it were. She has a graduate degree in clinical psychology, does not know Arabic or Hebrew, and 'has no political, academic, diplomatic or military experience' in or on the Middle East. A one-time gofer who set up lecture series for the American Enterprise Institute, she got onward and upward through friendships with Walter Cronkite and Peter Jennings.[184]

Fouad Ajami was CBS's consultant, appearing in Yasir Arafat-mimetic tonsorial guise to explain the mysteries of the Arab mind to Dan Rather. He would intone Arab aphorisms like 'the jackal is the lion in his neighborhood,' as if 'Confucius Say' were back in vogue. Meanwhile he cheerled for our American boys: 'we're going to stop this thug,' he said of Saddam Hussein, calling him every name in the book – 'thug' was mild; 'rampaging beast' was more like it.[185] Both Paul Gigot in the *Wall Street Journal* and William Safire in the *New York Times* marveled at his uncanny ability to 'read the Arab mind.'[186] Middle East expert Edward Peck revealed to NBC that Americans are 'New Testament' types who 'turn the other cheek,' but Iraqis are 'an Old Testament People.'[187] The war revealed George Bush also to be an Old Testament type, however, so I'm not sure Peck's distinction really captures all the variance.

TV's military experts often looked the part, like Anthony Cordesman, 'ABC's on-camera android for strategic affairs.'

Square-jawed, tight-lipped and broad-shouldered, wearing aviator glasses
that somehow seemed molded to his face, Cordesman looked as if he was
chiseled from a mountain somewhere out West . . . .

He, too, proved to be a celebrant of 'America's new military culture,' as he
called it in a *Times* Op-Ed piece.[188] Harry Summers (who didn't look the
part) made so many bad predictions as to win William Safire's booby
prize.[189]

The fairly wide (if mostly inside-the-beltway) spectrum of debate during
Desert Shield gave way to comical 'difference' during Desert Storm. In one
'debate' on the eve of the ground war, four experts outdid themselves to say
it would be won in days, hours, maybe even minutes. On CNN's *Larry
King Live*[190] a Congressman in Indiana argued for using tactical nuclear
weapons on the Iraqis to save American lives, with the contrary view
presented by my colleague John Mearsheimer, whose conservative views
and well-honed military expertise led him to think the ground war would
only take a week, and we'd barely 'get our hair mussed' (to cite Buck
Turgidson of *Dr Strangelove*). Mearsheimer was wrong: our troops won it in
four days, with the Iraqis desperately trying to cut it to three – and all our
hairs stayed in place.

Much attention focused on the anchors: Dan Rather and Tom Brokaw in
desert camouflage fatigues (but nowhere near the battle) and Peter Jennings
taking his ease at ABC central. Rather was at his hortatory, heart-in-the-
throat worst during the climactic ground war; he 'misted up a bit,'
according to Walter Goodman, and 'repeatedly praised every aspect and
element of the allied campaign.' Although David Martin was already
reporting from the Pentagon that 'the mother of all battles had turned into
the mother of all surrenders,' Rather was grittily grunting it out with the
granite-nosed good guys, regaling us with 'the determination and grit and
valor of the grunts and grits in the marines and Navy and the US Army.'[191]
Meanwhile Jennings was taking his lumps for his more balanced reporting
and for eschewing 'grunts and grits' *television vérité*, quickly earning himself
an 'anti-Israel' label from William Safire. Brokaw was less in evidence, or
maybe it's just that his baby-face is a bit mimetic: a GI in the desert
mistook him for Peter Jennings, prompting Brokaw to admit that 'we all
look alike.'[192]

The *reductio ad absurdum* of TV journalism, however, was reserved for Peter Arnett. Operating for CNN a curiously reflexive camera, both dependent on Iraqi censors and independent because we knew that fact, Arnett scooped the other networks time and again – even getting his microphone outside the window to catch the first bombs dropping on Baghdad, and later telling the world what the war-cum-Nintendo-game looked like on the receiving end. CNN backstopped every report with a proviso that his reporting was cleared by Iraqi censors (entirely appropriate, but the same was not said of the Pentagon-muzzled 'pool' TV from Saudi Arabia).

For his courage Arnett suffered the slings and arrows of a constricted journalism knowing best only how to cover its rear end. Saddam Hussein was Arnett's real editor, A.M. Rosenthal charged, harboring the sinister intention of denying him 'full, fair accounting of life in Baghdad.' CNN should 'tell the reader [sic] always that Arnett [was] . . . prohibited from seeing or reporting the military damage needed to put the civilian story into any wartime perspective.'[193]

For Walter Goodman, Arnett was 'Saddam Hussein's first line of rebuttal' in the Pentagon's case that its precision strike on a bunker housing hundreds of civilians (in which most died) was actually a military command post. The war had been 'bloodless' on TV until that event, Goodman observed correctly; 'then suddenly, like an animal that has been denied red meat,' TV zeroed in on the carnage.[194] For Wyoming Senator Alan Simpson, Arnett was an Iraqi 'sympathizer,' and one of those journalists who lost the Vietnam War for us; Simpson Red-baited him (in a war with no Reds) by claiming that his wife was Vietnamese and that her brother had been in the Vietcong. Reed Irvine's 'Accuracy in Media' went on a rampage against Arnett and CNN; suddenly hundreds of thousands of letters arrived on editorial desks, protesting biased media coverage of the war. Harry Summers was kinder, and unaccountably literate, in saying Arnett had succumbed to what he called 'the Lafcadio Hearn syndrome' – a man who 'became more Japanese than the Japanese.'[195] Presumably this made Arnett 'more Iraqi than the Iraqis.'

Only after the heat on Arnett subsided was it possible to learn (by sleuthing through the press) that Arnett had won a Pulitzer for his Vietnam reporting; that his (now estranged) wife had been separated from her brother since Vietnam was divided in the 1950s, and that he was a professor, not a guerrilla; that the flood of irate letters was orchestrated by a Republican National Committee appeal which Simpson signed; and that the Pentagon targeted the infamous bunker with a 'decapitation' laser-guided GBU-27 bomb (carried by the F-117 Stealth bomber and designed to wipe out the enemy command) because it was reserved for the Iraqi elite and their families. The goal of the attack was either to assassinate Saddam, or to punish the high command by obliterating their relatives.[196]

Unlike Peter Arnett, the free press outside Iraq was free to go anywhere: so long as it was in between their hotel swimming pool and the Riyadh press pool. There the Pentagon's anal-retentive press handlers massaged the 5 percent of the 1,000-odd journalists in Saudi Arabia lucky enough to get admitted, while smaller pools (seven to eighteen in size) herded everyone else around. The Pentagon took a 'tough love' approach to its wayward flock: it photographed, fingerprinted, and gave detailed marching orders to the reporters; it required all stories to be submitted for 'security review'; no one could report details of operations, numbers of troops, or specific locations; no journalists could report from frontline units, tank or artillery units, or from helicopters or other aircraft, except in small, press pools.[197] Even gung-ho *Soldier of Fortune* scribblers complained about being stuck in briefing rooms with a 'bunch of boobs and dorks.'[198] Pentavision restrictions went so far as to exclude private TV 'handcams' among the troops, lest they get too interactive and 'reflexive' with the enemy. Meanwhile Pentagon briefers parodied the television simulacrum by proffering 'simulated' TV pictures to the claustrophobic journalists, hand-drawn sketches meant to 'represent' targets and 'target hits' (the 'real TV pictures' might have violated security restrictions).

None of this is exaggerated. 'Annex Foxtrot' was the Pentagon's operative document,[199] developed to dance reporters away from any contact with the real battle. The majority of reporters operated out of the Dhahran International Hotel, in the Dhahran Airport complex; their daily routine was a grittily grunt-like task of rushing from daily briefings in the JIB (US Armed Forces Joint Information Bureau) to the locker room of the hotel's turquoise-domed swimming pool, where they did their 'stand-up' TV shots for the folks back home.[200] It would be like covering a ghetto riot in Detroit from Chicago's O'Hare Hyatt Regency.

James LeMoyne wrote that the pool officials

> decide which American units can be visited by reporters, how long a visit will last, which reporters can make the visit and, to some extent, what soldiers may say, what television cameras can show and what can be written.

Other Pentagon press officials busied themselves trying 'to sway coverage in the Pentagon's favor,' denying interviews to journalists deemed 'anti-military,' and reserving their 'most restrictive' ploys for television. LeMoyne had to wait nearly two months for an interview with General Schwarzkopf, during which time press handlers let him know whether Stormin' Norman liked his stories or not. Meanwhile the Pentagon let TV personalities like Hertz Rent-A-Car running back O.J. Simpson and jolly weathermorph Willard Scott travel hither and yon (they don't 'cause problems,' LeMoyne was told). Finally 'in desperation' over the ubiquitous controls, LeMoyne sped out into the pale of desert and located a US armored battalion. An officer asked him where all the reporters had been, and warmly welcomed him. 'Two hours later the officer, in acute embarrassment,' said he had been ordered to throw LeMoyne out.[201]

Malcolm Browne also got out to 'the front,' that is, the TV viewing room at an airbase for 'cockroach-shaped' F-117A Stealth bombers, where they let him watch videotapes of 'precision hits' taken automatically when the pilots aimed their 'laser designators' at a target, just before unloading 2,000-pound bombs in Iraq. He dutifully wrote up what he 'saw' and gave it to the pool censor, who found nothing wrong with it. Then he dispatched it to 'the outside world' and went to sleep, only to learn that a wing commander had later altered and excised some of his 'improper' text. Example: 'giddy pilots' was changed to 'proud pilots.' Browne nonetheless agreed to the changes, and sent his report off once again. His FAX transmission, however, ended up at Tonopah Test Range in Nevada (home of the Stealth bomber) where everything he wrote was deemed 'a breach of security.' But Browne was lucky. At least eight American reporters, including three from the *Times*, were arrested by American military authorities.[202]

Television's vaunted high-technology was nothing without access; the Pentagon 'accessed' the war for the networks using the same technology, and thus made them accessories after the fact of a violent war. Home television enveloped the war in a syrupy, homey, simulated American community that, it appeared most of the time, was united behind our President. The morning programs (which even by TV standards subordinate hard news to wake-me-up bromides) often opened with our stalwart sons and daughters hailing their parents or loved ones in countless sandy soundbites, the alien desert being the backdrop but also the surreptitious counterpart of the blank, cardboard conformity that was obligatory in the context: seldom was heard, a discouraging word, and the skies were not cloudy all day. (Imagine the opposite: 'Hi, Mom. It's really the pits here, this war is a disgrace, we're fighting for feudal polygamists and oil sheiks, and the media hype is one big lie.') The patriotic masses instead found themselves jammed into soundbite Procrustean beds which TV deemed appropriate to their status: they are the masses, one can't expect much from them, and so those who appear must seem generally dumb and inarticulate, in contrast to the well-spoken TV people. If this judgement seems harsh, the reader might remember that the sandy blip you see gets winnowed from the hundreds you don't: some of them must have had something intelligent or inapposite to say. (*Good Morning America* thrust microphones into the faces of eighth-graders in Virginia, asking their considered opinion on the issues of the war.[203] I saw many similar, equally cynical 'ask the kids' features.)

Perhaps more cynical were the 'polls' taken among the American people, in service to democratic debate. CNN and other programs frequently urged viewers to call in (forking over a fifty-cent poll tax) and register a 'yes' or a 'no' to some proposition about which next to no information had been provided, and about which a 'yes' or a 'no' was an impossibly simple answer even if there were any information. *Newsweek*'s 'Opinion Watch' asked this question, in the third week of February when the news blackout intensified: 'Is the military effort against Iraq going as well as US officials report?' – 69 percent said 'yes,' 25 percent said 'no,' and the truth was, 100 percent had no idea whatsoever. (But let the majority rule here . . . .) Such 'polls' are the *reductio ad absurdum* of Adorno's point:

> The effrontery of the rhetorical question, 'What do people want?' lies in the fact that it is addressed – as if to reflective individuals – to those very people who are deliberately . . . deprived of this individuality.[204]

The distinction between programming, patriotism, and commerce got blurred as TV joined the jingoes and commercials proliferated with war themes. CBS offered its clients program segments 'that were specially produced with upbeat images or messages about the war, like patriotic images from the home front.'[205] (Thus to assure Exxon and Preparation H that their commercials wouldn't air after any unbecoming bloody realism. But they needn't have bothered: we never saw a battle.)

CNN was better, in its round-the-clock coverage, the deadpan presentation of its broadcasters, and the courage of Peter Arnett. In Chicago, however, CNN tied up with 'all-news radio WMAQ,' where I followed the news when the TV wasn't available, in the shower or the car. Here the CNN audio played through a new type of commercial, mingling patriotism with advertising: 'This is WMAQ. All news, all the time. You give us twenty-two minutes, we'll give you the world. Today Americans are standing tall in the Persian Gulf,' ran the lead-in, and then we hear the President's voice: 'I ask only that all of you stop and say a prayer for all the coalition forces . . . who this very minute are risking their lives for their country and all of us.' And then, 'follow CNN's live coverage throughout the day and night on WMAQ.' Here was radio and CNN in the service of empire.

Meanwhile Saddam Hussein exhibited his paleolithic grasp of television style. Eager to show the world that he wasn't maltreating the women and children he had seized as hostages, he sat himself in front of the camera, simulated an avuncular grin, and patted terrified little boys on the back, or put his guests at ease by telling them that when they are posted at military targets to ward off bombing, they 'will all be heroes of peace.' A villain from Hollywood central casting, he never knew what hit him.

Pentavision's simulacrum encapsulated not just the war, and not just television, but also print journalism: the newspapers got the same news that CNN did, from the same Riyadh catatonics – but they couldn't print it for a day or so, by which time it was stale and old. Even our paper of record rarely had information that you hadn't heard before on CNN.

Although the elite news media complained about Pentavision constrictions, it was usually much after the fact. It wasn't until May 1991 that fifteen major news organizations petitioned the Department of Defense about the Pentagon's 'virtual total control' over the US press.[206] The television networks, to my knowledge, made no such complaint. Indeed, *éminence grise* cum wise man Walter Cronkite told ABC's *Good Morning America* that the Pentagon's guidelines were 'not unreasonable' and 'even workable.'[207] Prominent personalities like Barbara Walters busied themselves berating the forlorn Iraqi representatives in the US.[208] Furthermore the long background to and frankly political character of the censorship got little attention. Yet government studies of the role of the press in the Vietnam War had prepared the way years ago for herding journalists through 'new-type warfare' that would be too messy and violent for the uninitiates of the press.[209]

Most damning of all was the general response to the Pentagon's complete ban on several independent magazines. Journalists from *The Nation*, the *Village Voice*, *Mother Jones*, and even *Harper's* were 'excluded entirely' from the Pentagon pools. They banded together and launched a federal lawsuit on January 10, 1991, challenging the constitutionality of the Pentagon's proscription of their representatives, saying they blatantly violated First Amendment guarantees of freedom of the press, and constituted a prior restraint on publication.[210] One might expect a principled liberalism to fall in behind the beleaguered magazines. But the *New York Times* did not bother to mention the suit until three weeks after the war started, when R.W. Apple cited it in the twenty-fifth paragraph of an article on the 'credibility gap.'[211] I never heard mention of it on TV.

The Geraldo Rivera principle that if you don't like his brand of TV exhibitionism you're free to switch the channel has its counterpart in the print media. If you don't like the major 'networks,' like *Time* and *Newsweek*, you can buy *The Nation* or *The Progressive*. Unless you happen to be shopping at an airport, or a suburban mall, or a Waldenbooks: where you confront the print equivalent of the thirty-nine channels, a spectrum running from *The New Republic* to *The National Review*. It requires sleuth-like instincts to find the alternative press, unless you live in New York or an academic town. Unfortunately, it was in these American *samizdat* publications that one found a serious interrogation of the warmakers. And so the warmakers proscribed all their representatives. Neat trick, wasn't it.

The one large-circulation magazine which joined this suit was *Harper's*, which you do occasionally see at a mall or an airport. Its editor, Lewis Lapham, later unloaded on his colleagues in the Fourth Estate:[212] within hours of the start of the air war on January 17, he wrote, 'newspaper and television correspondents abandoned any claim to the power of independent thought.'

If there is one small-circulation 'highbrow' magazine that has done well under Reagan–Bushism, it is *The New Republic*. Needless to say, its reporters got into the pool. This magazine's neo-conservatism has played an important role in shaping television 'balance,' and thus in constricting the spectrum of mainstream discourse. People still think of it as 'liberal,' and even some academic Marxists still write for it (like Eugene Genovese and Benedict Anderson). Michael Kinsley not only does its flagship 'TRB' column, but plays the anemic 'left' foil to Patrick Buchanan on CNN's *Crossfire*. Other *New Republic* writers like Fred Barnes and Charles Krauthammer also appear frequently on TV. So let's briefly examine the magazine's coverage of the war.

The *New Republic*'s April Fool's Day issue might be taken as representative since it was the *post-mortem* issue, with six articles on the war. On the cover we observe an article entitled 'Pentagon 2001,' illustrated with pentagonal Stealth weapons flying through the blue sky. In the middle of this article is a two-page ad from Lockheed, where its black Stealth bombers also fly against a blue background. The ad carries paeans to Lockheed's high-tech weapons and still another message: 'Watch NOVA on PBS (sponsored by Lockheed)'. On the inside back cover we find another ad and another brooding black beast, the enormous C-17 airlifter, built by McDonnell Douglas. Is this *Aviation Week and Space Technology*, or the leftwing anchor of the American political spectrum?

Turning to the magazine's content, we find Conor O'Clery writing about the lengths to which some would go 'in curbing the power and autonomy of the media' – in Lithuania. (A Soviet hardliner argued that Lithuanian TV had to be controlled: 'it would be strange if state television were to use its huge resources to attack the president.') Congressman Dave McCurdy (Democrat – Oklahoma) argued that we need a strengthened CIA owing to 'the newest threat to American interests: authoritarian, often wealthy, anti-Western regimes that seek to overturn the international order . . . .'

Michael Kelly wrote about the turkey shoots as Iraqi troops sought to withdraw, in his article 'Highway to Hell.' But Kelly uses his smarmy, disgusting style to write clichés about death in war ('even in a mass attack, there is individuality'), to glorify American soldiers ('I liked [Major

Nugent] instantly . . . he felt very sad for the horrors around him . . . perhaps, he said . . . divine intervention had been at work – "some kind of good against evil thing'"), and to praise Pentavision ('the Pentagon has been very, very good in controlling the flow of information . . . ').

Not one criticism of pressgag rules intruded the pages of this issue. The editors, however, had some cautionary notes for George Bush. Like Teddy Roosevelt, he 'sits astride public opinion like a conqueror.' (Perhaps it is the fully conquered who best understand this.) Bush was now marching to the tune of 'the old bipartisan consensus . . . an unabashed assertion of certain principles of internationalism.' But unless he 'governed' from now on, particularly on the domestic front, the towering conqueror might be headed for a slip. It was left for Charles Krauthammer (in a subsequent cover article) to call this internationalism by its proper name: 'pseudo-multilateralism.' An unabashed imperialist, he champions American unilateralism: 'why should the preeminent power on the globe invite such a needless constraint [internationalism] on its action?'[213]

As Congressman McCurdy's article indicated, *The New Republic* was looking for new, post-Saddam enemies to slay. The problem was, as Colin Powell put it, 'I'm running out of demons. I'm running out of villains. I'm down to Castro and Kim Il Sung.'[214] Leslie Gelb had called North Korea 'The Next Renegade State' in a *New York Times* column on April 10, quoting Cheney as saying North Korea might soon possess nuclear weapons, and was the most probable source of 'a no-notice attack against US forces'; rumors also bubbled up about a budding Cuban nuclear capability. And thus it was that *The New Republic* dutifully published, also in April, articles on Castro and Kim – labeling the former an 'old caudillo' (translation: Cuba's just a banana republic and he's the horseback dictator) and the latter 'weird.'[215] Only specialists understood that the earliest scenario for a Korean nuke was 1995, a more likely time the year 2000, and some in the 'intelligence community' thought the presumed plutonium reprocessing facility might actually be a textile plant.[216]

Television format not only intruded on print journalism, but into books as well: thus it was that the Gulf TV docudrama, like Korea and Vietnam, had a 'book of the series.'[217] The 'book' began on a patriotic note about 'our kids over there' (Corporal Pulliam from Texas, Navy Seabee Oliver of Indiana), peddled soundbite inanities ('Will the Arab world ever be the same? Or will America?'), undertook the chapter entitled 'The Legacy of Nebuchadnezzar' by intoning that 'Saddam's unhesitating use of terror to solidify and justify [sic] his rule is deeply rooted in history,' and sought to stifle any speculation (such as that of Milton Viorst in *The New Yorker*) that Kuwait and the US had developed 'a strange conspiracy to destroy Baghdad' (which was a shameless but predictable misrepresentation of what Viorst and others had said). Just like Stanley Karnow's book-of-the-series, nary a footnote graced the pages. This 'book' illustrated how television composition rules increasingly inform 'literature' itself.

The result of television's complicity with its own irrelevance was that the more you watched, the stupider you got. An academic survey among 250 respondents in the Denver area conducted two weeks into the war found three groups of TV watchers: light (less than ninety minutes a day), medium (ninety minutes to three hours) and heavy (more than three hours). Knowledge of the issues varied inversely with television time, and varied directly with opposition to the war. 'Despite months of coverage,' the study concluded, 'most people do not know basic facts' about the Middle East and US policy in the region.[218]

It may be that Pete Williams, the Defense Department spokesman, got the last word when he said the pools 'gave the American people the best war coverage they ever had,'[219] if we recall our definition of the business as an entertainment medium dedicated to selling things. You could watch this war movie and be assured a happy ending. Or maybe it was a gay group in New York who had the last word, by 'outing' the Pentagon's macho manipulator of the Fourth Estate shortly after the war ended.

With all this as preface, the gratuitous violence of the ground war unfolded in a vacuum, a virtual television blackout. I felt a kind of sick numbness on Saturday, February 23, when it became clear that Iraq would be out of Kuwait shortly no matter what the US did, indeed that its army had begun the pullout, followed by the bulletins that the ground war had been launched. And then there was nothing to see.

Defense Secretary 'Dick' Cheney materialized at the Pentagon to tell reporters that 'we've been as forthcoming as possible' with you nosy folks, but now all briefings had to stop. The Riyadh Retentives disappeared, too. Television had no pictures, so out came simulations of the simulacrum: maps, experts, and huzzahs of patriotism. Tony Cordesman told ABC viewers all about tank warfare, NBC's Harry Summers tutored us on infantry tactics, CBS's Fouad Ajami chided Saddam for thinking 'we didn't have the guts' for this fight. Over and over network anchors allowed as how they 'understood' the need for the Pentagon blackout, fearful as ever that the silent majority might awake from its stupor and find them soft on Saddam. Fatuous toady Charles Kuralt assured Americans that 'CBS would do nothing to hurt American troops' (in Walter Goodman's paraphrase). Goodman noted that 'opponents of the war were not much in evidence,' and that the first day of the ground war looked 'distinctly rosy' on TV.[220]

College basketball was winding down to the climax of the play-offs, so that took precedence over the pictures of the ground war (had there been any). But at half-time Dan Rather broke in grittily to report that 'the Allied fast-break offense is running, gunning and going good.' Tom Brokaw, also good only for half-time, deemed it 'a blowout for the allied forces.' TV military experts deployed the 'Telestrator' (a sports TV invention) to draw electronic blueprints for squashing the evil enemy, or used computer-generated graphics in repulsive 'illustrations' of the fighting. Every once in a while a video image from the war would squiggle through, but still there wasn't much to see (they were all cleared by censors).[221] Finally Stormin' Norman squeezed onto the telly, to say that 'friendly casualties have been extremely light.' He didn't say anything about evil-enemy casualties, which mounted hourly by the thousands.

The running and gunning Allied forces met 'the mother of all surrenders,' and it was over in 100 hours. There followed an orgy of television patriotic triumphalism, the likes of which could never be imagined. Not one television reporter, in my viewing, was able to resist the call to wave the flag and backslap for 'the kids.' Not one paused to say what had been said 100 hours earlier, that no war was necessary. Few showed any concern for the tens of thousands of needless casualties. 'The war had a movie script happy ending,' wrote one White House correspondent; 'the good guys won, and a supporting cast of millions felt the future looked a lot better than they had hoped.'[222] It was the *Wall Street Journal*, however, which headlined the real story: 'Victory in Gulf War Exorcises the Demons of the Vietnam Years.' The lightning-quick victory is sweeping the Vietnam war from the forefront of the American consciousness. For nearly two decades, Americans . . . have brooded about its contradictory lessons and the air of defeatism it bred . . . many of these cobwebs have been cleared away.

'We are the most influential nation on earth,' Ben Wattenberg exuded; 'this may be the beginning of the second American Century.'[223]

THE GULF BEFORE THE GULF

The television discourse of the Gulf War could not mimic Vietnam as Vietnam (until 1968) did Korea; getting 'Vietnam' behind us was the goal, but the real Vietnam was poor surrogate for a war in the desert with no remotely civil or revolutionary aspect to it. This occasioned a revised television text. Nonetheless that text was mimetic, if not of Vietnam.

A peculiarity of the empiricist mind is to require that unpalatable truths well documented in one situation must then be well documented in similar situations: otherwise the truths are aberrations. It could not be assumed in our documentary, for example, that well-known aspects of the Vietnam War had anything to say about the Korean War: if Dean Rusk proved untrustworthy time and again in regard to Vietnam, that was no reason to question his veracity on Korea. If McGeorge Bundy was an architect of the Vietnam disaster, that did not disqualify him from being the historian of the Korean disaster for anniversary treatment in the *New York Times*.[224]

It is instructive therefore that television treatment of the recent Gulf War can be carried over virtually whole cloth to the Iranian hostage crisis in 1979–80. Both crises began with an act that was an undeniable outrage: instead of the invasion of Kuwait, the invasion of the US Embassy and the seizure of hostages. In both cases television then abstracted the event from its origins and background, from its context, so that it could function as original sin for the duration of the crisis.

The place of Hitler was taken not by Saddam Hussein, but by the religious leader Ayatollah Khomeini. Like Saddam, he threatened our control of the Persian Gulf and Middle Eastern oil; like Saddam, he was a fanatic – that is, his politics were not the outcome of understandable and knowable processes, but beyond rationality. (The networks universally assumed that we were rational, developed, modern people with reasonable goals, and the enemies were antediluvian, passionate people with outlandish or outrageous goals.) Khomeini was not a Sunni Muslim like Saddam, but as a Shiite he nonetheless had a 'penchant for martyrdom.' America was treated not as 'a complex system,' but 'as if it were an injured person'; barely touched was the sordid background of US policy a few years back (American complicity in arming the Shah to the teeth and in the terrorism of his Savak secret police, just as we sold arms, grain, and preferential loans to Saddam). When the hostages finally returned, network coverage was 'frequently intrusive and maudlin,' focusing on personal ordeals, the joy of reuniting with loved ones, 'celebrations of American heroism and Iranian barbarism.'[225]

Television coverage was not as blanketed then, of course (CNN was not yet available), but it was similarly 'misleadingly full,' with streams of geopolitical strategists and Middle Eastern pundits, but barely any sincere and thoughtful discussion of the origins of American involvement in the region, the legitimate grievances of the Iranian people, or the endless privileging of 'the West' at the expense of 'the East.' This was true both of mass programming and the elite shows like *MacNeill/Lehrer*, which in a three-month period in 1979–80 had two serious critics (Richard Falk and Eqbal Ahmad) and a handful of Iranians sprinkled among a host of government officials, corporate spokesmen, and docile academics.[226]

In 1979, however, the series of recent 'oil shocks' made the hegemonic linkage between US policy and Persian Gulf oil more prominent. Brzezinski referred many times to 'the arc of crisis' and the Persian Gulf as 'the third zone of containment,' an updating of Acheson's 1940s link between East Asian containment and a 'Great Crescent' stretching from Tokyo to Alexandria. Insider/wise man Clark Clifford, himself an architect of the original containment doctrine (but in 1991 tainted by a scandal involving a Middle East banking concern), journeyed to the region on behalf of President Carter, to declare on television that should the Soviets move beyond Afghanistan toward the Gulf, this would mean global war.[227]

The other significant departure in 1979–80, when compared to the recent coverage, was the close scrutiny of Saudi Arabia – which happened primarily because it was not playing ball with the US over the Camp David talks and other issues (only Edward Luttwak carried the anti-Saudi line through to the Gulf crisis). The regime's anti-democratic and feudal tendencies were given a big airing, the highlight being PBS's screening of the documentary entitled *The Death of a Princess*. Television depicted this regime, too, as an Islamic insult to liberal standards, a peculiar throwback to the pre-modern; if its peculiarity was distinct from Iran's, it was still peculiar.[228]

Shortly after the Gulf War began, with its vaunted precision and imagined violence, I happened upon a cable show in Arabic. A full, rounded woman in a flowing gown stood alone in the middle of a room draped with satin curtains, singing verses from the Koran which ran in Arabic subtitles as she sang. Unaccompanied by any music, hands folded across her stomach and bereft of dramatic gesture, she sang beautifully and hauntingly about I know not what. The crystalline solo wafting over the airwaves counterpointed everything on the network stations, which did not show the war, but also did not elucidate the Arabic enemy or the Arabic ally. The enemy was demonized, and the ally elided.

Not once did I see a serious inquiry into the depth and longevity of Arab culture. Not once, an investigative report on the Saudi or Kuwait regimes and societies which we defended, or on the Iraq of the 1980s which we armed. Never, the empathetic courage of a Nietzsche, who a century ago contrasted 'ancient Asia' with 'its protruding little peninsula Europe, which wants by all means to signify as against Asia the "progress of man."'[229]

Sometimes television's stereotyped representation of the 'other' went beyond prejudice and beyond parody, however, really beyond one's capacity for invention. Deborah Norville and Bryant Gumbel, for example, got into a rollicking repartee over the weird languages those people speak in the Middle East. 'Did you understand a word he said?,' Gumbel asked her, after one Colonel Yacoub finished speaking. This reminded him of the time he interviewed someone high up in the Afghan mujahideen ('a big muckety-muck,' Deborah suggested): the guy started talking and Bryant had no idea what language he was speaking. 'Blubbedyblubbedyblubbedy!', Deborah suggested[230] – which, come to think about it, was one of the more intelligent things I heard her say on *The Today Show*.

PANOPTICON: THE FIRST TELEVISION WAR

The advance of American technology allowed us to sit in our living rooms and watch missiles homing onto their Baghdad targets, relayed via nosecone cameras that had the good taste to cease transmitting just as they obliterated their quarry, thus vetting a cool, bloodless war through a cool medium. Here was 'a kind of video press release,' said a pioneer of the use of images to manipulate pubic opinion:[231] a bomb that was simultaneously image, warfare, news, spectacle, and advertisement for the Pentagon. The success of this warfare obscured the memory of Vietnam, but it also prepared a future in which the assumptions of positivism, the technology of smart weapons, and the unseeing but conforming eye of television combine to make a new form of war, simultaneously surveilling the home front and an unruly world.

Vietnam was what we might call an interactive or 'intersubjective' war, a story with a dilated beginning, middle and end, in which both we and the enemy came to know each other as human beings, locked in a highly mismatched and uneven contest over incommensurable goals. Tet and the street protests opened an interactive space where the war's purpose could be examined from top to bottom (even on TV occasionally), and thus we came to know ourselves and our enemy.

In the process the Third World got off the reservation, and US policy had to contend not just with the Kim Il Sungs and the Ho Chi Minhs, but with Chinese titans like Mao, Arab militants like Quadaffi, African socialists like Mugabe, Islamic fundamentalists like Khomeini, and yet more Central American Marxists near our shores like Daniel Ortega. The Carter stalemate over Iran and the Reagan stalemate over the Sandinistas[232] did nothing to change this pattern. But with the decline and fall of socialist systems, the only remaining security threat to American global interests today lies in the Third World, domination of which seems now to be in the interests not just of the advanced capitalist nations, but the former Soviet Union as well.

The utilitarian notion of 'the Good' is the greatest good for the greatest number. By that standard, a major redistribution of the world's wealth ought to ensue: First World reparations to the Third, in repayment for several centuries of imperialism. But, as Nietzsche noted, there was always 'a touch of Tartuffe' about Jeremy Bentham's idea of 'the happiness of the greatest number';[233] far more representative of the modern positivist project, as Foucault and others have shown, were new power grids and techniques of surveillance and control by which the rational, 'modern' individual, understanding himself as the only important subject, held sway over the object – the irrational, the pre-modern, the colonized, the feminine, the heterodox. Heterodox human objects, indeed, get defined, constituted and controlled by 'rational' human subjects, their interaction being purely instrumental rather than interactive and dialectical. Bentham's Panopticon was the logical outcome of such thinking.[234]

The Panopticon is a prison in which the individual cells surround a watch-tower, arrayed in circles that admit light and thereby silhouette every single inmate for the guard in the center. The guard, however, cannot be seen by the inmates, creating 'an effect of constant, omniscient surveillance,' and thus the prisoners police themselves.[235] The ubiquitous closed-circuit TV cameras that now monitor so much of American public life are a contemporary analogue, carried to an extreme in regard to the Third World in our midst, the ghetto war zone – even structuring the 'Martin Luther King Center' in the midst of one of our biggest ghettoes.[236] But the recent television war propelled utilitarian logic to its conclusion: a war to end all wars inaugurates a 'new world order' in which the whole Third World must behave and police itself, or suffer the consequences from an omniscient, omnipresent, technologically-omnipotent 'Big Brother.'

This was not an 'intersubjective' war, but a one-way ticket to oblivion for the uncomprehended adversary. Although the Gulf War was less afflicted than previous conflicts by stereotypical views of Arabs (probably because so many were on our side), it was no less governed by an Orientalism that wants either to know that the 'other' is just like us, or does not want to hear about them: a hegemony of uninterest, which gains power precisely as it places the object beyond the pale. This was the essential reason for the virtual absence of any Arabs on the TV, besides the Uncle Toms like Fouad Ajami, and the lack of interest in 'our' Arab allies, let alone the Iraqi enemy.

Most remarkable in this respect, however, was General Schwarzkopf, the media's war hero. Several times he told TV journalists that, in his view, there were no experts on the Middle East. None of them knew what they were talking about. Even the Arab experts were wanting. The epistemo-logy here seems to connote this: even the object does not know itself, so why need I be detained in doing with it as I will? My totalizing subject-position might be affronted by real people, real history, real difference, so why bother? Schwarzkopf unconsciously acknowledged the judgement that 'the Orient was not Europe's interlocutor, but its silent Other';[237] a decorated Vietnam veteran, he revealed the emotion Benedict Anderson spoke of, 'a rage at Vietnamese "inscrutability,"' a desire to penetrate an opaque, alien, recalcitrant entity with whom one could not even con-verse.[238] Better just to forget about them.

This is precisely what happened when the human wreckage occasionally entered the camera's eye: forget about it – it's Chinatown. Foreign correspondents told Christopher Hitchens of their incredulity at the 'absence of revulsion' in regard to the air raids on the 'Highway of Death,' where American forces, he wrote,

> caught a convoy of fleeing Iraqis, bombed the vehicles at both ends and then returned to shred and dismember the resulting traffic jam time and again. Everybody sat and watched those pictures. Yet for public and historical purposes, no memory or consciousness of the incident exists.[239]

In place of sincere inquiry into exactly what the weapons were doing to Iraq, television proffered yet another hero: however deaf, dumb, and blind the medium may have been during the Gulf War, the weapons were smart. Since this was one of the few new technologies Americans could be proud of in the recent period, it also got wrapped into the patriotic aura. And here, television for once was also 'smart': the weapons were TV-guided or TV-observed.

Take for example the 'SLAM Walleye' – a Standoff Land-Attack Missile with a Walleye video in its nosecone. Laser guidance was more common, but often accompanied by a videocam in the nose, to record the precision hit. The networks accepted both the 'eyewitness' evidence of the nosecams and Pentagon claims to perfect accuracy. The Patriot missile, of course, was the star of the show: *USA Today* (a postmodern soundbite newspaper) presented it in 1950s nostalgic–phallic terms: 'Length: 17 feet, 5 inches; three inches longer than a Cadillac Sedan de Ville.'[240] We all lined up to watch a game called the Patriots vs the Scuds, as if two teams had been added to the National Football League. Only the Scuds, however, had television there to record the havoc wreaked when they hit the ground – in Israel, where we witnessed graphic testimony to the awful human residue of Saddam's aimless, useless missile terrorism.

Readers of the fine print of our newspapers, however, later learned that our weapons weren't so smart after all. TV's Patriots vs Scuds game masked an Israel sorely upset with Patriots that, sources said, destroyed only one of twenty-five incoming Scuds in mid-air, as they were supposed to.[241] (This gave heart to some in the US, since the electronic guts of the Patriot are Japanese . . . .) The Air Force quietly reported in March that 70 percent of the 88,500 tons of bombs dropped on Iraq missed their targets. How so? It turned out that only 7 percent of the tonnage was 'smart.' Of that small percentage, which occupied all of television's attentions and praise during the war, 10 percent also proved 'dumb' and missed its target. Fully 62,137 tons of all types of American bombs missed: and where the tons fell, nobody knows, least of all television journalism.[242]

Michael Klare was about the only weapons expert who pointed out that the Pentagon used 'a new breed of munitions designed to duplicate the destructive effects of tactical nuclear weapons,' with firepower so devastating that it left many corpses beyond recognition, fried to a crisp. The BLU-82/B 'Daisy Cutter,' for example, was a 15,000-pound bomb so heavy that it had to be pushed out of special C-130 transports; a 'fuel-air' weapon, it turns battlefields into vast seas of fire. The Air Force's new deep-penetration 'decapitation' bombs (like the one used in the February 13 attack on the underground bomb shelter in Baghdad) grew out of new technologies designed to go after the Soviet leadership, which throughout the 1980s destabilized the arms race by leading many to believe that the US was developing a first-strike capability.[243]

In May 1991 I heard an off-the-record lecture by a recently retired, formerly high-ranking Army general who said that the military wanted to move out of nuclear weapons as fast as it could, because with precision guidance and new high-yield explosives you could get a similar bang for your buck, but without the moral and other problems occasioned by nukes (like irradiating your infantry).

This new 'conventional' destructive capability was the main reason why a United Nations observation team reported after visiting postwar Iraq that 'the recent conflict has wrought near-apocalyptic results on the infrastructure of what had been, until January 1991, a rather highly urbanized and mechanized society. Now, most means of modern life support have been destroyed or rendered tenuous.'[244]

Erika Munk, a New York writer, had a different point to make about the urban rubble. She visited Baghdad and found less human wreckage than she expected; some later assailed her observations about that, but she correctly intuited the meaning of 'smart' weapons even when they do what they're supposed to do:

> When a capital city's communication centers can be destroyed with little damage to the surrounding buildings or people; when a nation's infrastructure can be crippled so that the deadliest effects appear long after the world's eye has moved elsewhere; when high-tech, low-gore war can be combined with heavy censorship – then any nation willing to forfeit its social and economic development to weapons can exert power at will, deny moral responsibility and avoid popular revulsion.[245]

If you have nosecone cameras, laser-guided weapons, infra-red beams, terrain-mapping cruise missiles, AWACS surveillance aircraft, high-resolution spy satellites, Patriot anti-missile missiles, and a Telestrator to explain it all on TV, realizing 'ubiquitous orbital vision of enemy territory,'[246] what need have you for morality, or empathetic knowledge of the 'other'? If you have cooperative TV networks that limit debate to fleeting soundbites and a constrained, consensual politics, with anchors who patriotically rejoice in their own impotence and irrelevance to the very war they are reporting, who dutifully black themselves out and then celebrate (and help to create) a victorious national community, why worry about 'living room wars'?

Here television becomes not just an accomplice, but a two-way Panopticon: from the battlefield, through the Pentagon, into the home and back again – ubiquitous orbital vision of the enemy and the living room, a magical Stealth weapon of our own making. The state succeeds in realizing the 'armed eye' Vertov imagined: 'I am the camera's eye. I am the machine which shows you the world as I alone see it.'[247] And the TV cyclops doesn't get to see the war: the medium is the only message.

Was this Fiske's 'reflexive,' 'interactive' viewing experience? I think not. In *Signatures of the Visible* Jameson writes a great deal about how the photo registers the Event, and how film as a medium alters the Event historically and dialectically, as 'the production process becomes an event in its own right and comes to include its own reception of it.'[248] What was the Event of the Gulf War? It cannot have been the war. It was not the photo or the film. It was television itself, but then we can only intuit its production processes, particularly in regard to a Pentavision shrouded in secrecy. All that is left, therefore, is 'the reception of it,' the passive, easy-chair apprehension of an 'Event' so many times removed as to be incomprehensible. This event than passes quickly as memory, because there is no recess in the brain to locate it as 'what I saw in the war,' or as 'what I thought about it,' but only as 'identity,' as 'facsimile,' as simulacrum: and thus it locates alongside *M*A*S*H*, *Hogan's Heroes*, and other military sitcoms — last year's hit series.

The postmodern facsimile procreated and recombined and spawned again in the months after the war, too, while television memory still had its quickly disappearing half-life, with *Desert Storm: The Miniseries* on the 'Arts and Entertainment' network, CNN videocassettes on sale in supermarkets (videos of the videos as it were), video biographies of Stormin' Norman for rent in the video stores, comedian Jonathan Winters cloning Schwarzkopf in TV commercials (equally portly in his Desert Storm fatigues), and everyone but everyone draping themselves in the American logo, otherwise known as Old Glory.

The victory celebration in New York was distinctly postmodern, befitting our first postmodern war. First came theme music from the film *Star Wars*, then a sky battle between simulated Scuds and Patriots over the East River, than a colossal fireworks display inaugurated with the stirring tunes of *Thus Spake Zarathustra*, which Americans knew only as the music from Kubrick's *2001*.[249] Our paper of record foregrounded the megashow with an entire separate section, featuring on the cover a wife welcoming her soldier-husband home, Old Glory hanging in the background and he tightly gripping in his fist a small reproduction of same. They were African-Americans, limbing a new multicultural and multiethnic ventriloquy that had its greater symbols in Supreme Court nominee Clarence Thomas and celebrated intellectuals Fukuyama and D'Souza: behold, even the disadvantaged ethnics celebrate America and above all its New Right climate (so who are you to protest this war)? Although the *Times* labeled this section an advertisement, it allowed many of its own Gulf War articles to be reproduced throughout.[250]

Soon, however, it became last season's hit show, a mere summer re-run, and by the fall it was another in a lengthening list of America's 'forgotten wars.' More troops came home, more parades, more hoopla, and television duly covered it – but in a curiously attenuated and slightly bored way. It all seemed vaguely anachronistic, like something consumed and digested already. Memory was receding with the speed of (television) light. We now can appreciate the new principles of television war: crank up the hoopla and open the television window, whereupon the hoopla is magnified and the war (because censored) is unseen, and the party of forgetting wins an instant victory. Who can remember the Falklands or Grenada or Panama? Does anyone still remember the Gulf War? Memory cannot form amid the unseen, the images cannot become 'indelible.' This, in essence, was the formula for the Gulf War.

CHAPTER FIVE

BEFORE TELEVISION:

THE UNKNOWN WAR

Every day we saw dead Americans, dead Vietnamese, bombings, all
kinds of rather interesting things, but never one program on why;
never one program on the history of it; never one program
attempting to place it in context.
EMILE DE ANTONIO[251]

The quarrels in which the artistic experts become involved with
sponsor and censor about a lie going beyond the bounds of
credibility are evidence not so much of an inner aesthetic tension as
of a divergence of interests. The reputation of the specialist, in
which a last remnant of objective independence sometimes finds
refuge, conflicts with . . . the concern which is manufacturing the
cultural commodity. But the thing itself has been essentially
objectified and made viable before the established authorities begin
to argue about it.
THEODOR ADORNO[252]

Knowing what I know about television, why did I agree to work on a TV
documentary? Britain is the first, and in some ways the whole, answer. The
home of the first bourgeois revolution, that country has not yet exhausted
the great fruit of that revolution: the public sphere not just as an arena for
the entrepreneur looking for the main chance, but also for an informed
citizen-like discourse. To the unending shock of an American like myself,
this informed public shows itself on TV, and has the effrontery to expect
viewers to use that vestigial television-era organ, the brain. Even the
British television critics are serious theorists, like John Fiske or the late
Raymond Williams.

For all its obvious faults, it can be said that one needs a certain intelligence even to watch British television, let alone participate in it. Part of it is the preservation of a respect for language. This is, after all, a country where most cab drivers are more articulate than US university professors. Let me give an example. Once when I flew over to London I took the late and lamented 'People Express' to save Thames some money, and found myself sitting in the midst of a coven of Hell's Angels, off to make some mayhem in Britain. They were on their very best behavior, I was happy to find, in spite of (or because of) their black leather jackets, chains, engineer boots, and poor-white-trash molls.

The night passed with nothing more than a few grunts and belches here and there, and the wafting odor of unwashed flesh. When they met their British counterparts at Heathrow, who were costumed alike, I heard the following conversation: 'Oh, hello, jolly good of you to fly all the way over; sorry though, seems to be a bit of a queue getting out of here.' To which one of the Americans said, 'Hey Joe, whaddafuggisa Q?'

Britain is a country of choice also because it had little to do with the Korean War, other than allowing itself to be herded into it by Dean Acheson. My judgement was that an objective documentary on the Korean War could not be made in the United States, at least not with the needed funding and any hope of a wide audience. I had the history of such documentary efforts to guide me to my conclusion: the existing American documentaries on Korea are interesting only as a confirmation of the proposition that the camera not only can lie, but that an entire war can be encapsulated by unspoken rules of ideological discourse. All the ones I have seen are period pieces, indistinguishable from the time they were made. Herewith a couple of examples.

David Wolper made his Korea film in 1965, and it perhaps could not have been made at any later time; even by 1966 it seemed foolish. It is a fairy tale of American 'policemen' chasing communist 'criminals,' in which Koreans barely make an appearance; wounded soldiers are always American. The narration is often not historically accurate; fake or inappropriate footage appears at several points. It gives one or two minutes to the pre-1950 background. The Chinese entry brings into Korea 'a human sea.' Wolper's fable of the POW camps meets or perhaps surpasses 1950s communist treatment of the same issue. Our POWs are tortured and brainwashed, but their POWs (in our hands) are shown happily playing sports, reading, or painting. Haydon Boatner, the bull-headed commander who subdued North Korean POW camps with flamethrowers, is called 'an old China hand' who 'speaks Chinese fluently.'

The politics of this film, however, are middle-road Cold War Democratic. MacArthur is blamed time and again for every failure of strategy, trying 'again and again' to take the war to China; only a courageous Harry Truman reigns in the General's madness.[253]

Lou Reed's deftly titled *Korea: The Forgotten War*, narrated by Robert Stack, is quite similar, with unintended laugh lines like 'Vietnamese Communists [were] threatening French rule' in 1950, or that Korea was 'the invasion route' to Japan (Japan has invaded Korea at least three times, and only the Mongols departed from Korea in Japan's direction – only to be blown off course by the famous *kamikaze* or 'divine wind'), or that American forces in 1950 were 'weekend warriors,' 'sadly deficient' (five years after defeating Japan and Germany, and just as Acheson's NSC 68 military buildup took wing). Unfortunately this film plays all the time on cable TV, and I've been asked three times by one of our department secretaries if this was the film I helped to make . . . .

Another caution to the idea that America could produce an objective documentary was that the guardians of the Korean War Holy Grail in America were people like General Richard Stilwell, head of the national committee to get a memorial to the Korean War in Washington (a worthy cause), CIA chief for covert operations in Asia in 1950, 8th Army Commander in South Korea during Park Chung Hee's worst repression, staunch Reaganite, and early organizer of the 'Contras' in Honduras (all unworthy). I figured that by the standards of American television, he would be seen as the rightwing anchor of a responsible, consensual view, and I would be seen as a troublemaker. (I was proved right.)

Another reason for crossing the Atlantic was my respect for the British documentary. The origin of this, I thought, was the superb world reporting of the BBC, an organization that I deeply revered – until I got to Britain and learned a little bit about it. My respect was reinforced by a great documentary product, the 26-part *World at War* made by Thames Television. When I first saw that series in the mid-1970s, I was amazed by its depth, its courage, its commitment to unpalatable truths about 'the good war.' Furthermore some enlightened businessmen somewhere also buy commercials on Thames Television, I knew, which makes more and better documentaries than all our public stations combined, and even has the effrontery to parade them by in prime time.

Filmmaker Valerie Ross, a former student of mine, had given me a book that included interviews with several of the Thames people who worked on *The World at War*,[254] which I found impressive and refreshing. Jerome Kuehl, an associate producer on the series, explained the 'bottom up' quality of the documentary, in which the accounts of ordinary folk (footsoldiers, peasants) were given equal weight with the 'revered figure' or 'public personality' who, in ordinary documentaries, holds forth telling the audience what to think about what they are seeing. Kuehl also located the problem of American television at the appropriate point, the executive producers who fear controversy in the same measure that they fear their sponsors. He thought *The World at War* was too controversial to be made in America:

> We say the Russians could have beaten the Germans on their own. That the British didn't really win the Battle of Britain . . . these things are really quite extraordinarily offensive, not to the professional historians who have known them for thirty years, but offensive to American executives and producers who simply would not wish to commit . . . resources to that kind of series.

Kuehl went on to point out, however, that the series was 'an enormous success' in America, and asked this question: 'Why is it that in order to make serious programs which ordinary US audiences find attractive, Americans have to come to Britain? It's very curious.'[255]

Anyway, it was a good reason for me to come to Britain. Even more cogent were the remarks of David Elstein, a rising star in London television circles who had worked both for the BBC and Thames, and who in the late 1970s produced the popular documentary series *This Week*. The BBC was public and, an American would think, independent. In fact it was 'exceptionally wishy-washy, cautious [and] conservative,' according to Elstein, and usually lodged on the side of authority. Thames was commercial and, one would suppose, therefore dependent on its advertisers. In fact by an act of Parliament 'advertisers have no access to program makers at all,' and thus problems of sponsorship rarely arise.

So public television was skittish and private television independent, an amazing inversion of American expectation. Elstein could launch a scathing critique of Phillip Morris (a sponsor) and get away with it, whereas in the US even the National Archives helps Phillip Morris peddle its cigarettes by letting it parade the basic enabling documents of our nation through its television commercials, a kind of hucksterism-as-history.

Elstein subscribed to the de Antonio theory of documentary making, if in more measured terms. Standard television fare like BBC weekly business programs, he said, were 'monstrously biased' in the way they present issues, yet the BBC 'lays claim to some kind of objectivity.' As for Elstein himself,

> I have never subscribed to the myth of objectivity in journalism or in television current affairs. I'm a great believer in committed programs. That doesn't mean that people have to be overtly socialist or fascist or whatever it might be. It's just that the reporter, the interviewer ought to have commitment . . . it can be anger . . . it can be the passion for caring about a subject.

A committed position, even one consistently pursued through an entire run of programming, is not a problem: 'If someone is thought to be right-wing then someone socialist . . . will use a filter and interpret what that chap says and vice versa.' However, 'if you abandon your editorial standpoint then the audience has no means of assessing whether it's being got at, brainwashed, or whatever.'[256] It all seemed perfectly reasonable to me.

My last and most important reason for doing the documentary was not Britain, but a person who lives there, Jon Halliday. I first met Jon in 1976, but I knew about him from 1970 when he wrote a prescient article on Korea in the journal *Socialist Revolution*. In 1975 he produced an excellent study of Japan, *A Political History of Japanese Capitalism*. He and his brother Fred have divided up the world of small but interesting countries. Jon takes Korea, Japan, and Albania (he edited a wonderfully funny and interesting selection of Enver Hoxha's memoirs). Fred takes South Yemen, Afghanistan, Ethiopia, and the like, while writing provocative and important books on things like Reagan's 'New Cold War' of the early 1980s.

Jon is the older brother (if not the eldest). By the time I met him he had a restless collection of white hair sticking out from under a flattened maroon porkpie hat, small rectangular sunglasses with a purple tint, a mod sportcoat that seemed still to be slightly akilter on its hanger even though it was on his shoulders, dark pants, and a pair of colorful socks. These textiles all sat imperfectly on a bent body that nonetheless conveyed vigor; he hadn't passed forty by then, anyway. I once made the mistake of telling him he looked like Alec Guinness, which merited the immediate come-back, 'I hhhaaaaaate Alec Guinness!' But the first impression of Jon, to the average American or to me, would suggest an eccentric Englishman. (In fact Jon is part Irish.)

Since just about everything to do with our documentary turned out to be political, let me begin with politics. Everything I have just said would convince television moguls in the US that Jon and his brother are running dogs of the Soviets to be avoided at all costs, which indeed some Reaganite publications sought to maintain about Fred in the early 1980s, placing him at the top of the KGB hierarchy in Europe (to great mirth among his friends, although he rightly didn't see the humor in it). The Halliday brothers would have a chance of running a major documentary in America roughly like that of their being chosen for the next space shuttle. (I invited Fred to give a talk at the University of Washington once, prompting one of my Soviet-specialist colleagues to storm that he should not be allowed to speak under University sponsorship. This university had also prevented Robert Oppenheimer from speaking in 1956. Oppenheimer got off the plane and heard two things: he was disinvited, and Einstein had died while he was in the air.) But we are speaking of Britain, fortunately; quite fittingly, Fred has emerged as a prominent television commentator on foreign affairs, and has a chair at the London School of Economics.

I immediately liked Jon, both for our common interests and for his unfailing courtesy, good humor, and *savoir faire*. He is a gentleman, which turned out to be one of his difficulties in working at Thames. He has long had an interest in film, doing interview books with Douglas Sirk and with Pasolini, the latter under the name Oswald Stack (Oswald from Lee

Harvey, Stack from Robert); he also edited a study of the psychology of gambling.

His weekends were spent at a home south of London, to which he invited a congeries of guests to share his very considerable hospitality. I spent one weekend playing ping-pong with Clare Peploe, screenwriter (*Zabriskie Point* and other films), brother to Mark Peploe (who did the script for *The Last Emperor*), and wife to Bernardo Bertolucci (who directed it). I spent another playing tennis with Stephen Frears, director of several fine films including *My Beautiful Laundrette* and *The Grifters*. This definitely beat my usual American weekend.

Jon also used his time to glean information about the Korean War from a wide and discerning reading of the literature. For Jon the war literature was really just about any book or article that might have something to say, from a major account to a little tidbit. He read with the close attentions and studied skepticism of an I.F. Stone. We were friends and saw eye-to-eye, and so from the beginning (around 1982) he sought to involve me in his plans for a documentary.

Just for the record, let me say this about that: it was *our* documentary. Jon thought of doing it in 1982, I signed on, and when David Elstein brought Thames Television aboard in 1985 (after much spadework by Jon), the only names listed besides his and Phillip Whitehead's were Iain Bruce, a producer from Octagon Films who helped get the documentary started and then sold it to Thames, Jon Halliday ('writer'), and Bruce Cumings ('historian'). This was also the skeleton crew that WGBH/Boston agreed to support and fund.[257]

Jon was not simply the originator of the documentary, but was at the center of everything, from developing early ideas for the film to searching out funding to cracking open participation from the communist countries (through trips to the USSR and the DPRK in 1985). He put much more time and effort into it than anyone else, and was much closer to the daily grind of making it than I was. I have sheaf upon sheaf of letters from him over the period 1982–90, many of them running eight to ten pages, seeking out this person to interview or that obscure book to check, discussing the substance of the film, and the difficulties of being an outsider working in Thames production.

Jon's position throughout the process might be called the originator as outsider, because every day he had to fight for his standing. The executive producer, Phillip Whitehead, was established as filmmaker, journalist, and Labour Party activist. Scholars brought in as consultants had their university posts. The camera crews were not just Thames employees, but union people who could not be pushed around. Thames employees like Tony Lee or Isobel Hinshelwood, however good or bad they might be, were deemed 'researchers' and that was that.[258] Jon, of course, had published at length about the Korean War and had wide respect as an independent historian, but he hadn't a university post or a regular staff position at Thames. And so every day Jon had to reinvent his role, and justify his standing.

My participation in the making of the documentary exposed me to things I rarely have to put up with at the University – my credentials as historian challenged by those who have none, know-nothings on the Korean War telling me where to get off, character assassination by people of no character, highly political charlatans working a sleight-of-hand whereby I was deemed political and they unbiased. But I always returned to the University, where my colleagues (whatever some of them might think of me) do not challenge my standing or assail my character.

Jon, however, was exposed to these things incessantly, his motives under suspicion by everyone, a death of a thousand cuts with no escape. During the many seminars Thames held, he was forced to sit silently with the staff employees, silenced by Whitehead lest he taint the documentary with his presumed politics. Thatcherite Farrar-Hockley could rail on at any length, saying anything he wished, and never be challenged as to his motives. South Korean apparatchiks working for a ruthless authoritarian regime were treated with kid gloves, wined and dined, even as they slandered Jon (and me, of course). Strangers passing through the Thames offices felt free to Red-bait Jon, question his motives and his competence, or dismiss him as biased.

There is something I call liberal nystagmus. Nystagmus is a term used to describe an involuntary phenomenon in animals like pigeons: a spinning prompt will cause the pigeon to flip its head, but once the prompt stops, the pigeon's head will keep flipping much longer than one would expect. Like the hidden prompter in an opera, deeply imprinted notions ('durable dispositions') keep liberal heads flipping in the same direction, too. One of them is that bias is a problem of the Left. They may acknowledge that it's a problem of the Right, too. But that doesn't flip their heads, doesn't cause them to challenge credentials and assassinate character, because no one is going to accuse them of sympathizing with the Right. But since someone might accuse them of sympathizing with the Left, they must keep their nystagmus turned on.

Phillip Whitehead was an exception, I came to believe, although Jon may not agree with me (and since he worked more closely with Phillip than I, perhaps he is right). Phillip was a liberal without nystagmus, and a politician. His compromises on the film were political ones, for the most part, necessitated by accommodations to this or that constituency having a required voice in the film. But he wanted a film on a spectrum wide enough to accommodate South and North Korea, the US and the USSR, Richard Stilwell and KGB operatives in Korea, weighted toward the well-documented judgements Jon and I had come to about the nature of the war. American nystagmus would start by excluding Jon and including me – but only because of my undeniable 'standing' – and then work its way rightward, finding ballast at the point where a Dean Rusk is not unduly discomfited.

So, Phillip was different – difficult, exasperating, elusive – but, at least in my American experience, different. Jon and Iain Bruce could have produced a documentary on the Korean War. But Phillip was essential to bringing Thames on board, raising money well beyond the capabilities of Octagon Films, and making a film that would reach a much wider audience. That was my judgement at the beginning and my conviction at the end, and it is reflected in the Thames film being, all things considered, of lasting value.

Jon also knew David Elstein and introduced me to him, although it was only much later that I realized this was the same person whose interview I had read and admired some years before. Elstein was open and friendly, and when he became executive producer at Thames in 1986, he brought our Korean War documentary project along as his inaugural flagship program, with Phillip in charge of it.[259]

Our idea was to do a balanced documentary: balanced from a world standpoint, not an American or British or Western one. In America, objectivity connotes a construction in which those within the liberal realm agree to disagree, and the perceived enemies of liberalism are shown to be wrong. Jon and I had the illiberal premiss to take the liberal (or the emotivist) at his word, and find a means to let all relevant parties have their say, in the way they want to say it. For our purposes that meant above all clear, balanced presentation of the diametrically opposite views of the two Korean sides since it was, after all, a *Korean* war. Accomplishing that meant equal participation by representatives of South and North. That was our first premiss of balance.

This undercut the existing situation since the Korean War rather badly, however, in which South Korea has benefited from every sort of special pleading, with North Korea giving off the silence of the grave (we reverse the totalism of the North: there is not one serious person in the US who will take North Korea's 'side,' the conception of it having an independent point of view being difficult to grasp in the first place). Meanwhile we have many pundits, government officials, and professors unwilling to depart one iota from what the South Koreans want said about this war.

Another, less conscious premiss was that objectivity is in the eye of the beholder, that is, the documentary would be objective as we perceived it, it would be balanced as we determined it, on the basis of our knowledge of what happened. We knew more about the Korean War than anyone else connected to Thames, so why tolerate false views?

If someone was allowed to rail on about North Korean atrocities, for example, it would be incumbent upon us not simply to point out that there were also American and South Korean atrocities, but to establish the meaning of atrocity (a bullet to the back of the head? a village obliterated by napalm?), and then a hierarchy of who was more and who less atrocious, thus to allocate the precious seconds of time available to us, but more importantly to honor truth.

In other words we had a point of view. It was to be our documentary, not someone else's; let them do their own. (Indeed, within a short time after the announcement of our project, the BBC did get going on its own, with Max Hastings at the helm.) This premiss cut against another icon of television praxis, especially in the US. In principle, there is nothing wrong with airing a documentary made according to 'a point of view'; to say otherwise ends up in censorship. In practice, however, the reigning doctrine is that there should be internal balance in each documentary, not first this documentary, and then that one.

The point is that *everything* has to have 'balance,' otherwise someone (usually a neo-conservative) will have after you. But internal balance according to what standard? The standard is the known but hidden parameters of what is acceptable to the consensual positions held and reinforced by the media, and what the media people think is the consensus of their relevant public. And with that we are back to what Dan Rather, Ted Koppel, Tom Brokaw, McNeil/Lehrer, and Henry Kissinger think is appropriate.

Why should I talk about 'balance' as an American problem, instead of, for example, a North Korean problem, where everything is 'balanced' by reference to what's good for Kim Il Sung? Because North Korean solipsism can be taken as a given, and worked around; the only people we would run into who did not acknowledge its existence would be the North Koreans themselves, and even they are well aware that few believe what they do, outside their country.

The real problem is liberal solipsism, precisely because it is said not to exist. The American liberal's overwhelming and unacknowledged blindness is in grasping the world view of the non-liberal. The more one believes one's view to be self-evident and universal, the less tolerance there is for anyone outside that universe; the more one thinks that everyone, given a chance, would choose one's system, the less credence one can give to those who do not (who nonetheless constitute the vast majority of humans). The more unexamined one's own position, the less possible it is to understand another.

We wanted to represent the one, the two, the many solipsisms involved in making the Korean War, but to avoid complicity with any of them. The proper word for what we sought is encompassed by the German term *verstehen*. It carries a connotation of empathetic comprehension, of fathoming what someone thinks and why they think it, without regard to whether you believe they ought to or not. It is apprehension without false morality, that is, objectivity in the best sense. This means critical awareness of the other, and of oneself – of what might stand in the way of one's comprehension, for how else can one hope to know the other, to put yourself in the other guy's shoes?

Nietzsche begins his magnificent remembrance of his teacher, Schopen-hauer, with a discourse on human complacency. People are timid, lazy, they hide behind custom and opinion; they 'fear most of all the inconve-niences with which unconditional honesty and nakedness would burden them.' Yet in his heart of hearts, each person intuits that he is unique, a 'strangely variegated unity,' and, more dauntingly, so is everyone else: he intuits 'the law that every man is a unique miracle,' and in so being 'is beautiful, and worth regarding, and in no way tedious.' People shrink from this discovery, however, and bind themselves 'to views which are no longer binding even a couple of hundred miles away.' And then Nietzsche drops a line so rare in Western literature as to be virtually non-existent: 'Orient and Occident are chalk-lines drawn before us to fool our timidity.'[260]

Verstehen for Korea is not just a matter of taking the blinders off unthinking liberals, but of disabusing an entire Western tradition of its conceits. If anyone in the world fits the stereotype of an Oriental despot, it is of course Kim Il Sung; but one cannot be in South Korea for a minute without finding Westerners drawing upon the same bag of Orientalist nostrums to explain what they see.

The ubiquitous prejudice I speak of is perfectly revealed in Trotsky's amazing, unexpected first line in his biography of Stalin: it was the old revolutionist Leonid Krassin, he says, who 'was the first, if I am not mistaken, to call Stalin an "Asiatic." '[261] A brilliant mind like Trotsky's unwittingly shows itself to be merely provincial – the province of 'the West.'

So our standards were high, ridiculously so if one wanted to set right 'West' and 'East.' But I considered such standards nearly met by Thames Television's *The World at War*. In the fullness of that film one could sample everything from the brilliance of Franklin Roosevelt to the stark, gut-wrenching drama of Stalin flinging his white-coated Siberian tank corps against Germans at the gate of Moscow; to the Russian woman general still so happy to have been among the first into 'the viper's lair' of Berlin, even to an empathetic hour on wartime Japan which could never be produced in the US, especially not today when Japan rises as a new enemy, just as Russia recedes. Furthermore the producers had achieved this success by thinking through the knotty problem of bias.[262]

But even were we to produce a documentary that satisfied these high expectations, if we were to have our way, there were still hosts of problems. South and North Koreans rarely sit at the same table for any purpose; usually if one side is invited, to anything, the other side first tries to block the affair and then, if also invited, refuses to attend. How could we get them to sit together through a Thames seminar, where the issues would be hashed out? How could we get one Korea to let us film and interview if we had already been to the other one? Standing above all this was the simple fact that both Koreas would pull out all the stops to influence the substance of a film dealing with the great, defining event of their recent history. In spite of this, the only principle could be balance and equivalence, so we would have to figure out ways to get it.

We agreed that it was much more likely that we would get North Korean participation if we went to them first; if Seoul were already involved, the North would refuse any participation. But if P'yôngyang were already involved, we still thought it likely that South Korea would participate. So we contacted the North first, which ultimately proved the correct way to go. We also had the problem of the vastly superior weight of South Korea and its point of view in the West; indeed its 'point of view' merely made amendments to the American position, which had had the full resources of the US government and most scholars and pundits behind it for three decades.

So, put this way our task was considerable: but that's the only way to put it, if one wishes to do a serious documentary on the Korean War – this 'forgotten war' that resists its obscure tethering in Western memory. The making of the documentary was a daily expression of our original paradox: an unknown, unseen war that, upon retrospective examination, proves so unsettling.

RESEARCH, SEMINARS, POLITICS

Thames Television has the admirable and expensive practice of holding several long seminars during the course of documentary production, to hash out the issues, seek the truth, and arrive at consensus. The seminar format was one of the few Thames practices entirely familiar to me, of course, and I welcomed them. They bring together participants of all ranks – scholars, experts, pundits, and most of the production people; transcripts are then circulated for comment and for the use of the staff, especially the researchers. I had decided that for the role Thames had given me, and for what they were paying me, I would make available to them whatever I had come up with in fifteen years of research on the Korean War.

I was soon disabused of the notion that this would make much difference. At a preliminary meeting I had told the Thames researchers that I had a 1000-plus-page manuscript that I would be glad to let them see,[263] and got in return polite but glazed looks. They had already gotten their hands on the 600-page first volume of my study, and that was indigestible enough; it was apparent when I worked with them that they hadn't read it.

For example, one Thames researcher on the project heard during an interview with Donald MacDonald, an American foreign service officer with much Korean experience, that 'people's committees' had sprouted all over the peninsula in 1945. 'People's committees? You don't say! How interesting – tell me more about that.' I had written about two hundred pages on these committees, they were one of the major themes of the book, but I learned never to mention indelicate things like that. I mean, after all, I was only the principal historical consultant. (I just determined to fight to keep MacDonald's clip on the American suppression of the committees in the final version, which I did in spite of WGBH/Boston's anxiety that it was of little relevance for the Korean War.)

Isobel Hinshelwood, one of the researchers, was a married woman in her fifties, blonde, wiry, and somewhat neurasthenic in appearance, but the appearances hid an energetic, even indefatigable, sleuth when it came to unearthing interviewees, especially war veterans. She had worked on *The World At War*, and thus I initially held her in high regard. She had given me a blank but pleasant look when I mentioned my manuscript, however, and later I noticed her carrying a dog-eared copy of Joseph Goulden's *Korean War: The Untold Story*. I knew this to be a thrice-told tale, of dubious reliability, not to mention Goulden having signed on with 'Accuracy in Media.' I later found a way politely to say this to Isobel.

'But it has such a good index,' she responded. 'What's the worth of a good index to bad information,' I countered, regretting as it left my lips that I had said such a boorish thing. It was downhill, however graciously downhill, with Isobel from that point on.

Thames has a reputation for vast and diligent research,[264] but given time and money limitations, the absence of research training to any scholarly standard, and the vexing nature of the war itself, the researchers came up less with something new, than with the received wisdom many times over. This should not have surprised me, since I frequently have the experience of assigning the literature on the Korean War to bright students and finding that they rarely pick up the real faultlines of debate (the average undergraduate today finds I.F. Stone's *Hidden History of the Korean War* a delightful book, but can't see why it's controversial).

But I was surprised to learn that the researchers had little idea of, or interest in, what might be found in an archive, and extraordinary, credulous trust in the memories of witnesses – and the more august the rank of the witness, the deeper the credulity. Having in some cases compared current interviews with those recorded by military historians at the time of the war with the same person, I had next to no trust in individual memory – which was usually a mix of badly remembered event, politically determined context, and contemporary desire to say the proper thing, all of it overlaid with wish fulfillment.

Having watched Dean Rusk on television in the late 1960s, for example, it wouldn't have occurred to me to credit his veracity on the Korean War. But the Thames researchers and the people we dealt with at WGBH/ Boston seemed to find the retrospective judgements of people like Rusk compelling, and preferable to that of independent historians. Or, they distrust Rusk on Vietnam but only on Vietnam, and not Korea. Thus in our film Rusk not only reconstructs his own role for the viewer, but is relied upon for a number of crucial historical judgements.

To give an example, I would point out that in the archives one can find ample evidence of an American-sponsored coup being run against Chiang Kai-shek in the last week of June 1950. With some prodding I got one of the main movers, the same Mr Rusk, to admit in an interview that a coup was in motion (while attributing responsibility for it to elements in the Chinese military). I then sought to explain why this was important for the outbreak of the Korean War, that no one else had put this together, and that therefore Thames had its own coup, its own television scoop, in the making.

But then Isobel would thumb through Goulden, or David Rees's old book (*Korea: The Limited War*), and not find anything about it; her sidekick, Tony Lee, less accomplished as a researcher, would reinforce her sense that there wasn't much to this story, and their preferred producer, Mike Dormer, responsible for program hours two and three, would listen politely to me, but also hearken to Rusk's disclaimers and his implication that there wasn't really much to this story. And then, to make me and Jon happy, he would both use the coup story and bury it in a place where its significance was lost – which is exactly what happened in program two, no matter how much Jon and I squawked.

As usual, however, the real problem with the researchers was politics. They wanted to run the Korean War as a series of military battles, overlaid by their complacent notions about its politics. That politics, it seemed to me, was a marriage of whatever they had in their heads when we began, which was thoroughly conventional and unexamined, and the professional and bureaucratic prerogative they sought to protect within the Thames organization. They were 'researchers' and therefore they had to produce research results, even if Jon and I had heard most of it years ago.

The reader who has already tired of my arrogance will know what the Thames people were up against. But then the reader may not have had the experience of thinking through something for much of one's adult life, researching it in materials unavailable to an earlier generation, coming to certain fairly unshakeable conclusions, and then hearing the same, flawed conventional wisdom fly back in your face time and again with the regularity of the next sunrise.

People who collect stamps, or baseball cards, or batting averages, won't give the time of day to the ignorati who have never heard of the 1918 upside-down flying Jenny, or who think Luke Easter is a religious ceremony, or who say that Ted Williams's .406 wasn't much to write home about. So why do I have to listen to ignorati on the Korean War?

VICTORY TO THE PARTY OF FORGETTING

Let us now define this conventional wisdom, which may be done simply: What do we call this war? What's in a name? That is, what do Americans call this war, since their verdict has carried the day throughout the 'free world'? The Korean War is called 'the forgotten war' in America. Thames Television producers, with ineffable intuition and insight, also wanted to call our documentary 'Korea: The Forgotten War.'

The Korean War *is* of course forgotten in the US, if not in Korea where 40,000 American soldiers and 600,000 South Korean soldiers still confront Kim Il Sung. The war's having vanished at home explains the experience of a North Korean official who came to New York on Olympic business, finding that people could barely recall when the Korean War occurred, that cab drivers thought communists ran South Korea (since human rights were so violated), and that Americans were friendly and innocent of the antagonism he expected to find. He rightly called it a form of amnesia, but thought it might be useful in starting a new relationship. (Once I gave a lecture on human rights abuses in South Korea, to the American Friends Service Committee in Philadelphia. A tiny white-haired lady with 1890s pince-nez came up afterward and said, 'I want to shake your hand, young man, for having the courage to denounce those communists in Seoul!')

Still, this title is a way to think about the Korean War. By calling the Korean conflict a 'forgotten war,' we both name it, and we remember it – a paradox: What is it that we are remembering to forget? We do not remember history but particular verdicts, integral to and shaped by the raucous domestic politics of the 1950s. The war is forgotten and buried. But what is the *epitaph* on the American tombstone?

The tombstone has two messages: for the Truman Cold War liberal, Korea was a success, 'the limited war.' For the MacArthur conservative, Korea was a failure: the first defeat in American history, more properly a stalemate, in any case it proved that there was 'no substitute for victory.' The problem for MacArthur's epitaph is that if MacArthur saw no substitute for victory, he likewise saw no limit on victory: each victory begged another war. The problem for the Truman liberal is that the limited war got rather unlimited in late 1950.

So we need another verdict: a split decision – the first Korean War, the war for the south in the summer of 1950, was a success. The second war, the war for the North, was a failure. Thus Dean Acheson produced a schizophrenic epitaph: the decision to defend South Korea was the finest hour of the Truman Presidency; the decision to march to the Yalu occasioned 'an incalculable defeat to US foreign policy and destroyed the Truman administration'; this was 'the worst defeat . . . since Bull Run'[265] (another interesting analogy). Acheson assumed that the latter happened not to him but to his *bête noire*: Acheson squares the circle by blaming it all on MacArthur, and mainstream historiography has squared the circle in the same way.[266]

The Korean War happened during the height of the McCarthy period, and it was the handiwork of Dean Acheson and Harry Truman; McCarthy attacked both, and so the experience of the war disappeared in the shaping of the Cold War consensus – Truman and Acheson were the good guys. Cold War debate was almost always between the middle and the Right, the consensus anchored by the McCarthys on one end and the Achesons or Hubert Humphreys on the other. Furthermore the Korean War is no icon for the conservative or the liberal, it merely symbolizes an absence, mostly a forgetting, but also a never-knowing. The result is a kind of hegemony of forgetting, in which almost everything to do with the war is buried history.

The forgetting perhaps has a deeper reason, one found in the pathological realm of amnesia: as the intimations of American decline have multiplied, so has nostalgia for the 1950s. Reagan was the first two-term President since Eisenhower, his smiling persona drew on Ike's public mastery, and the Reaganites made frank comparisons with that quintessentially Republican era. If this rerun had a B-movie and even a Brumairean first-time-tragedy, second-time-farce quality to it for Reagan's detractors, it clearly drew on a wellspring of mass nostalgia for a lost time when America was Number One. The Korean War is errant counterpoint to the rosy memories, and so it vanishes.

A rule of this amnesia might be, 'all of so-and-so's paintings (or photographs, or books, or cinema) are interesting except those done about Korea.' Thus I found out only by reading the fine print of Picasso's obituary that he did a mural in 1951 in the genre of *Guernica*, titled *Massacre in*

Korea; I put it on the cover of my first book and then saw the original at the grand Picasso exhibition a few years ago in New York . . . and then read Hilton Kramer's review of the exhibition, where he referred to the mural as 'Stalinist trash.'[267] I asked a friend if it would be good for the cover of my book: 'it would be for the Vietnam War, but I don't know if it would be for Korea.' Picasso seemed guilty of a curious displacement.

It took years of reading to find out that Margaret Bourke-White had her camera-eye trained on the unconventional in Korea, literally the 'unconventional' guerrilla war in the South, or that filmmaker Chris Marker produced his marvelous picture book on North Korea in the late 1950s, or that Marilyn Monroe's career owed in large measure to her being the Betty Grable of the Korean War, 'discovered' during its height and nicknamed 'Miss Flamethrower.'[268]

Journalists reported Korea not just in the McCarthy era, but under military censorship. Foreign reporters (usually from the British Commonwealth) covered the war in much more depth and honesty than Americans, with the remarkable exception of I.F. Stone. Reginald Thompson, an Englishman, authored *Cry Korea*, a fine, honest eyewitness account of the first year of the war. War correspondents found the campaign for the South 'strangely disturbing,' he wrote, different from World War II in its guerrilla and popular aspect. 'There were few who dared to write the truth of things as they saw them.' Koreans were dehumanized; GIs 'never spoke of the enemy as though they were people, but as one might speak of apes.' Even among correspondents, 'every man's dearest wish was to kill a Korean. "Today," . . . "I'll get me a gook." '[269]

Before censorship was imposed on them, American journalists also described a similar war, if without Thompson's emphasis. Charles Grutzner of the *New York Times* said that in the early going, 'fear of infiltrators led to the slaughter of hundreds of South Korean civilians, women as well as men, by some US troops and police of the Republic.' He quoted a high-ranking US officer who told him of an American regiment that panicked in July 1950 and shot 'many civilians.'[270] Keyes Beech wrote in the *Newark Star-Ledger*, 'It is not the time to be a Korean, for the Yankees are shooting them all . . . nervous American troops are ready to fire at any Korean.'[271] Complete control of the air was achieved within days, and produced a certain air of indulgence, which no doubt contributed to

Korean casualties. As I.F. Stone put it, the air raids and the sanitized reports 'reflected not the pity which human feeling called for, but a kind of gay moral imbecility, utterly devoid of imagination – as if the flyers were playing in a bowling alley, with villages for pins.'[272]

Korea is an ellipsis in television and film discourse, too, just as it is in the American mind. It is not just a forgotten war, but a repressed, occluded experience, what Nietzsche called *historia abscondita*, what Pierre Macherey called a 'structured absence.'[273] Television was in its infancy during the war, and Hollywood constructed Korea in the patriotic, heroic modes of World War II. Because the fit of that genre was so poor in Korea, however, with the exception of Sam Fuller's *Battle Helmet*, there is barely a memorable film among the many produced in the 1950s;[274] the best, like *The Bridges at Toko-ri*, just happen to be set in Korea – it might as well have been the bridge at Remagen. The 'structured absence' is none other than the script of World War II itself, for in Korea an American army victorious on a world scale five years earlier was fought to a standstill by rough peasant armies.

The one and only classic film of the Korean War is *The Manchurian Candidate*, whose genius was to wrap the Orientalism and communist-hating of the fifties in the black humor of the sixties, thus making both palatable; the film allows one to be chic in one's prejudices. The one clear exception to the hegemony of forgetting, *M*A*S*H*, is no exception because it was a series about Vietnam, once removed to Korea. I thought about all this when *The New Yorker* ran a short but poignant account of some Korean-American students who held a hunger strike for several weeks in the fall of 1989 in front of the United Nations, to protest the UN's continuing role in Korea's division and to call attention to the division itself, amid all the sudden talk of German reunification. The thrust of the article was that they had held a hunger strike and no one showed up, save one *New Yorker* reporter.

Yet the amnesia masks a reality in which we all are a product of Korea whether we know it or not; it was the Korean War, not Greece or Turkey or the Marshall Plan or Vietnam, that inaugurated big defense budgets and the national security state, that transformed a limited containment doctrine into a global crusade, that ignited McCarthyism just as it seemed to fizzle, and thereby gave the Cold War its long run.

Forgetting, Nietzsche said, is no mere result of inertia: 'It is rather an active and in the strictest sense positive faculty of repression.' This human animal *needs* to be forgetful, he says; forgetfulness is 'like a doorkeeper, a preserver of psychic order, repose and etiquette . . . . there could be no present without forgetfulness.'[275] So it is not for nothing that the Korean War is called the Forgotten War. There is more than a little wisdom in the final episode of the television show *M*A*S*H*, where Hawkeye opens a bottle of cognac and remarks, 'We drink to forget.'

Heidegger, following Nietzsche, found an intimate connection between memory, the naming of things, and that process we call thinking. By naming we locate or 'call' something for the memory, rescue it from oblivion, retain it and keep it for thought. We war against 'that passing away which allows what has passed only to be in the past, which lets it freeze in the finality of this rigor mortis.'[276] If that finality is buried, we should dig it up and think about it, even if it shocks us. Fredric Jameson writes,

> The past always is assumed: we are not free to have no attitude toward it. It cannot be changed; but we always lend the changeless facts a meaning in terms of the lives we lead and even the forgetting of them . . . .[277]

The American split verdict on the Korean War is an agreement to disagree, a stitched-together mending of a torn national psyche. Above all it is a compact to forget – a selective forgetting that preserves psychic order. You remember one verdict, and forget or condemn the other. Each verdict implies a corresponding amnesia. 'Better a mended sock than a torn one,' said Hegel; 'not so for self-awareness.'

Here the reader may now grasp what a big victory it was when Jon Halliday and I prevailed upon Thames to call the documentary *Korea: The Unknown War*. Anyway, in this repression and forgetting there is nonetheless a text of the Korean War, a conventional wisdom, and it is this paleosymbolic that was in the heads of Thames researchers, and just about everybody else's in the free world, however consciously or unconsciously (usually the latter). Now back to the seminars.

Thames' first general seminar, held in September 1986, met a fine standard and was most encouraging. I remember it as a high-minded and well-informed discussion of the period leading up to the war, and the transcript perused years later bears this out. A number of scholars were there, including Lord Max Beloff, Laurence Freedman, John Gittings, and Peter Lowe. Phillip Whitehead was kind enough to turn first to me, and I gave a summary of my view that the origins of the war went well back into the pre-1945 colonial period, back to divisions begun in the 1920s really, and that this history allows us to understand that it was fundamentally a civil war of long genesis, not a thunderclap exploding in 1950. This met with little dissent and God knows what level of cognition, and the rest of the day was equally pleasant – both the stimulating discussion, and the beneficent, supremely polite way in which the Thames staff kept us well-fed and happy. It was an auspicious start, and only later did I learn that the Thames researchers seemed not to have been attentive during the seminars, nor to have read the transcripts,[278] judging from the questions they later put to me.

The seminar also, however, illustrated the absence (or fear) of what we have called reflexivity on the part of television people. My views (and Jon Halliday's) about the war were available in any library. I and the other consultants were asked again to present our views, which inevitably led to controversy because the war itself is unsettled. These views, furthermore, were transcribed and sent around to all concerned, including the South and North Korean governments, which have life-and-death stakes in the war's representation. But the Thames and WGBH producers were not required to give their views.

Phillip would occasionally make a comment, but the other producers, Mike Dormer and Max Whitby, were mostly silent, except to ask questions. Austin Hoyt of WGBH rarely spoke, and his colleague (and boss) Peter McGhee mimicked the Sphinx. The producers merely carried on a subliminal chorus of impassive mien, twiddled thumbs, well-camouflaged knowing looks, and occasional raised eyebrows of indeterminate meaning. Hardly ever did we get a sense of what they thought about the Korean War. Never were they forced to defend their views. Yet as the assemblers and editors of footage, they were to end up the authors of our text.

The second seminar, held a month later, was less inspiring than the first. Its constituency held fewer scholars and more participants in the war,

including my military counterpart Sir Anthony Farrar-Hockley, veteran of
the Imjin campaigns and two years in North Korean and Chinese prisons,
onetime British commander of NATO, official historian of British participation in the Korean War, and, as I told you earlier, 'principal military
consultant' to our documentary. Lord Gladwyn Jebb was also there, a
former British Ambassador to the United Nations, plus Robert Oliver,
Syngman Rhee's jovial sidekick and biographer, and one Kim Chong-Whi,
listed as 'Director, Korean National Institute of Security Affairs,' Seoul.
Our plan had been to have Mr Kim pitted against an appropriate North
Korean representative, but none showed up. So Phillip thoughtfully called
on me to play that role.

Peter Lowe, the well-known and erudite British historian, started us off
by dropping a big piece of fat in the fire: 'At a rough guess I would assign
responsibility about equally, between North and South Korea, for the
provocative actions which had occurred previously' to June 1950, a
judgement amply confirmed by declassified documentation.

His next point was that 'people don't know exactly for certain what
happened immediately before the outbreak of the war.' Clearly North
Korea was preparing major military action, but:

> What we don't know, I think, is whether there was provocative action
> immediately beforehand by South Korea and I think that's still an area of
> uncertainty on which we have to suspend judgement – perhaps that will
> never be fully resolved – but I think we have to leave a question mark there
> for the moment.

Peter Lowe both is, and looks like, the soul of diplomatic-historian
probity. From his work I knew him to be a scholar who would not depart
one iota from the evidence before him, and when I finally met him this
judgement was repaid to the degree that I would even buy a used car, or real
estate, or life insurance from him, so level-headed is his external aspect.

Nonetheless this same mild-mannered, scholarly professor had the
temerity to utter these heretical words, and from all sides came such a
cacophonous dissent that within minutes he was scrunched into a small ball
of red-faced discomfort. Lord Gladwyn thought the South Koreans,
'however unfortunate their policy may have been,' should not 'be regarded

as in any way responsible for the aggression by the North.' Sir Anthony chimed in, saying the earlier squabbles between North and South were as different from the events of June 1950 as 'the difference of chalk to cheese' (a distinction I could not sustain, since the previous seminar dinner was brought to a close with some English cheese, but Sir Anthony reinforced my view that Englishmen like to talk about cheese – 'hard cheese' for 'bad luck' – precisely to the degree of their inability to make it). Quite to the contrary, the General opined; the North Koreans had carried off 'a brilliant piece of surprise.'

Dr Oliver strode forth with his memory, to the effect that Dr Rhee's Austrian wife had told him how weary her husband was, just before the war, and therefore looking forward to hard-earned repose 'at a little summer cottage' on the southern coast (otherwise known as the summer residence of the former Japanese naval commander, at Chinhae). Kim Chong-Whi held forth to the effect that all the North Korean training manuals, now captured and in the archives, stopped precisely at Saturday, June 24. (In fact there are many that do not: many project ordinary military drill well into July.) He then digressed onto what his cousin had told him about the outbreak of the war.

At length I sought to intervene on Dr Lowe's behalf, acknowledging that 'to do so is rather difficult after four or five comments which are essentially saying that Peter Lowe is trafficking in absurdity.' Instead, I said, Dr Lowe was 'trying to pursue the historian's craft, which is quite different than to be at a particular position, say, in the United Nations [Jebb] or in Korea [Kim] in June 1950 and to think that therefore . . . you know what happened.'

It is human nature to assume that if you were somewhere around a historic event, or witnessed some aspect of it, you know more about it than someone who was not there – especially some arrogant younger 'scholar' who was assembling plastic airplanes when the skin of one's back (in this case Farrar-Hockley's) was serving as the ash tray for North Korean cigarette butts. Sounding like the pedant that I must have become, I went on to recommend thorough reading of the reams of declassified documents, intelligence reports, and the like that we now have, before coming to a judgement about what happened on June 25 (the reader is free to peruse all this in the second volume of my book on the war, thus detaining us no longer here). At best Professor Lowe and I succeeded but momentarily in holding up the steamroller of received wisdom, now crunching through our best laid plans and hopes for the documentary.

This sort of exchange became par for the course. Periodically I would assert my documents, and the witnesses would assert their experience. When it got hot, as for example when I pointed out that the vast flow of refugees from North Korea was in large part an urban population fleeing before the Americans' systematic demolition and firing of their cities, or in some cases herded southward by Rhee's police, Farrar-Hockley's admirable and gentlemanly reserve would break down and he would repeat his vaunted 'My deah boy, I was theah' line. But I got to like the General, even if we both held each other at a good arm's length. He was a gentleman, with a far more supple mind than the few American generals I've met. He was effective, too.

On the bus to lunch one day, he sat next to me and had me teary-eyed with his stories about the humiliations of his captivity and his heroic attempts to escape. 'It was only a couple of years ago that the cigarette burns finally disappeared from my back.' Whereupon I had the nasty empiricist gall to think, so how do we know they were there? (I have no doubt, of course, that they were there; Sir Anthony also was a model prisoner of war, staunch for his fellow POWs and game for an escape whenever he got the chance.)

It was also at the second seminar that I first met Austin Hoyt, erstwhile representative of WGBH/Boston and gatekeeper for the easily bruised American psyche. Austin passed his fiftieth birthday around this time, but looked much younger. By virtue of his important role in the PBS 13-part series on Vietnam, Austin was positioned throughout the 1980s in the gunsights of Reaganite Reed Irvine and his vaunted 'Accuracy in Media,' an organization so ill-named as to make Heidegger flip in his grave.

I was never quite clear on what Austin thought about the Korean War. But from our first meeting, it was clear how much he wanted to avoid flak on the documentary. That flak seemed most likely to fly, he intimated, because of Jon Halliday's presence on the crew. Almost the first words out of his mouth to me, as we sat munching one of Thames's outstanding seminar banquets, had to do with Jon's leftwing politics. After I trotted out my recipe for dealing with that question, there came the next: 'In the seminar, you seem quite convinced of your own positions on the war, and, er, you seem somewhat intolerant of people who disagree with you. Have you learned much about the war from your association with this project?' To which I answered, all things considered, no – for reasons I have already given to the reader.[279] Austin seemed both amused and discomfited by this response.

Austin had the habit of blurting out things that he would later deny: for example, looking at early rough cuts depicting American atrocities and remarking, 'we can't have that in, my phone will be ringing off the hook.' Jon and I heard him say that, Callum McDonald heard him say it, but Austin later claimed no memory of it.[280]

Over time it became apparent to Jon and me that Austin was in many ways the best public television producers in the US had to offer, and that he was sincere in wanting a documentary that was both truthful (within the bounds determined by his world view) and pitched such that it would only suffer the slings and arrows of Reed Irvine if that was absolutely necessary to the integrity of the film. This not unreasonable (but, like Whitehead, politician-like) message was delivered with eyes like those of a deer caught in your headlights, however, which I did find disconcerting.

Seminar two gave way to seminar three, held the next day (October 23, 1986), and on the previous evening Phillip had taken Kim Chong-Whi to dinner to see if he could cajole him into arguing on behalf of allowing a Thames film crew to come to Seoul, once he returned to his country. Phillip had let on that Kim spent much of the evening disparaging me and Jon; the South Korean Embassy had gotten involved, too, trying to bring pressure on the Thatcher government to take an interest in the documentary and help to shape it. There were rumors that Seoul threatened to disrupt relations if things came out bad. At one point the Korean Ambassador to the UK, General Young Hoon Kang – who left the US under subpoena in the 1970s rather than testify about the Koreagate scandal, in which he was deeply involved[281] – turned up at the Thames offices in his limousine, and urged that Jon be fired; getting no satisfaction, he roared off to the Foreign Office. The minimax solution to the Thames problem, for the Seoul regime, was to eliminate first Jon, and then me.

I hadn't held out much hope for Mr Kim, well before I heard this news. He had received a Ph.D. from Columbia, like me, but that made him less a friendly alumnus than a useful go-between in Columbia's attempts to get millions of dollars for its Korean studies program from the Chun Doo Hwan 'Blue House,' where Kim was ensconced with Presidential access and security clearances altitudinous enough to make him an interrogator of the woman who allegedly blew up a South Korean airliner in 1987. He stayed on with the mildly renovated Roh Tae Woo regime, Assistant to the President for Foreign and National Security Affairs.[282]

Phillip had asked the South Koreans to send to London an eminent expert on the war, but, much like the North Koreans, they sent instead someone eminently reliable. Kim Chong-Hwi's contribution to the seminar was thus not that of someone who knew the issues of the war, but rather one who combined a seat-of-the-pants anecdotalism ('my mother told me this, my cousin said that') with all the hoary but safe South Korean shibboleths handed down since 1953. When I gave an outline of the guerrilla struggle in the South and its indigenous roots, for example, I ended by saying that the ROK point of view, of course, was that not even one guerrilla came from the South. Whereupon Kim, without a trace of irony, piped up and said that not even one guerrilla came from the South.

But I would not have predicted the alacrity with which he took the seminar down to the malicious depths wherein the South Korean elite likes to place discussion of the war – although I should have expected it, since this is a country where a McCarthyism far more ferocious than our own has held sway for four decades. This memorable exchange occurred when I complained to Phillip that

> I am being put in a position of representing the North Korean viewpoint which I do not like at all . . . they themselves have never dealt honestly with their history . . . I'm trying to sit here and tell you what I found in the archives, not what I got from Kim Il Sung when we talked last week.

Our plan had been to have a North Korean representative to go along with Mr Kim. This did not happen, of course, because the South Koreans (and perhaps the Thatcher government) had succeeded in blocking any North Korean participation. In one of the strangest episodes of all, a North Korean representative said they would not participate, because Phillip had disparaged Kim Il Sung at the South Korean Embassy in London – in the process implying either that they had the capability to monitor the Embassy, or that someone in the Embassy was talking to them. Anyway, we just got Mr Kim.

After I was done saying I wasn't Kim Il Sung's lickspittle, Mr Kim leaped forward, his face beclouded, and blurted out, 'I think you are a perfect representative of North Korea.'[283] 'Well, now you're insulting me,' I said. I looked around at a table full of red-faced Thames staff, and learned once again, to my considerable comfort, how much weight the English put on bad form, and rightly so.

During a break Mike Dormer remarked that he didn't know how I put up with such people, and I said something about it being modal behavior for those who have ruled South Korea. But good manners are little defense against a raging bull, and at the visceral level Mr Kim had carried the day, intimidating just about everyone, including Phillip Whitehead[284] – even if that didn't show up until we got to actually roughing out the documentary.

At this seminar I also had the pleasure of meeting Major Ellery Anderson, who had sought to run South Korean guerrillas into the North, without much success – something he was the first to admit. Everything he said squared with the documents I had seen, but more than that, he had a guileless and candid, heartfelt view of the war from the ground's-eye-level that perfectly validated Thames's method of interviewing the high and the low.

With his thick accent he allowed that he was 'feeling very 'umble, not least because I'm sitting opposite this chap' (meaning General Farrar-Hockley, and perhaps intending some irony); 'I'm only speaking from a very low level,' he said. The Koreans he met were peasants,

> Simple souls, and frankly they were all bloody unhappy . . . . They were frightened of what was going to happen and their whole mentality was to keep their head down, look after your own path and don't get involved [with] any of them.

The southerners he sought to mobilize

> weren't the slightest bit interested in fighting against communism, they wanted to stay alive, they wanted their children to stay alive and they wanted their property to be left alone.

There was no feeling of North and South, he said, they were just all Koreans. Foreigners had come and gone, Koreans told him, but 'we've got our own religion, we've got our own culture, we have always wanted this bloody nonsense to stop.' Of course, they would give lip service to whatever their leaders wanted – 'Oh my God yes. They would all fight for democracy and this, that and the other. But the point of fact is they didn't want to do anything at all.'

As for Anderson, the unholy bloodbath he had witnessed caused him to hire onto a crew bound for Antarctica, so desperate was he from his years in Korea to avoid the human species and its terrible capacity for violence. After listening to the discussions at the seminar, he said it was the first time he had been told what the war was about.

At the fourth seminar in November 1986 we met Tibor Meray, who would become one of our wisest and most experienced informants on North Korea. He had been a Hungarian war correspondent in the North who later, after the failed 1956 Hungarian revolution (in which he played an important role), renounced communism and Budapest for Paris, where Jon Halliday located him. Meray clearly had absolutely no use for the Kim Il Sung regime or for communism, which gave corresponding weight to his judgements. Meray is a witty, worldly man, who struck me as very like I.F. Stone in being sick to death of official lying.

After an extended discussion of atrocities in the war, who did what to whom, and so on, Meray broke in after I made a statement about South Korean atrocities, to the effect that[285] as an American it ill-behoved me to talk about anyone's atrocities. He went on to say that however brutal Koreans on either side might have been, 'I saw destruction and horrible things committed by the American forces':

Everything which moved in North Korea was a military target, peasants in the fields often were machine gunned by pilots who I, this was my impression, amused themselves to shoot the targets which moved.

His party crossed the Yalu in August 1951 and witnessed 'a complete devastation between the Yalu River and the capital,' P'yôngyang. There were simply 'no more cities in North Korea.' The incessant, indiscriminate bombing forced them always to drive by night:

> We travelled in moonlight, so my impression was that I am travelling on the moon, because there was only devastation . . . every city was a collection of chimneys. I don't know why houses collapsed and chimneys did not, but I went through a city of 200,000 inhabitants and I saw thousands of chimneys and that – that was all.

Meray was our best eyewitness to the most awful history of the Korean War, three years of genocidal bombing by the US Air Force which killed perhaps two million civilians (one-quarter of the population), dropped oceans of napalm, left barely a modern building standing, opened large dams to flood nearby rice valleys and kill thousands of peasants by denying them food, and went far beyond anything done in Vietnam in a conscious program of using air power to destroy a society, a society 'of a new type,' as it was called in the 1950s. This well-documented episode (by the Air Force itself[286]) merits not the slightest attention or moral qualm in the United States. But Meray's testimony, and Max Whitby's adroit use of documentary footage, brought this episode home dramatically to many viewers of our film.

Meray also was taken around to photograph alleged incidents of American germ warfare, observing 'thousands and thousands' of flies moving on the snow near a peasant hut, even breeding on the ice, which local peasants said were dropped a week earlier from low-flying planes; North Korean specialists told him they were infected with cholera germs. He believed the allegations to be true at the time, but upon his return to Hungary and especially after he fled to Paris, he began to doubt the explanations he had been given.

'I consulted six French scientists,' he said, 'and I told them every detail of what I saw.' They pointed out various discrepancies, and eventually he came to believe he had been tricked. Among other things, they told him flies cannot live on the ice for as much as a week, but 'should have died immediately.' Meray thus came to think it was all a plot by Stalin. Shortly thereafter we took a break, and Jon Halliday and I told Meray that in fact flies are very hardy creatures and can live that long on ice, whereupon he waved at us with his hand, smiled with a pained look in his eyes. 'Please don't tell me this, I'll begin to believe it all again.'

Meray's formal interview with Thames ended with the question, 'who were the real heroes of the war?' I urge the reader to ponder his response:

> I would say something without wanting to be too pathetic or sentimental. During my stay in Korea . . . I made long walks. I was often sitting on the hillsides and I saw Korean peasants working in the fields, especially the women, since most of the men were soldiers. And I saw these women planting rice and ploughing and working from morning 'til night, and their children on their backs . . . the real heroes were these simple people, the peasants and especially the women . . . . The Korean people are not as sophisticated as the Chinese and are much less organized than the Japanese. But it is a fine people and I would express all my sympathy and my admiration for these people, who survived this war.

I also first met Theodore R. Conant at the fourth seminar, son to former Harvard President James Conant and once the head of the US Information Service in South Korea. He had brought with him some excellent early color footage of Korea at the end of the war. The first impression was of a congenial fellow with some interesting experience in Korea; the quickly arriving second impression was of an overbearing schlamazel, literally so in that at about 6' 8" he towered over everyone else, tending to hover above, thence to droop his long face directly into yours. Phillip took an instant dislike to him. We used some of his film, but he added little to the seminar.

Some weeks later Phillip showed up in New York to have a look at more of Conant's films. We picked Conant up outside his Carnegie Hill Park Avenue apartment, and took him down to the Asia Society where he screened some footage for us. The whole ride down he was in Phillip's face, and if not that, then in my face. He showed us some films in a small room, all the while jumping up and down to fiddle with the projector, the sound, the screen, or to offer running commentary on what we were endeavoring to watch. I watched Phillip do a classic slow burn, but Conant was oblivious. Then it was back in the cab and back up Park Avenue, Conant drooping over Phillip and Phillip fending off asphyxiation. We waved goodbye to him and turned back down 5th Avenue, Phillip now furious and convulsing me by storming that never, ever, as long as he lived, would he submit himself to Ted Conant again. But we will hear more of Mr Conant.

At the fifth seminar, November 28, 1986, Jon and I were anxious to meet Captain James R. Graham, described as 'Mr Korea' in the CIA, where he was reading the communist tealeaves in 1950 when the war began. I was interested in him both because he was reputed to have seen the North Korean attack coming, and because I had found in William 'Wild Bill' Donovan's little diary[287] the notation 'call Graham,' just when the war broke out.

Alas, Captain Graham was a disappointment. He was a retiring, mild-mannered pipesmoker, wearing tweeds and looking a little depressed; he had the reserve of the professor, not the reticence of the spy. That is, he was just like my academic colleagues, or my aunt's CIA friends (my father's sister spent her whole career in the CIA after getting a Ph.D. in French). Furthermore he had never had any contact with Donovan, or so he said; he had sensed that something might happen in Korea shortly before the war, but didn't push his views on his superiors; his Korean pronunciation was so execrable that he obviously had never attempted to learn the language. Captain Graham was a hard lesson for my delusion that there is in Washington someone, somewhere, who knows all there is to know about Korea.

After the film assemblage was roughed out Thames held more seminars, where we again discussed and debated the issues of the war, and principles for inclusion and exclusion in the film. By this time, however, the glow of novelty was off and the film was basically complete; although we argued mightily over some things (the germ warfare episode, for example), we were arguing at the margins of the film. I had learned a truth of documentary filmmaking: the editors are the authors.

THE INTERVIEWS

Our Thames producers had years of experience in on-camera interviewing and I had none, but they were kind enough to have me do many of our interviews (and all the ones in North Korea). This art requires presence of mind and subtle skills at getting people to say things on camera that they wouldn't otherwise, if they had time to think about their implications. I had admired, for example, the account of how Thames coaxed Karl Wolff (who helped build the Nazi SS) into relating on camera how Himmler stalked the edge of the death pit as people were murdered and thrown in, at Minsk.[288] Somehow Thames had a different approach to the Korean War, however, and rarely sought on-camera unveiling; furthermore their technique was to eliminate the questions from the soundtrack used in the documentary, so that hectoring the interviewee was bad form, technically and otherwise.

My first interview was with Dean Rusk in his office at the University of Georgia. From his TV appearances in the sixties I had imagined him a short and mousy man, but in fact he is very tall, with the courtly manners of a southern gentleman. He ushered us in with an air of resignation and a look at his watch: 'I hope this will be quick.'

I put a bunch of questions to him, which he answered in perfect, effective soundbites as if he were reading from a tape running behind his eyes. In discussing Acheson's Press Club speech, he repeated nearly verbatim what he had told an earlier interviewer. His memory only lapsed when I asked him what he was doing at the Plaza Hotel on June 23, 1950: 'no recollection of that.' During a break he asked me if the archival materials I had seen squared with what I was hearing from him. Before I could give my diplomatically negative reply, he remarked that the documents were useful, but far more important in knowing what happened were the innumerable daily conversations, phone calls, coffee breaks, gossip, knowing looks, pats on the back – all lost to the record. He's right, of course: but it's a bit damaging to the historian's craft, and to empiricism; that level of awareness only fits an epistemology of 'durable dispositions' growing out of the 'myriad "small perceptions" of everyday life.'

Henry Kissinger was next on my menu of interviewees. We arrived early in the morning at Kissinger Associates, occupying what can best be called an unmarked floor some fifty stories atop a skyscraper on Park Avenue. The elevator opens onto a lobby with no name, surveilled by closed-circuit television and one forlorn but cordial receptionist. In my memory she is sitting behind bullet-proof glass, but I can't vouch for that now.

Inside we observed a number of secretaries, a couple of bushy-tailed eager young men, a Japanese woman engrossed in combing through a pile of Tokyo newspapers, and Lawrence Eagleburger, bustling back and forth with the endomorphic somatotype of Henry at his heftiest. It wasn't just the girth, either, that was reminiscent of Henry. Eagleburger chopped the air with his hand and held his head as he talked just like his beloved patron, although he stopped short of mimicking his German accent.

My wife and I were joined by Austin Hoyt, who had arranged for the crew and who, my devious mind thought, was there to make sure I didn't say something untoward to Henry. As we waited for the Great Man to appear, Austin informed me of his worries about 'Accuracy in Media.' Reed Irvine had called him up and intimated that if our project did not interview certain people, he would charge it with bias. The first person mentioned was General Richard Stilwell, whom Hoyt agreed to interview, telling me that they would have done him anyway. Stilwell then recommended we interview James Hausman, who recommended his good friend General Paek Sôn-yôp. And there you have the minimum winning coalition on what happened on the morning of June 25, 1950.[289]

We sat around looking at the nondescript walls of Kissinger Associates, when all of a sudden in popped the man himself: 'Vy dit I akree to do zis inderview? Vat iz it zuppozed to be about?' He hadn't really the time for it, he continued, he had no involvement in the Korean War . . . and thus within seconds he had us all on the defensive, fearful that he would throw us out.

Then he suddenly warmed, and took his place in front of the camera. Up close Kissinger resembles a head that just happens to be supported by a lower body, and by legs that carry the assembly from here to there. His brain occupies most of the space between his shoulders, and constitutes perhaps a quarter of his body height. He couldn't be taller than five-five, but he projects enormous weight and presence. His eye-nose configuration looks just like Woody Allen, yet the penetrating eyes, guttural delivery, and consummate arrogance provide a formidable front. His hands depart restlessly from his ample midriff, frequently mobile before his lips, as if to draw out his thoughts. The overall effect is one of sovereign intelligence.

He was pleasant enough with me, not knowing me from Adam, and did a great interview (which I grudgingly admit). Every comment, however mainstream it might be, had a twist, a sidelight, or an unexpected take; every thought was well put, and seemingly spontaneous; much of it was embroidered with dry humor. We mined more nuggets (i.e. soundbites) with him than with most of our interviews. He readily admitted, for example, that as a Harvard graduate student he had been involved in an intelligence project[290] on Korea in 1951: 'It was sort of an absurd assignment because I knew nothing about Korea,' he said, and later on, 'I don't know what I thought'; being just a graduate student 'all I could affect was a group of undergraduates at Harvard.'

Nonetheless he went off to observe the war. 'The Americans had the same disdain for the Koreans that I later saw them have for the Vietnamese.' He never met Syngman Rhee, but knew he was an exile politician and, no doubt drawing on his experience with such people in Europe, etched a perfect portrait of the South Korean leader:

a special kind of single-mindedness, obstinacy . . . the people who do this are not the most attractive human beings to deal with . . . having achieved independence against all probability [Rhee knew] that if he just stuck to his guns he had as good a chance of achieving his objective as by bargaining with nations that were much stronger than he.

North Korea, he said predictably, was 'a combination of feudalism and communism with . . . a cult of emperor worship'; unpredictably, he remarked that it 'had made some extraordinary achievements' in industrial and military capability, if only by regimentation of the population. He also revealed that Kim Il Sung had been visiting Chou En-lai in August 1971, when Henry got his famous tummy ache in Pakistan and materialized in Beijing. However, he told us, he had no discussions with Kim.

I gave him but one uncomfortable moment, I'm sure Austin was happy to note, when I dared to mention books by Roger Morris (a former, hated aide) and Seymour Hersh (loathed beyond measure for *The Price of Power*), to the effect that Nixon was drunk during the EC-121 mini-crisis in 1969, and that he and Kissinger ordered the Air Force to take out a North Korean airfield in retaliation, relenting only when the Joint Chiefs countermanded them by pointing out that this would start the Second Korean War. Kissinger's eyes narrowed and fixed me with contempt: 'It is absurd to say that a President is overruled by the Defense Department.' Instantly his eyes were back to their modal state, of Henry being shrewd and witty before the camera.

Toward the end he confounded everyone by saying that 'on balance' he thought that the US had 'suffered' as a result of the Korean War:

> North Korea attacked the American ally and was not defeated . . . [it] destroyed the aura of American invincibility and showed that there were psychological and political limits to the use to which an American force could be put.

(This paraphrases Kim Il Sung's dictum on the result of the war, by the way.) He went on to say that he now thought the North Koreans had instigated the war, not the Soviets – although perhaps Moscow acquiesced in it.

When it was over he turned to look down the long table at my wife and in self-parody asked, 'Who iz da beautiful voman?' A conversation ensued, whereupon Kissinger told us an anecdote about finding himself standing on a podium next to a Vietnamese general in Beijing, after the war ended, something his Chinese hosts enjoyed doing to him. 'Vat is your name,' Henry asked him, getting an incomprehensible reply. With consummate timing the general waited a bit and then said, 'And what is yours?' 'Zons of bitches zose Vietnamese,' Henry said, 'real zons of bitches.' And then a turn toward my Korean wife: 'No offense meant, of course.' We shuffled out, the closed-circuit cameras whirring.

THE HIDDEN HISTORY OF I.F. STONE'S INTERVIEW

The late I.F. Stone was to be filmed at the Tabard Inn, a charming if drafty hotel on the English model, located near DuPont Circle and furnished with expensive antiques and old windows that don't fit. This place was Max Whitby's favorite, and I loved it myself; I often thought we were back in England until someone spoke who was not on our crew. The inn creaked a lot, though, and now and then a plane could be heard coming into

National Airport, so it gave fits to our sound man, Eric Brazier. Eric was a wonderful companion, good drinker, strong union man, and all-round gentleman. He exemplified the technical professionalism of the Thames group: as we sat in the Tabard about to begin an interview, he would hearken to his earphones, listen and think a bit, and then point to a mantelpiece where a small glass was vibrating, asking that we move it. Or he would get a buzz, and go over to a bookcase and uncover a rattling metal bookend. I was always amazed at his discernment.

Izzy was to be our fourth interview on a Friday, the crew ensconced in a nicely refurbished attic atop the inn. The first take was a handsome, friendly, WASP American Marine officer with a sunny disposition, and without a clue or a care about the destructiveness of American firepower in Korea. Next was Keyes Beech, a crusty war correspondent for the *Chicago Daily News* with (as he told us) good intelligence contacts. Isobel really liked Keyes; he was with the Marines up near 'frozen Chosin' (the Changjin Reservoir) in November 1950, and kept saying 'we' when he meant 'them,' the Marines. Beech had a good ear for a good yarn, and told us all how cold it was up there, when the howling sub-zero Siberian blasts became Kim Il Sung's 'divine wind,' and combat-hardened Marines who had fought at Iwo Jima were down on their knees and crying for Mother.

Off camera he told me a good one, too, about how when Park Chung Hee made his coup in 1961 the first person Beech called to get the story was James Hausman, who gave Beech to believe that Hausman had advance knowledge of Park's overthrow of the elected ROK government. He also said on camera that the head of the South Korean National Police told him in early July 1950 that they had killed 12,000 political prisoners in the two weeks since the war began; Beech later called up to say the figure was actually 1,200. Whether 1,200 or 12,000, this bit didn't make its way into the film.[291]

Isobel did three or four clips with Beech (a clip of film running about twenty minutes before a break to get a new one), even though most of what he told her was the same old stuff we had gotten from many others; at one point I broke in and asked that he comment on the 1948 Yôsu Rebellion, which he also observed and which nearly started the Korean War two years early. Isobel consented to ask the question with this preface: 'Bruce has another piece of minutia here.'

With a long lunch break and the Beech interview, it was late afternoon when I sat down to interview U. Alexis Johnson, who was mostly useless except for some remarks on his youthful days in the late 1930s as a consular official in Korea. He did supply me with a moment of levity when I quoted to him, from his memoirs, a passage about how corrupt and authoritarian Syngman Rhee was; he had been going on about what a great patriot the old codger had been. Now he eyeballed me with the outraged look that diplomats like him reserve for people like me (as if I had said it). He backed and filled for a while, and then murmured, 'I guess I did use [such] term [s] in my book.' (His memoirs had been written with a co-author.)

Johnson told us that the Geneva Conference in 1954, designed to replace the Korean armistice with a durable peace, was to the American delegation merely an empty exercise to be gotten through. 'How does one prepare for a conference . . . when you have no hope that negotiations are going to change anything?', I asked him. 'Oh, you make your speeches and you also try to make sure that Korean foreign minister P'yôn is well established and knows what he's supposed to do and . . . don't let Syngman Rhee, er, sabotage it.'

By this time we were into the fourth or fifth clip with Johnson, and the skies outside had darkened. I thought him worth no more than a clip or two, but Max kept suggesting more questions. At some point I spied in the background none other than I.F. Stone, who had been quietly ushered in and was attentively listening to Johnson's replies.

Izzy had been scheduled for about 5 p.m., but it was getting on 7 or so. Johnson droned on some more, finishing his fifth clip, and at 7:30 we got to Stone. I had met him just once before, at a conference in Washington in 1983. He looked just the same: cherubic is the word everyone liked to use to describe him, and it fit, with the angelic giving some way to the feminine – from a short distance Izzy looked just like a twinkling, kindly grandmother. Up close the quadri-focals that mediated his near-blindness disclosed flashing, shimmering eyes, dancing over a firmly set chin. Both of them communicated a resolute message: the bullshit stops here.

But unfortunately the bullshit did not stop there. We got him situated in front of the camera and finished the first clip, which took about twenty minutes. I looked to my notes for the next set of questions, whereupon Max announced that the interview was over. 'Whaaattt?', I gasped. 'When we go past 8 p.m.,' Max said, 'Thames has to pay the crew triple-time, because it's a weekend. So we have to end it.' I protested mightily, while Izzy looked on like a pleasant sphinx. 'I'm taking full responsibility for this,' Max said, as the crew folded up its equipment. And well he should.

This was the worst decision I saw Max make in all my time with him; had it been anybody else I would have attributed it to political distaste for Stone's views, but after the heat of the moment I chalked it up to Max's stringent and occasionally autocratic style, a well-masked youthful insecurity pushing him toward unnecessary displays of command. Or maybe he just thought Izzy and I were enjoying things too much. Whatever the reason, we spent all day with the fatuous and twenty minutes with Stone.

To appease the both of us Max took us down to dinner at the Tabard, where Izzy showed not a trace of discomfort or hurt feelings about the interview, and regaled us for two hours in his curiously spellbinding way. Max, well read in philosophy (he studied Wittgenstein at Oxford), found particularly interesting the Greek and Latin learning that had occupied Izzy's past few years, and the book on Socrates that he was about to publish. I satisfied myself that what Stone said about John Foster Dulles in his book, suggesting that he might somehow have been involved in touching off the war (which I thought unlikely), was essentially a matter of hanging Dulles for the wrong crime. What Izzy really hated him for was the glacial pace at which Foster became an anti-fascist, dealing with German firms right up to and through Pearl Harbor.

When it was over I drove Stone back to his home in Northwest Washington, over icy and empty streets. As I helped him up the slippery stairs, waiting at the door was his wife and copartner of fifty years, Esther, wearing a nightgown and a look that said, Izzy was talking a lot again, wasn't he. 'Let me introduce you to a wonderful young historian,' he graciously said to Esther, and I drove back to the Tabard thinking that no compliment had ever meant so much to me.

Stone also told us how terrible he felt at the way an earlier interview was cut by the makers of a documentary on Huey Long. I had seen it, and the only appearance by Izzy has him saying, out of context, that maybe Long's assassination was for the better. 'I sat watching it in the theater and felt like a murderer,' he exclaimed. But he needn't have worried about Thames.

They didn't use a bit of his interview, nor did WGBH in the American version, no matter how loudly Jon and I squawked. Just as his *Hidden History* was elided from his obituaries in June 1989, so was he elided from *The Unknown War*. So let's remember a couple of his points, unfit for Thames/PBS print.

About his *Hidden History*, he said, 'I didn't really have a thesis in the book. I felt that just as with the Spanish–American War there were unanswered questions, [among them] the possibility of a [South Korean] feint across the border . . . . But I didn't have a theory and I still don't have a theory . . . I still don't know what happened, [and] I'm still not satisfied . . . . I still think there's a lot we don't know.' The book itself, which he could not get published until a chance meeting with Leo Huberman and Paul Sweezy in Central Park got it out through Monthly Review Press, 'was simply ignored. I think it had about two reviews, one called [Stone chuckling] "Fictive History of the Korean War." '[292]

On the Senator from Wisconsin, who barely takes a bow in the documentary, Stone told us, 'McCarthy in some ways was a product of the China question' and the 'corrupting influence' of the China Lobby, which dropped a lot of money around Washington. Izzy met him once: 'I remember one night waiting, as dusk fell over the capital, waiting for a taxi and McCarthy . . . was coming across the street and he saw me, and his eyes lit up in a friendly fashion, and I stiffed him. I still feel badly about having been rude, but I couldn't help it.' Of his downfall, Stone remarked, 'McCarthy was fine as long as he was harrassing the Democrats. But once the Republicans came in McCarthy couldn't be a team player. He was an adventurer . . . he began to attack the military establishment and got himself some powerful enemies.'

If there is such a thing as cherubic nobility, I.F. Stone had it.

UNTOWARD MOMENTS

Our interviews, however frustrating they so often were, nonetheless produced delicious moments when the truth of Stone's formulation hit home: there's a lot we don't know about the Korean War. If the sober and sedate Peter Lowe did it for the seminars, the Australian Col. Stuart Peach, peering over a stiff brush moustache as if it were a backyard fence, did it for the interviews. He was one of two United Nations military observers who concluded a famous inspection of the Ongjin Peninsula two days before the war began, the report of which was crucial to the United Nations' first resolution condemning North Korea as an aggressor, and cited ever since by scholar, pundit, and statesman alike. (It found the South Korean army entirely in defensive formation, with nary a hint of impending conflict.)

Col. Peach himself, however, told a Thames crew that he 'never quite knew what went on' that sudden Sunday morning when the war began. The Ongjin commander was Paek In-yôp (brother to Paek Sôn-yôp), 'a get-going sort of chap' who bossed the 'twin-tiger' 17th Regimental Combat Team:

> I, I never quite knew what went on. There's a bit of a mystery still about Haeju, I think it might have been Paek and his merry men, the 17th Regiment, attacking it . . . . We didn't hear anything about it until the war had been going for a while, and I never quite knew what went on. It's been said that they attacked there and that the North Koreans responded.

Peach went on to say that he didn't think this version held much water. (Note also that if the South Koreans attack, it is 'Paek and his merry men'; when the North Koreans do the same, it is heinous aggression.) This clip, with the demurral, survived into the final version of the film, but without the context that would make it explicable to the viewer: for example, that the 17th Regiment was part of the crack Capitol Division, that it was full of soldiers of North Korean origin who had served in Japan's Imperial Army (not to mention many members of the terrorist, paramilitary organization called 'Northwest Youth'), that Haeju was the headquarters for the leftist underground in the South, that it commanded a direct route to P'yôngyang, and that the southern army had sought to occupy it more than a year earlier, attacking across the parallel from Ongjin.[293]

Then there was John Burton, mild-mannered professor of Political Science at George Mason University, who had been the very young head of the Australian Foreign Office in 1950. He told us of telegrams coming from South Korea to the Foreign Office just before the war broke out, reporting South Korean patrols crossing the border, trying to provoke the

North Koreans; Dr Burton took these straight to the Foreign Minister and the Prime Minister, 'and we sent a very strongly worded telegram to the State Department,' asking them to curb South Korean adventurism. Before a reply came back from Washington, the war began. Burton opposed Australia's support for the American war, and subsequently resigned. Thereafter the telegrams, according to Dr Burton, disappeared from Australian Foreign Office files.

I spent an afternoon with Dr Burton before the interview, and came to the conclusion that he was entirely sincere in his recitation of what happened thirty-five years before, somewhat beclouded on names and dates (as he was the first to admit), and inured to not being believed. I have seen this last quality many times in older people who were open to the Left and who suffered through the 1950s; it is the written-on-the-face residue of a thousand indignities.

This quality intruded ever so mildly in the filmed interview the next day, causing Isobel to object that Dr Burton wasn't credible. Then Phillip, in London many months later, also told me Dr Burton wasn't credible, he was grinding an axe, and that there was no evidence substantiating his story. The Australian cables disappeared, I responded, which puts a bit of a burden on us to find them. But in the British Foreign Office records, I said, you'll find a cable, nicely preserved, saying that the Americans were trying to restrain hot-headed South Korean officers along the parallel, a few weeks before June 25.

Furthermore, I continued, half the people we've interviewed look perfectly credible while saying erroneous things, and a few more even look *in*credible while saying erroneous things, but we use them. We've interviewed people of great weight and power who honed their axes long ago, so why is an obscure person with no obvious interest in lying, nonetheless 'grinding an axe,' lacking in 'credibility'? As you will already have surmised, however, Dr Burton hit the cutting room floor with the speed of light.

Even James Hausman was a bit tantalizing about the start of the war, not a small matter since it was Hausman that Roy Appleman, America's official historian of the war, relied on for his account of what happened at Ongjin. Hausman told a Thames crew that Paek In-yôp was at Ongjin 'and when the war broke out as you know he was there not only defending his

line but counter attacking' (i.e. across the parallel). As for 'those who think
that the South may have started this war,' he went on, 'I think . . . I think
they're wrong.' I think, I think . . . that's just a bit too tentative.

Ultimately these untoward moments were errant blips on the Thames
radar screen, because they subverted rather than bolstered the paleosymbolic text of this war, forged long ago in the intense 1950s heat of the 'Cold'
War. This text rested dormant in the viscera, not the mind, disclosed only
by this spasm or that knee jerk. The untoward moments unearthed by
Thames became gaps in an interior logic, obstacles to an intuited consensus, enigmas that must remain enigmatic. Here was the opposite of Stone's
studied method, which took the one small thread that didn't fit, and used
it to unravel a tapestry of lies woven by the powerful, who always have the
most to hide.

THE MYSTERIOUS MR WADA

An index of the state of knowledge about the Korean War is that many still
believe Kim Il Sung was some sort of imposter, who stole the name of a
famous anti-Japanese guerrilla. The South Korean regime put this line out
in the 1940s, and has pushed it ever since.[294]

Kim's original name and birthplace were given in the newspapers when
he returned to Korea in October 1945, and subsequent scholarship in
Japanese police records turned his name up frequently during the 1930s
and early 1940s, as a guerrilla fighting the Japanese in Manchuria. Jon and
I knocked the imposter canard down about fifty times, but it kept coming
back up, like a plastic dummy with sand in the bottom.

The leading authority in the world on Kim's past is Wada Haruki, a
scholar at Tokyo University who has researched the question in five
languages. Like I.F. Stone, he is a person of unquestionable integrity and
honesty, and also a very funny man. But he doesn't quite look the part of a
professor, especially not a professor at the most prestigious university in
Japan. Or perhaps he looks the part of a professor in the 1930s, with his
long hair, thick glasses, and wispy moustache. When I invited him to be a
visiting researcher at the University of Washington, a colleague who
teaches Japanese politics remarked that 'he's the type you see on a plane

from Tokyo to Moscow,' which was the most creative piece of Red-baiting I'd ever heard.

When I took Wada-san to the airport for his trip back to Tokyo, we were talking intently at the gate, so much so that they nearly closed the gateway door before he realized it was time to go. As I waved goodbye and started off, a woman at the security checkpoint motioned me over: 'Can I ask you a question?' 'What?' 'Are you gay?' 'Not the last time I checked.' 'Well your friend looks gay.' 'He's a Japanese communist,' I said, and walked away.

Dr Wada reciprocated these reactions: he found America an odd place. One morning when we were eating breakfast, watching the TV news, along came a story about Baby Faye, who lived for a time with a chimpanzee's heart in her chest. Wada-san looked at me and said slowly, 'The modern world: wonderful world, or terrible world?'

At any rate, we got the crew to interview Professor Wada in Japan, and he gave a very nice account of Kim's background. Phillip was happy to use the interview at first, because he had mistakenly thought, after getting the translation done, that Wada had said Kim Il Sung did in fact steal the name of a legendary hero. When we pointed out to Phillip that Wada said just the opposite,[295] somehow the clip never got into the program. Instead Phillip began referring to him as 'the mysterious Mr Wada,' and substituted a clip on Kim Il Sung from our interview with anti-communist scholar Chong Sik Lee.

Ultimately you don't get much from interviews, a fact I learned early on in my research. But you do get 'talking heads,' which was what Thames was looking for, and the heads have to look plausible. The Mysterious Mr Wada had got Kim Il Sung's background right, but he never appeared, which merely illustrated a television principle: it wants not accuracy, but the semblance of accuracy.

CHAPTER SIX

ACCESSING THE 'OTHER':
WE MEET ROSA KLEB
IN BEIJING

You may think you know what you're dealing with, Mr Gittes, but
believe me, you don't.
JOHN HUSTON TO JACK NICHOLSON in *Chinatown*

How does the low-tech 'other' handle inquisitive television crews and nosy
scholars? What happens to 'the unknown war' when it becomes the well-
known war?

If the Korean War becomes sensitive and political when it is dredged
from the depths of the American psyche, it is a point of endless neuralgia
for both Koreas. The war is still the touchstone of politics, and one can go
to jail in both halves of the country for getting its history wrong (although
in the North, typically, things are harsher: denouncing the official view is
like turning up the wrong card in 'Monopoly' – you go directly to jail).
Americans can intuit the problem, perhaps, if they imagine an armistice to
our Civil War rather than the submission at Appommatox, followed by a
Korean film crew showing up on the Mason-Dixon line with lots of prying
questions about Fort Sumter, Andersonville, slavery, and the aborted
union.

In the summer of 1987 we were despairing of getting any cooperation
from North Korea, and not doing too well with South Korea. Although
Thames had gotten a film crew into the South, it received only minimal
cooperation from the authorities. Bureaucrats would sit the producer, Mike
Dormer, down in their offices and ask him (1) who was the originator and
writer of the film, and (2) who was the historian? Mike would answer (1)
Halliday and (2) Cumings (which they already knew all too well),

whereupon they would throw up their hands and say, 'why should we cooperate with you?' The Thames interpreter found General Paek Sôn-yôp rather stony, too, when she called to request an interview – until he found out she was from a prominent family in Seoul, whereupon he exclaimed, 'Daughter! What are you doing running around with these communists?' Halliday and I didn't make this trip, of course; through his own wits and resourcefulness Mike brought back a number of interviews, but very little film and strong memories of how tightly controlled was the southern system.

But then, Mike hadn't been to the North. Thames did get to the North in 1987, however, but not without a struggle that, looking back on it, I still find hard to believe. I will relate this bizarre travail for you here.

The summer of 1987 I spent in pleasant isolation in the slightly displaced New England village of Hamilton, New York – home to Colgate University, but given back to the natives and the quiet of the hills and lakes with the annual departure of the students. On a somnolent day in July the phone rang: it was the cheery voice of Jill Service, at Thames Television: 'Hullo, Bruce! It looks like our friends in P'yôngyang are finally coming round, so won't you hop a plane and be here next week? Have your passport and be all ready for a long trip.'

I jammed myself into the cramped seats of a British Airways jet, already tired but happy for the polite crew. On arrival I had terminal jet lag and vertigo, barely able to navigate through customs. The officer asked me what I was doing in London. 'Making a documentary for Thames.' 'Oh really? What about?' 'It's about the Korean War.' 'The old one, or the current one?' Obviously a reader of newspapers, this man, since at that time several hundred thousand folks had filled the streets of Seoul demanding the overthrow of the Chun regime. 'The old one,' I said. 'Splendid,' he remarked for some reason, as he stamped me into the country.

I checked into the White House Hotel, opened the convenient mini-frig for a beer, and called Jon. This time it was the real thing, he related, the North Koreans having said our visas would be ready in Paris the following day. Come into Thames at 9 a.m., and we'll call P'yôngyang. Call P'yôngyang, I thought? That means I have to talk to them at nine in the morning, in Korean, and I can't remember how to speak English because it is the dead of night, my time.

In the morning I had an English breakfast which consisted of a bloody-side-up egg and some indeterminate black meat swimming in grease, a meal which by now was entirely familiar to me. Thames Television was just a block away from the hotel, and the staff all greeted me with the British cheer I have come to prize and respect, and to contrast with the rampant and purely gratuitous rudeness of Chicago and New York (although New York more than Chicago).

Phillip wasn't in yet, but we were going to put through the call anyway. We gathered around the phone, and Jon noted that I looked nauseous: 'Feeling alright, Bruce? Long trip, was it?' 'Yeah, yeah, I'm okay.' The operator began the laborious task of connecting London to P'yôngyang.

Twenty minutes later we were still sitting and Phillip had just brushed in. 'Goddammit, why can't those crazy North Koreans join the twentieth century and get a decent phone?' Suddenly there was a hush, as the operator got a voice at the distant end. 'What should we tell them?', someone asked. 'I'll say their twenty pizzas are ready and how would they like them to be delivered,' I responded.

But in the event we did not get through to our party, and we were back to the waiting game. Another telex was sent, and copied to Paris. In the afternoon, a response from Paris, but not from P'yôngyang: they had the visas. Sue Lockett, the most efficient person in Thames Television and probably paid the least, dashed off to Paris to pick them up. She was back the next morning, and Phillip and I boarded a London–Hong Kong–Beijing flight the next day.

North Korean visas are issued on blue cards, a bit bigger than an American passport. Because I hate having a bulging coatpocket, in the London hotel I left my small passport in the pocket but put the blue visa in my valise, with several other documents, including the nice bundle of expense-cash Thames always thoughtfully provides. In Hong Kong we picked up a direct flight to Beijing, and arrived on a hot, sticky Sunday afternoon.

As we exited customs, a smiling man ran up and asked us if we needed a ride to Beijing. I looked at him. He had the high cheekbones of a Korean, but so do some northern Chinese; he was speaking English and Chinese and

I thought nothing of giving him my bags, while I got some Chinese money from the bank. We rode in from the airport in the man's Shanghai sedan, which appeared to me to be an amalgam of a 1953 Plymouth and a 1954 Willys. It had the same yellowing plastic trim on the dashboard, the same smell of thick cotton cushions, the same sound of gears meshing not-too-well, the same thwack of the clutch banging back to position.

We arrived at our hotel, the Great Wall Sheraton, a gleaming palace that marked the distance between my first visit to Beijing in 1981 and the schizophrenic China of 1987. At that time I stayed at the 'Friendship' Hotel — a creaking Soviet creation of the 1950s on the model of an Indianapolis railroad hotel of the 1940s, with cantilevered plumbing catacombed by roaches, swaybacked beds and food that seemed like Chinese cuisine vetted through Soviet cookery. (And probably was. One morning some beefy American businessmen shouted at the top of their lungs to a waitress, 'Whatever you do to the egg, don't open the shell!' And then they muttered, 'otherwise they'll just screw it up.' All this was observed closely by a lonely Japanese businessman at the next table, breaking into a concrete egg fried in crankcase oil as if he liked it.)

Our vaguely Korean-Chinese taxi driver arrived at the hotel with his eyes darting at the rearview mirror like Robert De Niro playing Travis Bickle. He handed our bags to the bellboy and rushed off, refusing a tip — so I thought he must be one of the old Maoist cab drivers, doing it for the revolution. The bellboy showed us to the check-in counter, and said our bags would be in our rooms.

We dawdled around and gawked at the displays, and at the Chinese girls in the restaurant with skirts slit up to mid-thigh (Jiang Qing, Mao's proletarian-clad wife, being safely in jail). We both needed a shower and a nap, so we agreed to meet for dinner. When I got to my room, for some reason I pawed through my valise to make sure my papers were in good order. I couldn't find the blue North Korean visa.

For the next half-hour I proceeded to subject every last pocket and bit of paper to intense scrutiny, but it was gone. Yet the papers it was ensconced with were untouched, as was the wad of cash. My memory then paced back over the past two days. I had a picture in my mind of the White House Hotel, where I placed the visa in the bag. The zippered bag didn't leave my hand thereafter except to reside in the bin over my plane seat, so I called the airline and asked them to search both planes for it. No one opened it at customs, so I couldn't call them.

I called Phillip with the distressing news, who arrived in my room instantaneously, and none too pleased: 'I always keep my papers in my passport and my passport next to my chest,' he announced, patting his vest pocket. He gave me a certain Fabian socialist beady-eyed look which I equate to the same look among my Calvinist- or Jewish-Mother-influenced friends. We both agreed to call London and see if Jill or Jon might have somehow found it. No luck there, but more astonished talk about how could one lose it. (Indeed.) I told Phillip I would see him at dinner, after I went over every inch of my effects, and my recent activity, once again.

As I dozed on the bed, a Korean-Chinese face appeared in my mind: the way he immediately singled us out for a ride, his darting eyes in the taxi mirror at the hotel, his refusal of a tip, the simple fact that my bag had been in his hands for ten minutes and the bellhop's for twenty. The visa was stolen, that was the only explanation.

But who would steal it? The South Korean security services popped to mind first; it would have been easy for them to place an agent at the airport. If so, it was mere harassment since the North Koreans would be happy to replace it at their Embassy the next morning. The next candidates were the Americans and the Chinese, both easily dismissed.

That left the North Koreans. In 1981 I had noticed how one of their agents materialized within seconds of my purchasing a ticket to P'yŏng-yang at the main Chinese air terminal. Obviously the Korean and Chinese secret services could work together to steal my visa. But why? I told all this to Phillip over a marvelous Szechuan meal at the hotel restaurant, and we agreed that the proof would be in the pudding at the North Korean Embassy next morning.

Monday morning was gray and the city was gray-on-gray as we boarded another Shanghai/Willys/Plymouth and weaved our way through vast gray masses of proletarians bicycling to work. We arrived at the stolid DPRK Embassy, a typical but not unpleasing Soviet-style rectangular building. Outside the gate a youthful PLA soldier in baggy green uniform stood desultory guard, but inside the building it seemed as if a neutron bomb had hit, for there were no signs of human life in the grand foyer – other than a massive portrait of Kim Il Sung.

Shortly, however, a kindly, rotund old woman materialized behind a window and stared at us, probably unsure about which language to try. I stated our business in Korean, which brought from her a benign smile and little else – quite unlike South Koreans, who fall all over themselves to say how good your Korean is, even when it's wretched. She disappeared and we were again alone with the fifty-foot ceiling and the Fatherly Leader's visage.

A bit later a rather different person stomped across the carpet toward us, a hard-eyed, sharp-faced woman packed into a cheap but tight blue dress, whom within seconds we dubbed Rosa Kleb. She was about thirty, and had an air about her that I had seen in fledgling North Korean diplomats before – a look as if to say, 'Aha, some capitalist swine have appeared, just watch me handle them!'

'Hello,' she spit out, 'what do you want?' For all the many days we spent with her, she always prefaced any sentence in English or Korean with the attention-getting ejaculation 'Hello!' I answered in Korean that we were due to catch the afternoon train for P'yôngyang, our counterparts were waiting for us to arrive to work on a documentary film, but my visa had disappeared. She escorted us into an anteroom filled with low overstuffed chairs with doilies on the arm, and racks of DPRK literature in various languages along the walls.

She continued in English: 'You lost your visa? That's pretty stupid' – this time with a meanly drawn smile. 'Maybe the South Koreans stole it,' I lamely suggested, to more laughter. 'Who are you supposed to meet in P'yôngyang?' Mr Pok Sông-gyu, I replied. 'Pok? You mean Pak?' No, I said, his name is Pok and he runs the Documentary Film Studio. (One-third of all Koreans are named Kim, and it seems that most of the remainder are Paks and Lees. Pok is a name that I had rarely encountered before.) This brought another narrow-eyed search of my own eyes, and a request that I go over once again the story of where we got the visa and how it was lost.

Rosa asked for our passports and disappeared. We sat for an hour or so perusing the latest magazines from P'yôngyang: 'On the Juche Idea' by Kim Il Sung; 'On the Juche Idea' by his son Kim Jong Il; an anonymously authored book, 'Kim Il Sung is a Legendary Hero for All Ages'; color pictures of a tractor factory that had increased production by 6 percent over the previous year; a cement complex that at Kim Jong Il's behest was bringing forth a new kind of silicate brick to be used in workers' housing; short stories about American imperialist atrocities during the war; a commercial magazine showing long billets of rolled steel, ginseng tablets, and pictures of Korean fish for export. I busied myself brushing up my Chinese by reading Kim's works exported for Chinese consumption. A young, demure woman served us ginseng tea.

Once again Rosa trooped in, this time with another 'responsible official' who did in fact look responsible; he also took in our story, start to finish. They then told us abruptly to return in the afternoon for my visa. 'But then we can't catch the train.' 'There's a plane tomorrow.'

Aha, we ruminated over lunch, they didn't want us to take the train because we'd see too much, so they just wanted to delay us until the Tuesday plane flight. We returned in the afternoon, but were told the visa was not ready. So, we spent the rest of the day walking the dusty streets of Beijing. Phillip was enjoyable to be with, with his sense of humor and interesting observations. Old workers squatted in the alleyways, and speculated on who we were as we passed. 'That one with the red beard's probably an Englishman,' an old voice correctly observed. We bought a watermelon at absurdly inflated prices (bringing it to about a quarter of what it would cost in Chicago); the street sharpies could not contain their glee at our foolishness, but we happily dug into the cool, sweet red meat.

As we walked, Phillip gently brought up the 'subject of Jon,' the Halliday problem which now surfaced in the liberal mind with the predictability of the next sunrise. I granted him that Jon was too involved with office politics at Thames, but restated my now-accustomed position, that no one was more sincere in his views, or committed to the success of the documentary, or knowledgeable about the problems of presenting the Korean War, than Jon; that he was only a 'problem' because various people with far less sincerity, commitment, or knowledge had singled him out, above all the South Koreans, who were interested in nothing more than grinding an axe which, once it cut down Jon, would aim for me next, and once it got me, would go for Phillip. Phillip listened carefully, silently, and without a glimmer of disagreement. He is smart, I thought to myself, but above all he is politic.

Beijing streets were now festooned with billboards advertising the consumer goodies of the capitalist world; unlike my previous visit in 1981, it seemed that many urban Chinese could afford them. Hardly a single Maoist slogan was visible, in contrast to 1981 when they were faded but still, and embarrassingly, present. We finally spied one in the underground walkway near the railway station: 'seize the time, march forward to greater victories!'

When we emerged above ground on the other side of this vast intersection, we saw hundreds, perhaps thousands of peasants from the countryside, with pathetic bundles of their worldly goods wrapped inside ricecloth. They talked or slept in groups throughout the station, or made the curbside or the shade of scarce trees their temporary home. They arrived day in and day out, with some ending up beggars in the streets.

Still, the *mise-en-scène* had none of the rank pathology of New York's Grand Central Station or Port Authority terminal; this human traffic was 'progress,' Deng Xiao-ping style. In this way Beijing in 1987 had a curious resemblance to Seoul in 1967, when I first went there; the detritus of the war still hung over the city, and peasants surged off the trains looking for work in the burgeoning industries. The similarities were reinforced by the side streets and four-cornered courtyard homes, which mimicked older Korean homes because Koreans had for centuries taken their models from China.

That evening we ate Peking Duck on Thames money, at another fine restaurant reserved for foreigners; I returned to my room and watched Cable News Network from Atlanta, took a shower under a high-tech pulsating head, and easily dialed a crystal-clear call to the States. China had joined the high-tech late-twentieth-century world: that miniscule part of 'China' represented by the Great Wall Sheraton Hotel, a sheltered complex grafted onto a suburban block near the diplomatic community, with no more relationship to the average Chinese than the Plaza Hotel has to Harlem. (It was the central staging area for American journalists covering the Beijing spring in 1989.)

Tuesday morning we had another go-round with Rosa Kleb. My tale was restated for the fourth or fifth time in Korean and English. More long waits in the anteroom with the Kim father-son duo. More ginseng tea. At length Rosa came in to give us the bad news: P'yôngyang had not replied to her telegrams, so she couldn't issue the visa. 'We'll miss the afternoon plane.' 'Come back tomorrow,' Rosa shot back; there's another plane on Thursday.

Rosa retained her triumphant, put-them-in-their-place look, and we were ready to wring her neck. Yet she curiously softened when her cute three-year-old daughter suddenly bounded in and jumped in her lap. Rosa summoned uncharacteristic warmth and playfulness for her, we thought; maybe also for communist-bloc visitors (although we thought that unlikely). Suddenly she looked to me like any other devoted mother. But she remained unyielding to us: no visa.

We had the rest of the day to ourselves, so we hired a car and drove out to the Great Wall. It was a beastly hot day, and I've never been one for hiking in any climate. But Phillip mounted the wall and went heaving off to the nearest parapet, which seemed miles in the distance – or in the sky – to me. It was simply another example of his prodigious energy. I often wish there were two of myself, so my work could get done; Phillip seems to act on the principle that there are at least two of him, and they can expend the energy of two people, and be in two places at once. As I lurched along behind him, he gave a start and stared down at a pen where two Chinese handlers were whipping a camel to get it to walk in a circle. It struck me as a literal oasis. But as the camel turned, we could see that the whips lashed at bloody raw flesh on his hindquarters.

Phillip, to my astonishment but above all to everyone else's, bellowed down to the handlers, 'You there! Unhand that beast! I won't stand for you to maltreat an animal like that!' An old Chinese man next to us laughed uncontrollably, spitting out that 'they hear you but they won't listen.' Yet suddenly the two put their whips down and sat on a bench, looking contrite before Phillip's Fabian onslaught. The long neck of the camel slowly craned around in Phillip's direction, giving him a sustained look through pellucid eyes that had thought, up to now, that they had seen everything.

We continued up to the parapet, which surveilled the northern-barbarian hinterland for miles and miles; little windows and vantage points had Chinese grafitti scribbled on them and smelled of stale urine, rather a pale reminder of a New York telephone booth. We were the only foreigners at this point on the wall, and I heard from a Chinese group nearby the words 'yang guize' (foreign devil). At least some things never change in China, I thought.

Phillip took pity on me and merely strolled back down the long incline. As we reached the oasis, the handlers were still sitting on their whips. Again the camel craned his neck and his big, pool-like eyes toward Phillip. 'Come back in thirty years,' I said, 'he'll still be looking for you.'

As we reached the base a little urchin-beggar accosted us, grabbing at the pens in our shirtpocket. 'You want a pen,' Phillip said, 'here, have an official Thames Television pen.' The kid grabbed it and started running up the wall, sure that we would run after him to get the pen back. When we didn't, he returned and trotted along by our side as we made for the communal urinal nearby. As it became obvious that he would follow us in, we tried to shoo him off.

'Wouldn't look good on Beijing television, two foreign devils caught in the bathroom with a little boy,' I said. 'Rosa really wouldn't give us the visa then, would she,' Phillip responded. The boy held back until we got inside, then bounced in as we were urinating. He circled around Phillip, who lurched this way and that, spraying the urinal: 'I'll be damned if I'm going to give this little bastard a look at mine,' he yelled, 'he just wants to see how big it is.' I shared the sentiment and we both quickly finished. We motored back to Beijing, slowed here and there by peasants tending an oxcart, bicycling youngsters, or trucks laden with oversize and overripe eggplants.

Wednesday morning we presented ourselves to Rosa like prisoners awaiting execution. She was surprisingly friendly, perhaps because she caught our demeanor, or merely because her comrades in P'yôngyang had heard of us and therefore we couldn't be all bad: 'Okay, everything is alright, you'll have your visa tomorrow and you can take the plane tomorrow afternoon.' We brightened immediately, and went back to await a negotiating session at our hotel with Chinese 'responsible officials,' who had finally consented to see us in regard to filming in China.

Three of them showed up that afternoon, a pleasant interpreter, a taciturn man who kept his dark sunglasses on, and our counterpart from the documentary studio. The latter was polite and to the point, asking us what sort of cooperation we wanted from China and when we wanted it. We requested access to archival film and interviews with various sorts of people who fought in Korea or were connected to the war. They were all very friendly and open in saying that all this would be possible, once they convinced themselves that North Korea had really approved cooperation on the project. What would convince them, beyond our going to P'yôngyang the next day? An authoritative letter from a responsible official, they said, and made clear in their correct and cheery way that not an iota of help would be forthcoming until they had the letter. The PRC clearly thought its relations with the DPRK were far more important than our documentary, but we weren't really surprised and saw nothing to dim our happy Wednesday. So we had another fine Szechuan meal, and went off to bed – but not before deciding that if somehow my visa were still not available tomorrow, Phillip would venture off to P'yôngyang by himself, and then send for me.

Thursday we arrived promptly at 9 a.m., our spirits boosted by Rosa's continued aberrant friendliness. 'We're just waiting for the visa,' she said, and ushered us to our now familiar overstuffed chairs amid the Juche literature and the ginseng tea. 'What the hell,' Phillip remarked, 'we haven't really had such a tough time of it now, running around Beijing and the Great Wall and the like; we'll be off today to P'yôngyang, and we'll look back on all of it as a lark.' I hoped he was right.

At this point a delegation of Japanese showed up in the anteroom, about the first people we had seen there without Kim Il Sung buttons in their lapels; they conducted their business through a Korean interpreter whom they'd brought along (no self-respecting North Korean willing to be caught dead speaking the language of the former colonizer). They had just arrived from Tokyo and were off to Korea that afternoon on fisheries business. We were happy to see that Rosa treated them with no less contempt than she had us. She let her evil eye drift over them for a while, then left the room. The Japanese visitors perused the North Korean publications with apparent interest, and no smirking. Shortly Rosa was back with visas for all of them, and not an eye cast toward us.

More hours passed, and it got to be lunch, when as far as we could tell not a soul stirred in the Embassy – or in all Beijing, maybe all China – for the next two hours. We demanded to speak with Rosa. Instead a man showed up, looking responsible and solicitous, saying my visa would be ready after lunch. Phillip decided to leave me at the Embassy and go ready a car with our bags, to take us (or him) to the airport.

As the 'lunch hour' dragged on I paced the broad boulevard in front of the Embassy, exchanging errant glances with the fresh-faced, taciturn PLA soldier who had pulled guard duty that day. We eyed each other with the mute, expectant air of something about to happen, like de Antonioni's film *The Passenger*, where Jack Nicholson adopts the identity of a dead stranger and then goes off to keep the man's appointments. But nothing happened. I walked down and got some dumplings for lunch.

At 1:30 sharp the Embassy reopened, and Phillip swerved into the driveway in the car. We were welcomed inside by Rosa and the man we had met that morning, he grimacing and Rosa beaming, almost laughing. 'Your visa is not yet ready,' he said with a look of chagrin; Rosa continued beaming. Phillip and I declaimed our outrage for a few futile seconds. He grabbed my arm for a race to the airport. We roared out of the Embassy and down the boulevard. As we turned the corner, I saw through the back window a green Mercedes sedan turn out of the Embassy, followed by several black Russian cars.

The traffic was thick on the way to Beijing's surprisingly small and inconvenient international airport, and we arrived a little after 2 p.m., for a flight leaving at 3. As we pulled up to the door, across the way the green Mercedes arrived to our rear, and three men bounded out, leaving the doors open. I then saw the black sedans pulling up at a distance. But Phillip was already inside, beckoning us both forward. 'Just come through with me, you've got a ticket. To hell with the visa.'

We went through customs only to confront a Korean airlines baggage counter bereft of personnel. I asked a PLA guard what was going on. 'They closed,' he said. 'Maybe you can find them in their office downstairs.' We frantically plowed back through customs and down the stairs to a bunch of small airline offices; the Korean office was empty, with a half-smoked cigarette butted in the ashtray. We clambered back upstairs. Phillip was carrying much more luggage than I, and even his prodigious energy began to give out — but not before his temper: 'They can't do this to me,' he shouted to no one in particular; 'I was a member of Parliament, I don't have to put up with this.'

I saw a man with a Kim Il Sung button standing near the customs door,

PLATE 1 John Foster Dulles at the 38th parallel

PLATE 2 Bird in a cage

PLATE 3 Roundup time in North Korea

PLATE 4 Postwar reconstruction in North Korea

LATE 5   Reversals

PLATE 6   Three scenes from Vietnam

PLATE 7   TV cameraman in tow

PLATE 8   The Dear Comrade Kim Jong Il and the Great Leader Kim Il Sung

PLATE 9   Woman with pistol   PLATE 10   Couch potatoes in North Korea

PLATE 11   The 'harvest' station on the P'yôngyang subway

and asked him if he worked for Korean airlines. I actually thought he was one of the people who had piled out of the Mercedes. As I spoke to him I noticed several Korean thugs hanging over the railing above us. 'The office is closed, the plane is full, you'll have to come back Monday,' the man told me. 'We have tickets, and the plane is never full,' I said. 'You should have got here earlier,' he shot back; 'we close an hour before flight time.' He then turned abruptly and walked away.

By this time it was obvious that Phillip wasn't going to P'yôngyang, regardless of his ticket or his visa. We calmed down and strolled out to the observation deck, where the North Korean turboprop sat far out on the runway, the passengers serviced by a bus. It sat there for another thirty minutes and so did we, after which we returned to the airport lobby: just in time to see the Japanese fishery delegation rush through customs, out to the bus and onto the waiting plane. 'Probably the only passengers,' I told Phillip. 'Hope they sell them Japanese blowfish and they all get poisoned,' Phillip said.

With nothing more to do in China we left the next day for Tokyo, stopping over for a meeting with a would-be go-between with the North, Christine Choi. On the flight Phillip and I commiserated about our unproductive days in Beijing. A stewardess brought me lunch first, and I chose a chicken dish. When she got around to Phillip, he asked me how it was. 'Terrible – I think they killed and skinned the chicken by running a truck back and forth over it on one of those dusty streets in Beijing.' He took the beef. 'How was it?', I asked him later. 'I wondered what they did with the meat off that camel's thigh.'

Tokyo was pleasant because we didn't have to fight our way in from the distant Narita Airport, but observed it from the air and then stayed at a local hotel. Christine Choi joined us for dinner. She had been in the North recently, doing a film on separated Korean families, and had prevailed upon the authorities to welcome our Thames crew to P'yôngyang. She is a documentary filmmaker, whose recent work on the killing of Vincent Chin (a Chinese mistaken for a Japanese and beaten to death in 'the motor city') was nominated for an academy award.

A radical feminist with a gravelly voice owed to years of chainsmoking, her hair frizzed up in an unnatural 'natural,' bluejeans, no bra, no makeup, this tough-talking woman is also every Korean male's worst nightmare about what happens to 'their women' in the West. The North Koreans found her as agreeable as a teenage werewolf, but her startling incongruity to people from a country that reportedly has jailed women for smoking in public made it all the more difficult to fit her into the hierarchy.

The result of this and her irrepressible style was uncontrollability, and thus more access to average people in the North than any other filmmaker got. Chris had no immediate remedy for our plight, however, so we had sushi and a lot of sake, and we told her all about Rosa Kleb. As we drained one sake bottle after another, at length she piped up and said, 'Well, can't go into Tokyo, nothing else to do, I guess we'll all just have to sleep together.'

I looked down at my hands long enough to think that this was probably a setup of two middle-aged men, which she could laugh hysterically about with her women friends back at their documentary studio, which occupies a floor in a seedy old textile warehouse in the endlessly seedy garment district in New York. When I got the courage to look up, Phillip was eyeing her warily, and with a bit of a sardonic grin. Soon we were onto another subject.

Our week in Beijing had expanded the Phillip I knew from his fluttering presence at the Thames offices to a Phillip one could appreciate in his complicated fullness, during an enforced leisurely dilation in which we got to know each other. (More leisure than Phillip had had in years, he told me.) I came to the view that his haphazard shepherding of all of us did not owe to a dereliction driven by his overcommitment (although that was part of it), nor to a desire to set limits on the content of the program (although that was also part of it), but ultimately to his deeply political character: he is a politician, who saw himself maneuvering a dissimilar set of personalities, and balancing a diverse bunch of world views. This would result in a documentary the ultimate politics of which would be a representation of different claims to truth, rather than the necessary commitment to truth itself. The film would be an improvement on the literature, so to speak, but it would not have the coherence driven by a self-aware guiding hand.

As it happened we later got into North Korea, and when we were driving to the airport to depart P'yôngyang in late November, one of our

North Korean counterparts said to me in Korean: 'You know all that business in Beijing, well, we just weren't ready to accommodate you then.' So they did steal my visa. Left hanging was an explanation of why they could not have found a better way to let us know.

CHAPTER SEVEN

FILMING THE LAST

COMMUNISTS

'I really don't know what it is you people want,' he said pettishly.
'To have things called by their proper names, that's all.'
DORIS LESSING'S *Martha Quest*

Chicago has a few magical moments every year, usually in May and October, when its fierce weather mutates into crystalline days of pure comfort: no clammy humidity, no howling Arctic winds, no pollutants from nearby Gary, just pure comfort. On one of those days in October, 1987, I heard Jill Service's cheery voice again: 'It's the real thing this time, Bruce, so why don't you hop over and hear about it.'

In the schedule of the documentary it was the very last minute, several of the programs already having entered the 'rough cut' stage. But then the North Koreans always seem to wait until the very last minute. Visas were waiting in Paris, Max Whitby was waiting for me with our tickets (Phillip refused to go this time, understandably), and so off we went to P'yôngyang for 'negotiations' preparatory to filming.

North Korea was our enemy in the unknown war, and it remains as unknown today as it was then. If it ever gets any press, you can bet it won't be good. Take it from CBS, which, Dan Rather announced with his usual heart-in-the-throat portentousness, slipped a team into North Korea in the summer of 1989.[296] He introduced the eyewitness report with these words: North Korea is 'a society where individuality is the greatest crime.' Cut to masses marching beneath Kim Il Sung's gaze, and we hear correspondent Bob Fall – not since the Nazi storm troopers, he intones, have you seen anything like this: 'forty years of nationalism, state terror, and brainwashing' has turned the people into 'thousands of cogs in an Orwellian wheel.' More shots of the mindless masses, followed by a non-sequitur: 'disabled and deformed people are never seen.'

The next day *CBS This Morning* has Bob Fall in for an interview, more clips, more analogies with Nazi Germany, more talk about the absence of 'cripples,'[297] more discussion of individuality as 'the greatest crime.' All the people idolize Kim Il Sung, and all say they live in a utopia, says Fall, whereupon we see an interview with a guide whom I remember from one of our museum tours – a sweet, friendly woman whose English was exceedingly poor. Fall asks her in English if she will do anything her President, The Great Leader, says. She does not quite understand the question, but answers yes. 'Anything?' 'Yes,' she responds, her face a bit quizzical. Cut to more mindless marching masses. CBS News has unearthed the anti-liberal, still daring to raise its ugly head when the whole world is 'going American.' (Indeed, CBS filmed in the North during the annual 'Month of Struggle Against American Imperialism.')

Bob Fall of CBS News would never know that the kindly guide he barked English at in the museum would no more insult her President to a nosy foreigner than she would spit on her father's grave, and neither would her ancestors going back two millennia. Let's face it: for a Bob Fall, the horrors of Kimilsungian communism cannot, in the final analysis, be distinguished from the horrors of the Confucian doctrine of politics. They both enter the dusky realm of the non-liberal, where all colors take on the same hue.

In South Korea you don't have Kimilsungism, but you do have Confucianism, vetted for most of the postwar period through a militarist dictatorship modeled on 1930s Japan. My heritage is such that I just cannot comprehend the organic self-confidence that motivates a Korean father to discourse authoritatively to his children about any and all matters and to make all choices for them, especially whom to marry, or for Kim Il Sung to do that for his North Korean children, or for the South Korean President to throw a few hundred student protesters off campus and into military boot camp along with his morning rice. But it happens everyday.

What does not happen is anything organically liberal (I'll use that expression, but I'm not sure liberalism is ever organic). A student of mine once asked me how many liberals there were in Korea, North or South.

'About as many as we have Confucianists in the US,' I said, 'and they mostly hang out in departments of East Asian languages and cultures.'

I first visited North Korea in 1981, when they let in a number of American scholars working on Korea, for carefully guided tours. I was anxious to see it because I knew the other half of Korea much better, from having been in the Peace Corps and doing a year of dissertation research in Seoul. I had learned there not to take the surface manifestations of Korea for the reality, and that within the bowels of one of the toughest political systems in the world was a people of remarkable talent, a society that was admirable in many ways, one which contained a variety of associates, friends, and acquaintances who enabled a stumbling, inexperienced American to count on the innumerable kindnesses of strangers, and to count Seoul as a place I could call home.

Unlike Seoul, in P'yôngyang I couldn't go anywhere by myself; indeed, I had my own 'pool' of handlers and explicators taking me everywhere, as if it were Riyadh during the Gulf War. Even a stroll down the street required the organization of a delegation. One time I faked out my guides by walking briskly toward the hotel lobby door, only to hide behind a pillar and watch them frantically run outside looking for me. They justified this shepherding by saying 'Our people wouldn't understand if an American walks anywhere he pleases, and anyway, a lot of them are still bitter from the war and an unfortunate incident might occur.' I didn't believe this for a minute, and in fact those people I did speak with were nothing but friendly, polite, and curious about why I had come to their country – except for some little boys who were fishing, and who pulled up their hooks and scampered away when they spied me drawing near.

North Korea was a striking mix of the old and the new: demure women in traditional dress, bustling bureaucrats in Western suits; long-bearded grandfathers on bicycles and slick cadres in Mercedes sedans; flowing Korean roof lines fixed upon marble-pillared government buildings; modern conveyances (especially a showplace subway) amid the unexpectedly antiquarian atmosphere, broken by electric buses and a showplace subway. It had the same quality found in Moscow, of entering a time machine and returning to the technology and consumer-goods culture of the 1950s, with the round black-and-white television tubes in big wooden cabinets, neon signs announcing this or that communist advance, and hotel nightclubs with multi-hued plastic discs slowly orbiting in front of a spotlight. But P'yôngyang was both more advanced, and more antique, than Moscow. In the simultaneity of its images and the pastiche of its mosaic, it also is a postmodern city.

The high cadres with their Mercedes had world-class facilities at their disposal, like a circular barber-beauty shop I observed in the center of the city, or the handful of speedboats pulling waterskiers on the river, or the multi-storied restaurant I was taken to, to dine on shrimp, lobster, and succulent barbecued beef. Here was a proletarian country going first-class, so it seemed. In his New Year speeches, Kim Il Sung would call for another million tons of steel, but also for semiconductors and biotechnology. At the other end of the spectrum were simple working folk out for a Sunday stroll in the park, dancing to saccharine accordions or fishing with a string and a pole, accompanied by venerable elders in traditional garb.

In between was a vast mass of salaried employees, who would leave their high-rise, three-room apartments and flood into the subways shortly after the crack of dawn, put in their day and return in the early evening, the women carrying some fresh vegetables or fish for dinner; this could have been in Seoul, or Tokyo, or any other city where 'modern' means being a cog in some bureaucratic wheel. P'yôngyang had a general dearth of consumer goods, but otherwise it had long since traded the bucolic peace of the farm for the humdrum agglomerated existence of the city, at least that 10 percent of the population with the privilege of living in the capital.

The architecture of P'yôngyang expresses the same contradiction between functionalism and modernism at all costs, between proletarian, even bucolic, utility and world-class strivings. You get simplicity here and grandeur there, deprivation here and grandiosity there. The showplace Mansudae Theater, where I was taken on the first night to see *Song of Paradise* (about the DPRK, of course), is not a modern but a postmodern collage: mixed Korean themes with Romanesque and Louis XIV pillars, streamline moderne with Stalinism thrown in, all lavished with marble. Inside are fountains with colored water and great chandeliers, gaudy paintings in hot pink or lime-green, whirring neon creations, making one think Versailles was mixed with Disneyland (or merely with the Kennedy Center in Washington, which always struck me as a kleenex box lined with red velvet). The theater is what Koreans take to be high-class modern; there are many similar monuments in Seoul.

From my first encounter with Koreans I marveled at the schizophrenic contrast between 'Confucianism' and real life; between formal rectitude and informal abandon; it is one of the reasons I took a liking to the country. Kim Il Sung symbolizes this contrast. From his earliest 1930s guerrilla pictures you see him with an insubordinate smirk on his face, arms akimbo. He is the model for the Korean *capo di tutti capi*, slouching about while everyone else stands at attention. Easy and humorous in informal conversation, always laughing like Ronald Reagan when he's out pressing flesh, he is attended with extreme deference and elaborate protocol. Stolid and aloof in state portraits, Kim also exemplifies 'the mass line' by listening sincerely to the weal and woe of the peasants; Kim gets down on his haunches to take a simple meal with a worker's family, having arrived in a Lincoln limousine (or a close Soviet facsimile). Yet everything good in North Korea is said to come from the top down, not the bottom up.

My hosts showed me a long film detailing the 1980 6th Party Congress, a typically elaborate extravaganza which served as Kim Jong Il's coming-out party. When Kim mounted the podium in a cavernous assembly hall, the tightly packed delegates yelled themselves hoarse, tears streaming down their faces. Kim just stared back at them, deadpan, with a vague look of superiority. Like Mao, he has a feminine mouth and a curiously soft face. If you want to peg him exactly in that incarnation, giving a party speech at the age of sixty-eight, he's Marlon Brando playing a big oil mogul in a film called *The Formula*, walking with feet splayed to handle the weight and hands amidrift thus to pat the tummy, combined with the big head on narrow shoulders and blank, guttural delivery of Henry Kissinger. Earlier in his life, when he worked crowds and pressed the flesh, he reminded me of Muhammad Ali doing the same thing, with the same broad no-flies-on-me smile, the same cheeky chutzpah, the same airy sense that everybody loves me, and why not? In pictures in the 1950s he looked like Khrushchev, with a wide-brimmed hat and stuffed-shoulder overcoat. In the early 1960s, when he sided with China in the dispute with Moscow, he went round in Mao cap and greatcoat, looking just like the helmsman. A few years ago, though, he materialized wearing a Western business suit and tie, and I figured North Korea was ready to do joint ventures (which they were).

P'yôngyang seems to have erred on the Korean side of the formal. I was amazed in 1981 by the crisp energy of city traffic, and by the absence of human-drawn and ox-drawn carts. On Chinese streets, elderly peasants dangle whips over donkeys pulling carts loaded with produce or with five or six sleeping laborers. Phalanxes of bicycles serenely go forth into hailstorms of honking cabs and trucks. Traffic police make a pass at controlling all this, while trying not to offend anyone and thus touch off a row. P'yôngyang, by contrast, is an exceedingly orderly, smoothly functioning, and sparsely populated city (in spite of its two million inhabitants). Electric buses, half-ton trucks, and European sedans (mainly Volvos and Mercedes) ply the streets, with hardly any bicycles. Smart traffic police, men and women in sparkling white uniforms, controlled the flow with an iron hand, pirouetting this way and that. With its wide avenues, parks and rivers, immaculate streets (I never saw a piece of litter), and widespread use of color, P'yôngyang is anything but drab. It struck me that if the name of the game is effective urban management, the North Koreans had succeeded as well as anyone else, and far better than contemporary American cities. Maybe Lee Kuan Yew, a capitalist version of Kim Il Sung, has done better in Singapore. But P'yôngyang was impressive.

Because of my expertise, I occasionally get to savor delicious postmodern juxtapositions that others don't. In September 1991, when the American consensus had it that we were now into 'post-communism' (1.3 thousand million Asian communists notwithstanding), the newspapers sought out Gus Hall, octogenarian head of the Communist Party-USA. No, it wasn't the end of communism, he opined, just a lull and a drought. Besides, there were still communist success stories: take North Korea, for example. He proceeded to urge Americans to take their vacations in P'yôngyang – 'it's a beautiful city.' And he's right – at least about the city. But I wouldn't expect a rush of American tourists.

My first trip brought home to me the extent of Kim worship, which I had thought (or hoped) was mainly for external consumption. I was quickly disabused of that foolish notion. Kim is everywhere. He greets you from large murals in the foyers of government buildings and schools. Buildings and rooms within them have plaques over the door showing the dates of his visits, and lately, his son's. Family bedrooms have portraits of Father and Son on the wall. One story has it that a Japanese cameraman, unhappy with his Polaroid take of the Great Leader, ripped it up and started to snap another. He was set upon by a phalanx of retainers: 'you *never* destroy a picture of our Leader.' His photo is everywhere, and yet none can be ripped up: it is an extreme of Bourdieu's view that nothing is 'more regulated and conventional than photographic practice . . . stilted, posed, rigid, contrived,' and that every photograph connotes class ethos – or in this case, the maximum representative of a class state.[298]

Quotations are everywhere, ranging from rip-offs of Marxist-Leninist slogans to quaint homilies, reminiscent of *Mr Rogers*. In the finely arranged Folk History museum, next to a display of food was a saying from Kim: 'Koreans can hardly be Korean if they don't eat *toenjang*' (a fermented bean paste that is the most characteristic of Korean foods). In a school, an intelligent young girl played what sounded to my philistine ears like Bach, on a Yamaha piano. Over her head was a quote: 'It is important to play the piano well.'

Kim is 'always to be found among the masses,' so the saying goes, except when relaxing at one of his villas, or with Prince Sihanouk at his estate near P'yôngyang. Sihanouk, who calls Kim Il Sung 'my best friend,' had use during his exile of a villa sporting 200-square-foot bathrooms, with 'heated floors to take off the chill in winter, and half a dozen bottles of toilet water, cream, and deodorant – all marked "Made in the D.P.R.K." '[299] Sihanouk directed a film in North Korea, in which he played an evil WW II Japanese officer seeking the virtue of a Cambodian maiden, played by Princess Monique. It was shot in Korean and dubbed in Cambodian; I'm dying to see it.

We visited the Museum of the Revolution, with a sixty-foot statue of Kim towering over the entry plaza. I witnessed kindergartners assembling before it and bowing, chanting 'thank you father'. The alpha and omega of the revolution is Kim's life, which modern Korean history merely adumbrates. He is shown in the van of a mass uprising against the Japanese in 1919, when he was exactly seven years old. If it is not Kim on display, it's his mother, father, grandparents, or his first wife (mother of Jong Il), but not, interestingly, his second and current wife. Even his great-grandfather gets into the act, helping to torch the unfortunate USS *General Sherman*, an

American ship that ran aground just short of P'yôngyang while trying to teach the Koreans a lesson in 1866. (I guess the Koreans took revenge for an Atlanta that could not.)

I took the chance to converse with the waitress who invariably served my meals at the hotel – always in traditional garb, well-coiffed hair, a bit of lipstick, very polite. I was struck by how similar her responses were to ones I would get in South Korea: about how many kids to have (two, a boy first), when to get married (mid-twenties), divorce (terrible if not utterly unthinkable), teenage pregnancy (rarely happened, but when it did, the kids were given political education), husbands who stay out late (a cross wives have to bear), homosexuality (which she said did not exist in North Korea, to my disbelief).

The model woman is Kim's second wife: pretty, demure, seen in traditional Korean dress if ever seen. In other words she is no Jiang Qing in baggy blue pants, plain white blouse, bowl haircut, dictating what to wear and what to think. North Korean women spend a lot of time in beauty salons, and on Sundays turn out in silk finery, permanent waves, and spare but noticeable makeup. But I also saw brown-faced women being trundled out to heavy labor in the backs of trucks, a look of dreadful resignation on their faces.

North Korea classifies most of its important statistics, so it is impossible to know if one's observations have any real validity. But it seems to be more efficient, to work better, than China, the former Soviet Union, or the former Eastern European socialist states like Poland and Romania. It is stuck technologically in the 1960s, but the delivery of goods and services appears more rational and effective. Neither on my first visit nor the recent ones did I witness any long queues, although resident diplomats say they are common, and that there isn't much in the stores anyway. That is true for any luxury items or diversionary consumer goods but it did not seem to be true for daily necessities like vegetables, fish, ordinary clothing, silks for traditional Korean dresses, and the like. Buildings seemed to go up overnight, literally so in that construction went on round the clock on a couple of the projects I saw near my hotel.

Our 1987 trip did not alter these observations so much as reinforce them. In October Max and I went alone for 'negotiations,' and in November we brought back a film crew. Max and I had come to like each other and have a good professional relationship, so I looked forward to our adventure. We spent most of our two weeks in the P'yôngyang Koryô Hotel – a twin-towered structure with each side reaching up forty stories to a revolving restaurant; it is turned out in classic P'yôngyang-moderne, with a congeries of architectural styles – Soviet-style dwarfing of the human, a confusing mélange of building materials, late-twentieth-century American suburban unconcern for the scale of nearby buildings, the quality of a newer Japanese luxury hotel, and little that is noticeably Korean. But the architecture isn't anymore disagreeable than the average Marriott Hotel, and the rooms were entirely quiet and comfortable – and, of course, clean as could be.

What is traditional is what is nice in Korea, to mimic something R.H. Tawney once said about China; the lovely silk comforter on the hotel bed, for example, in contrast to the room's Western furniture, which was merely functional, a copy of a design with its soul extruded; the elegant Korean food, rather than the labored Western dishes; the decorous hotel staff.

I had brought with me an unread tome to pass the non-working hours, in this case the full unexpurgated version of Goethe's *Faust*, which I found immensely enjoyable, one perfectly turned phrase after another, and finished by the time we left. *Faust* reminded me of a student I had in Seattle, one of the generic blonde-haired, blue-eyed, translucent-complexioned Scandinavian types named Kristin Sundvelt or the like that we got in droves, who had been assigned to read an essay by historian Alexander Gerschenkron. She didn't get past his intoxicating first page before she was in my office asking questions: 'Who is Goath?' I answered that by referring her to a Woody Allen movie in which Goethe is mentioned. But I grew aphasic with the second query: 'Is Seneca an American Indian?'

The hotel lobby was nearly empty, and with its high ceilings voices ricocheted as if it were a mausoleum. An enormous dining room with mirrors to make it seem even larger likewise serviced a handful of guests. The staff was unfailingly polite, however, and the food was excellent.

The rooms all had television, a Korean color brand based on Japanese innards, which I flipped on immediately, although not expecting to find thirty-nine channels. Instead there were three, with a mix of didactic party programming, educational fare (including English lessons), Korean War melodramas, and emotional, family-based soap operas: all of it pitched at an adult audience, all of it within the circumscribed orbit of old Korean culture or the new Korean socialism plus what the regime thought appropriate, and all of it wholesome to a fault – nothing perverse, defiled, idiotic, insulting to a child's intelligence (with the exception of the Kim worship), or merely frivolous. Nothing very entertaining to a jaded late-twentieth-century Chicagoan like myself, either – and, I imagine, to more worldly North Koreans. Let me give you an example.

Some years ago I knew a North Korean staffer at their UN observer group in New York. I asked him what he did for recreation in their improbable penthouse atop a building in Manhattan, and he said they watched television. His favorite show? 'Charley's Angels,' he replied, a show with three girls playing detective, their jiggling breasts being the main attraction. And with this, I grasped the truth of Baudrillard's observation:

> Whatever happens, and whatever one thinks of the arrogance of the dollar or the multinationals, it is this culture which, the world over, fascinates those very people who suffer most at its hands, and it does so through the deep, insane conviction that it has made all their dreams come true.[300]

As expected our hosts took Max and me on some of the usual sightseeing tours, including the Namp'o 'lock-gate,' a project that made lakes and irrigation ponds out of the Taedong River estuaries near the sea, and that was uncomfortably reminiscent of the 'Oriental despotism' Polanski stood on its head in *Chinatown*. Max is a businesslike person, however, and was impatient with touring P'yŏngyang. We were there to hammer out an agreement that would let our film crew into the country, and we had negotiations to complete. So every morning we sought to 'negotiate' with our hosts. It was, I suppose, a bit like the interminable negotiations at P'anmunjŏm.

On Monday we would be introduced to a 'responsible official,' who would ask us to state our business, explain how the documentary came about, what we wanted from them, and what they could expect from us. This we would dutifully do, and then would follow a couple of hours of discussion and debate, where they would probe at all our points for holes and contradictions.

On Tuesday we would meet a different 'responsible official,' and we would start again from the beginning: restating all the points we made the day before. On Wednesday yet another 'responsible official' would be introduced to us – a stranger bearing a name very similar to the guy we had on Monday. He would proceed to point out inconsistencies in what we said on Monday, as opposed to Tuesday. We seemed to work our way up the hierarchy as the days went by, but never did we sense that we were with anyone capable of making a decision. Our interlocutors came and went, and seemed to merge together in our memories; sometimes we thought we had seen the same man twice, the same name thrice.

After several days of 'negotiation' we were taken to the headquarters of their state documentary outfit, and got an inkling that Big Brother was watching. Or, at least, little rotund Son: over every door was a plaque saying 'Kim Jong Il was here.' He has taken a 'special interest' in film (and is reputed to possess a library of 20,000 Western movies), and we had no doubt that the buck would not stop until it entered his door. Here we finally met the head of the documentary studio, Mr Pok, a handsome man somewhere between forty-five and sixty years of age.

This day our negotiations started off on a different tack. 'Who do you think started the Korean War?' Ah, yes, an idle question. Now I am sure that to prove ourselves unbiased and pursuers of truth, Reed Irvine would have wanted us to say, 'Why, of course, everyone knows it was Kim Il Sung who started the Korean War!'

That would have gotten us a quick escort to the airport (at minimum). Fortunately I was able instead to tell the truth: 'It was a civil war, and in a civil war the question of who fired the first shot doesn't matter.' This response energized a wiry, elderly man, no more than 110 pounds soaking wet, who had been watching us intently: 'It was not a civil war. It was a war of American imperialism waged against the Korean people. For nearly forty years, our party has maintained that position on the war. How do you respond to that?' His eyes had narrowed, his face had turned to stone: it was a full count in the bottom of the ninth and we had just one swing left, if we hoped to shoot in North Korea. So Max and I batted our response around for a while, hoping the question would go away.

Shortly Mr Pok motioned in my direction and said to one of his aides in *sotto voce* Korean, 'ask that son-of-a-bitch.' I said this: 'I am a scholar. I may be right or wrong, but the evidence I have seen convinces me that it was a civil war; that it started in 1945 with the division of Korea; that it was fought by unconventional means until the summer of 1949 when the South sought to invade the North, but was restrained by the US. In 1949 the North was not ready to fight, because its best soldiers were still fighting in the Chinese civil war. In the summer of 1950 those soldiers had returned, and now the North was ready to fight.'

To my surprise their side exchanged glances, faces softened, and the question was not brought up again. Perhaps they decided just to drop it, or perhaps they thought my answer was the best they were likely to get, from their standpoint. In any case it is the truth. Later on the skinny, wizened old geezer who had pinned us down became quite congenial; he had lived in the South until the national division and knew many of the people I had studied in my work.

From that point onward our hosts gave us to believe that we would have an agreement; Mr Pok's presence at the session meant that finally they were ready to do business. My guess had always been that whatever else they thought of us, they would go for the foreign exchange we were offering. Thames pays commercial rates for the use of film, and if they coughed up authentic footage P'yôngyang might make as much as $100,000 by participating. Soon Max and I were spending hours watching North Korean archival and newsreel footage shot during the war, which I found absolutely fascinating (never having seen a frame) and which Max found both fascinating and disturbing.

Max and his wife had a baby girl, and the harrowing footage of the destructiveness of America's carpet bombing, with close-ups of napalmed babies, shook him to his roots. It was a holocaust, and they had unimpeachable film to prove it. The Koreans had built an entire underground society to cope with the bombing: factories, hospitals, schools, and troop facilities were all moved into tunnels, caves, and mountain redoubts. This was new and shocking to Max, but to his credit he did not shy from presenting this evidence in hours four and five of the documentary.

Max telexed back to Thames that it looked like we had an agreement, and indeed it did; we drew up lists of the newsreels we wished to purchase and began to seek out interview targets for our filming. We had more meetings, more dinners, more sightseeing, and still no signed contract.

On our last night we had a fine banquet at the hotel, Mr Pok presiding in such good humor that we were sure we would sign an agreement. We all offered toasts to our agreement. Everyone agreed that we had an agreement. Max and I went back to London with no agreement.

Instead Mr Pok and a couple of aides showed up in London shortly thereafter: a visit that I missed, and sorely missed, since Phillip kept doubling over with laughter at the mere mention of it. When Pok's entourage visited his own home it was just one rollicking thing after another.

First it was the bathroom, which would show on the toilet seat the prints of Pok's shoes: he was used to a squat toilet, and was now squatting on Phillip's, if from an altitude. Then it was the money: when they brought the films we had requested and Phillip gave them a Thames check (for $50,000 as I remember it), and one of them jammed it into his shirt as if it were contraband. Then it was the interviews: we had 250 to show them, but they wanted only to watch the ones taken in South Korea – and watch, and watch.

And, of course, neither Phillip nor Mr Pok were alone: in good British fashion they were shown every courtesy, taken out to eat, driven around in Phillip's car for sightseeing, and the like. And in predictable KCIA fashion Phillip's car was briefly stolen and ransacked by an interested party, and while entertaining the North Koreans at a restaurant unknown people snapped photos and then quickly departed.

Unlike his easy aplomb and devil-may-care approach in P'yôngyang, Mr Pok struck Phillip as a frightened and weak man, deathly worried that we would say something nasty about the Maximum Leader in the film. Phillip finally hammered out an agreement with him, but only after a session in which he (in his telling) humiliated Pok in front of his underlings. But we had the agreement, and soon we were back in P'yôngyang with a film crew: Max as producer, Frank Haysom as cameraman, Eric Brazier as sound mixer, and Ray Jones handling the lights.

We were initially put into the P'yôngyang Hotel, a rambling, third-class older place that was well maintained and crystal clean. This is the fourth hotel I have been in in North Korea on two visits, and I have yet to see a roach, which would set a record in Beijing or Seoul, except for the internationally run megahotels; what is more amazing is that I never saw a rat, anywhere; many nights I have laid awake in older Korean inns in the South, listening to the rats play on the paper-thin ceiling, worried that one would gnaw through and splatter down on my face.

But even though we were all given suites, it was a distinct cut below the Koryô where Max and I stayed in October, which we attributed (accurately, I am sure) to the fact that the North Koreans were now picking up our tab, as per the contract and the $50,000 they had wound their mits around. My room had a 1950s-style black-and-white TV of the Taedong River brand, the picture flipping vertically no matter what I did to the controls. On the wall was a wholesome little painting of a chipmunk munching a nut on the limb of a tree, dabbed with bright colors and done in a vaguely Korean genre. Just across the street from this hotel was an older monumental building, not unpleasing to the eye; on the side facing us was an inlaid-tile mural, larger than life, of an attractive Korean woman, wearing a radiant orange traditional dress and seeming to leap forward. In her right hand was a pistol. The same woman is featured on the currency, in the middle of the one *wôn* note. (See Plate 9.)

We demanded that we be quartered at the Koryô, more out of a sense that if we didn't we would be in a bad bargaining position on other things than out of a desire for more comfort. We got the usual excuses about the Koryô being full up, which convulsed Max and me, who had strolled its empty corridors for two weeks. We ate a couple of meals in the big old dining room, serviced by a gracious staff with excellent food. It had a big fish tank with an arch inside it, shaped like the St Louis gateway; a lone goldfish spent his days climbing up one side and down the other of this arch, examining floating bits of matter for edibility. I thought we had the freedom of that fish in P'yôngyang – moving in a Mercedes capsule through the various sights, not having to wear a Kim Il Sung button like everybody else, but equally alone and out of touch.

Our hosts would not give into Max, so he took matters into his own hands, called a couple of cars and stuffed our bags in, and off we went to the Koryô Hotel. Our guide Mr Kim was nonplussed, but he couldn't do anything about it. We found the Koryô mostly empty, as we had thought. In the evening, though, a peculiar assortment of foreigners would collect around the bar and trade stories.

I chatted with a medical student from Africa, who had spent several years studying in North Korea. He did not utter a word without stutter-like hesitation, acompanied by rapid blinking of his eyes, making him look amiably shell-shocked. His Korean was pretty good, but I thought not good enough for medical studies. 'Oh, there's a lot of English in the textbooks, and I sit in my room reading them, then I go over it with my professor.' 'What do you do for recreation?,' I asked. 'I come here and drink, or I try to pick up girls on the street.' 'You're joking!' 'No, you'd be surprised,' he said, 'some will do it for money, and some will just do it.'

He asked what I did, and then shot a question at me: 'Why do you think all those students are rioting in South Korea?' I was giving him a stock professorial answer when he cut me short. 'That's not why. The students listen to the communist radio, that's why. They listen to these people. And these people, I tell you, they're just waiting for their moment, all they live for is to pounce on the South and put it under the rule of their Leader. That's why you can't take your troops out.' A few years in North Korea had turned him into a raving anti-communist.

Also at the bar, however, was a blasé Englishman in his twenties, who had answered an ad to come to P'yôngyang and teach English. He was red-haired and tall, a little slack while not being fat, of balmy disposition, with an eyelid that drooped halfway over the cornea. He rather liked North Korea, having been there a year or so, and took his African friend's tales and woes with a big dose of salt. He had a room in the P'yôngyang Hotel, and came and went as he pleased. He had no discernible politics, but could be counted around the hotel bar almost every night.

On this visit, too, I mostly read *Faust* and listened to the 'classical' music on the radio. To a philistine like me it sounded just like the Mozart and Bach and Beethoven I keep on in the background when I'm working, but it was not, it was all indigenous. It was immensely soothing, and I noticed Frank, our cameraman – utterly homesick the whole time – listening to it as he read the book he had brought, a local history about his village in England. This familiar volume supplemented Frank's marmalade, and both stimulated reveries about his much-loved dog, his children, and I assume, although he did not mention her, his wife. Occasionally the radio music would pause, and a bit of news would come on, some weather, or someone in a sonorous, hortatory voice intoning very slowly, in total seriousness, 'There are many fine cities in the world . . . but in all the world . . . there is no city so fine as P'yôngyang.'

Our concessions occurred at breakfast, where we ate from Frank's jar of marmalade, Eric's jar of some delicious lemon-flavored toast spread, along with boxes of cereal brought from home. Unlike the Chinese, the Korean staff knew how to make eggs properly; if you told them to softboil an egg for three minutes, it would come back perfect.

All this was disconcerting to Frank and Eric, who had been on any number of missions for Thames around the world, and had extorted combat-pay bonuses out of Thames for agreeing to accompany us to North Korea. They had recently been in Moscow, where the hotel was awful, the food was worse, and the staff all had advanced degrees in boorishness. Earlier they had been in Teheran, shortly after the revolution. Cars tore through the streets full of young men brandishing machine guns out the window. They thought P'yôngyang would be a cross between those two cities.

Instead they found a cross between the fastidious efficiency of Singapore and the bucolic pace of Alma Ata.[301] The street movement was controlled by pivoting hands holding electric batons, attached to the tightly packed bodies of iron-willed young women pleasingly poured into svelte traffic-cop uniforms, pirouetting around on pedestals with military precision in the middle of intersections.

Underneath all this was a spic-and-span subway system, the trains moving from one cathedral-like station to another. Each cathedral played out a theme, in lavish marble and painstakingly crafted inlaid tile: the 'harvest' station, for example, showed the Fatherly Leader standing in the midst of an abundant corn harvest, the shimmering porcelain lit by chandeliers made of glass goblets in lime green, hot pink, and bright orange, meant to represent bunches of fruit. (See Plate 11.) Another, newer station allowed the underground traveler to see what they were missing above, in the form of inlaid tile murals of prominent places in the capital city. Before the traveler ascends an enormous escalator, longer than the cavernous one at DuPont Circle in Washington, they notice at its base a set of three gigantic, ten-foot-spaced blast doors receded into the walls – no doubt intended to withstand atomic bombing.

Soon we met a delegation led by Cho Pong-jae, a tall, slender, angular man with large ears, who moved and talked with the deliberate pace of a James Stewart, albeit in a thick P'yôngyang accent, adam's apple bobbing along with the words. The only variation was when he mentioned Kim Il Sung, and his voice lowered almost to a whisper. Cho was said to be in charge of documentaries, and was certainly used to command. He started out on such a hard note that Max and I thought we were back in our October negotiations.

'Jon Halliday broke his promise to us, you know, he said this documentary would present our point of view, and now you talk about "balance," and you have filmed in the South. We don't know why we should trust you.'

He continued in this vein for some time, accompanied by his aides' somber looks. I said Jon would never have promised such a thing, since from the beginning he wanted both Koreas to have their say, not just one; Jon was not a liar and we resented this implication. Max agreed, and restated the principles of the documentary. I trotted out the experience Phillip and I had with Rosa Kleb in Beijing: 'Most people would never come back to a country which treats you like that, but now I've returned twice.' Mr Cho didn't say anything to that, just fixed me with a languid stare, a little like Phillip's camel at the Great Wall.

We began to wonder if we would do any filming at all. Shortly, however, he broke into his facsimile of a broad grin, and announced that we could start filming the next day. 'You will follow all my orders, of course,' he said, his grin now widening a hair more. All the aides laughed, too. I felt like we were in the restaurant scene of *The Godfather*, the next move being an abrazo and a kiss on the cheek.

Our filming counterpart was a 'cameraman' (more likely a director) named Shin, who was obviously highly trusted by the regime. He had filmed several exchanges with South Korea (in South Korea), and had traveled abroad extensively. Except for his Korean eyes, he was a dead ringer for the actor Harvey Keitel. He had a frame the same size, and the same balled-up, tightly packed, high-male-hormone intensity. He couldn't stand still, eyes hopping, grinning, a coil of energy. He also was a regular fellow with a good sense of humor, and we never had a bad moment with him.

One day he ticked off his global travels for me, mentioning Italy.

Having been to northern Italy for the first time myself in 1986, we compared notes on the cuisine, the people, the various cities. 'How did you like Venice? – the canals and all.' 'Oh, the canals were very interesting. But all those old buildings . . . .' I had a vision of Kim Il Sung taking over Venice, and getting his bulldozers out. The truth is all we have in the late twentieth century is two kinds of modernism, once called capitalism and communism, now called capitalism and post-communism, and they both tear at the few remaining vestiges of the past, only to put up a parking lot.

The next day we went out for filming at the Juche Tower, named after the ruling 'Juche' (self-reliance) ideology, and which the crew called Il Duce Tower. It is on the model of the Washington Monument, although not quite so tall, and with a fake red flame at the top. We took the elevator to the circular parapet just below the flame, which commands a panoramic view of P'yôngyang. While the crew was busy filming, I chatted with the tower guide. After a few questions she remarked in Korean, 'You're good-looking.' Taken aback and trying to think of something to say, I asked her where she lived. 'Oh, right over there, on the sixth floor of that red building.' There was indeed a big red apartment house where she pointed, and she was smiling up at me; I still wasn't out of this thicket, which flabbergasted me. But then Max came around the corner and that was that. Now I figured the African student knew whereof he spoke.

Sunday, November 15, was election day for people's committees. At dusk the night before P'yôngyang lit up with a thousand electric and neon signs – DPRK flags, paeans of praise and gratitude to the Great Leader, slogans for the masses, patriotic axioms, get out the vote exhortations. The main railway station, one of the only big structures clearly influenced by Soviet architecture, was a cornucopia of flashing bulbs and neon. So we went out and filmed, and then got ready for election day.

We had an archival clip from the first elections in 1946, showing a white box and a black box; you put your ballot in the white one if you wished to vote for the single candidate, or you blackballed him with a no . . . under the watchful eye of party cadres. Needless to say, the candidates got vote totals breaking all records in political science. Max was determined to get inside a poll to film the ballot boxes in 1987.

Our hosts were happy enough to let us record the hoopla at each polling place: brass band, young couples in their finest outfits dancing in the chaste way I remember from 'square dances' in the Midwest in the 1950s, little kids fooling around while their parents waited to vote. It was a holiday as much as anything else, but everyone (100 percent, or so the regime says) votes – the vote being a token of citizen belief in the system, not an election that decides anything.

As we mingled among the kids, the dancers, and the polling line (with some pretty old folks bent over their canes, even a 'cripple' here and there), I noticed a handsome middle-aged Korean woman wearing a mink coat. Along with the mink, she had the sharp eyes, fine makeup and typical carriage of a bourgeois woman, unlike anyone you see in North Korea. (Eyes may be sharp, but connote a different shrewdness.) She might as well have been shopping on Fifth Avenue in New York. I sidled over to her, and noticed she wasn't wearing a Kim button on her mink. When I spoke to her she waved me away. Who was she? Maybe a Korean from Japan, or maybe a member of the small number of protected bourgeois families living in the North, because they gave help at some point to the revolution.

The rest of the morning was spent moving from one polling place to another, asking to go inside, demanding to go inside, begging to go inside, being allowed to film at the door of the polling place, but never getting a look or a shot at the ballot box itself. So, it's probably still the old black/white routine.

North Korea has one undeniable freedom, a freedom disallowed during the colonial era, attenuated by the Sinified elite in the 500 years of the Yi Dynasty, and a freedom less easily exercised in the South: the freedom to be Korean. This would not be high on the American bill of rights, but it is palpable and, presumably, important to Koreans. You never see a foreign word in Korea, most of the foreign loan words in Korean having been eliminated (one of the remaining few is *ttank'u* for tank, as in T-34 tank), you never see a foreign publication, you rarely see a foreigner, and the only non-Korean communists on display are Marx and Lenin, in two lonely, forlorn, and mildly faded portraits hanging off a state building in the central plaza.

It was *kimjang* time in Korea, the point at which huge numbers of cabbages are sodden with garlic, onions, red pepper, fish heads, and what-not, and put in big pots to ferment, thus to make *kimch'i*, the fiery national dish, for use during the long winter. Trucks brought in big loads of cabbage and dumped them near the towering apartment houses, and the women descended upon the vegetables with an age-old intensity. Little kids bounded through and around the cabbage piles, pausing to see what was going on, helping to clean up, and then running off to play.

This child's play goes on in the middle of a great city; the streets are utterly safe for little kids, dawn to dusk, except for the roaring Mercedes sedans; no pedophiles here, no crime, nor any other sort of pathology that I could see. When a five-year-old happens upon a foreigner like me, they will give a bit of a start, with a mix of shyness and playfulness on their face, and then bow to the waist and say how-do-you-do.

The North Koreans are never quite sure what to do with their foreign charges once the usual sights have been seen, and so they have recourse to films. I watched a new feature called *An Chong Kun Shoots Ito Horobumi*, a technicolor docudrama about the Korean patriot who assassinated this great Japanese statesman at Harbin Station on October 26, 1909, just before Japan annexed Korea. When the date flashed on the screen my Korean guide nudged me and asked what day Park Chung Hee was perforated by his KCIA chief. I responded October 26, 1979 – and he sat back in his chair with an air of satisfaction.

In the course of our visit, it developed that virtually all of our guides and associates lost immediate family members in the war. Mr Pok lost both his parents, as did several others, resulting in their being sent to Eastern Europe (especially to Hungary, given the Uralic-Altaic language affinities) with other orphans to live with families and go to school. I thought for a while that this was why they were assigned to deal with us, there being no chance of security lapses or defection. But then our interpreter, Mr Yun, told me his mother, grandmother, and elder sister were 'captured' by ROK soldiers and taken to the South (all South Koreans with relatives who went North during the war also say they were captured and dragooned off); he was raised by his other grandmother, who merely got off with a clubbing on her back that left her stooped for life. When we later went on our trip to the demilitarized zone, Mr Yun was not allowed to go along: he had no 'passport,' we were told. The real reason: he was young and callow by Korean standards, and his mother was in the South.

THE NORTH KOREAN INTERVIEWS

Max Whitby, the crew, and I got twenty-five interviews with North Koreans about the war, the first ever shown in the West. The value of the North Koreans was not for 'balance,' although that was the justification for the effort to get them, and had they not appeared, the film would have been impossibly biased toward the American and South Korean viewpoint. Their real value is that they bring to the film an authenticity and immediacy that inevitably shocks the Western viewer. It is not just that they have diametrically opposite views on the war, although that is part of it. It is more that they come from 'The Brainwashed Republic,' as the *New York Times* called it in 1989, and yet speak from the heart; they clearly believe what they are saying, and yet what they are saying is said to be incredible. Or perhaps the modernist North Koreans have raised simulation to a higher artform than postmodernist American television?

The North Koreans come across like men from outer space, or Zeks from the Gulag, or a Malcolm X from the ghetto, in that they contradict our expectations, they refute a comfortable logic forged by state power, and thus counterpoint everything else in the film. It's what we wanted, and we got it. The contrast between the North Koreans and all the Americans interviewed for the documentary exemplifies Barthes' point:

> The oppressed is nothing, he has only one language, that of emancipation; the oppressor is everything, his language is rich, multiform, supple, with all possible degrees of dignity at its disposal; he has an exclusive right to meta-language.[302]

All this is not to say the twenty-five interviews were gotten easily. After our tortuous negotiations, we had few illusions about how difficult it would be to get the people we wanted. Except for a few well-known figures, we didn't even know who they were. So we presented the Koreans with a list of names, and of generic types (a soldier on the 38th parallel on June 25, a woman who worked in the underground industries).

Towering above everyone else on our list, as he does in his country, was the Maximum Leader himself, and if not him, then his Beloved Son. We very much wanted to interview Kim Il Sung, among other reasons because we thought he might talk more freely than anyone else. In the end we didn't get him, but we got more cooperation out of the North than we did from the South, which (with a couple of exceptions) presented us with people whose positions and views were predictable and common. The North gave us maybe fifteen turkeys like that, out of the twenty-five.

We were politic enough not to ask after someone like Mu Chông, a fiery general and rival of Kim's who reportedly went to China after he was purged; we were impolitic enough to ask for Pang Ho-san, a general of long Chinese experience like Mu Chông who distinguished himself in the early Korean War campaigns, and who some say was executed after the war. His name drew a blank, a stare of no recognition which the North Koreans specialize in. Max also wanted to find people we had seen in newsreel footage from the time so that their participation could be verified, and so we could run then-and-now shots. I hoped to find some of their historians, to see what I could get out of them.

We got a couple from both categories – a cameraman and a reporter we had seen in the newsreels, both of whom gave interviews, and a historian and a recording secretary to a military unit on the front line, both of whom I found to be authentic and interesting. The former showed me a massive internal (*naebu*) history of the war (but wouldn't let me make a copy[303]), and the latter showed me originals of reports on border fighting in 1949 that he sent up to his superiors, and that he did let me copy. In his interview he told us the war really started in 1949, not 1950, which is not the usual North Korean line.

Then there was the problem of what questions we wanted to ask. Our North Korean counterparts were not gauche enough to try to tell us what to ask, although they would have preferred that; but they didn't like surprises, either. Max and I always felt we were treading a thin line between trying to get what we wanted, and trying not to be put on the next plane out. Furthermore our guests wanted to know what they might be asked, lest they blurt out something untoward that would be preserved forever on film.

The language problem complicated all this, in that I was both the interviewer and the simultaneous interpreter (with occasional assistance from Mr Yun), the person who knew the issues and the one trying to remember under the hot lights how to refer to Kim Il Sung without insulting our counterparts or perjuring myself (or saying 'His Nibs' or 'Il Duce,' which is what we called him on the crew), not to say *Han'guk* ('South Korea') but *Nam-Chosôn* ('South Korea' said the North Korean way, thus not to offend North Korea – although they preferred '*Nam-panbu*,' i.e., southern part of the DPRK), so on and so forth, all of which I had told Max and Phillip I was not qualified to do, why didn't they get a simultaneous interpreter instead of a historian if that's what they wanted, blah-blah-blah to no avail.

Anyway Max and I would figure out what we wanted to ask in English, I would render it into Korean, give the interviewee and our counterparts a general idea of what we would ask, and start the cameras whirring. That process worked fine if we had some time to prepare, and so I could look up vocabulary like 'hand-grenade pin.' I preferred having written-out questions, since the Koreans were always trying to put words in my mouth. (Question: 'How do you say Sabre jet in Korean?' Answer: 'American imperialist plane.')

But frequently the Koreans would change the schedule, or substitute someone at the last minute. I even had the impression that, as with our negotiations, they switched names on the same person – although Max assured me that I was simply jet-lagged and having delusions. Finally, of course, the gnawing twinges of patriotic longing I felt during the whole trip (see below) came welling up when faced with a napalm victim to interview: 'Tell us about wolfish American imperialist atrocities, why don't you?'

Of the fifteen turkeys, I will always remember Ch'oe Tôk-shin and Li Wôn-gyun. The now deceased Ch'oe was a former South Korean general and one-time Foreign Minister who went to live in the US for many years, and then answered the call of the Fatherly Leader to come to P'yôngyang and head up an organization of Ch'ôndoggyo believers, that being a native religion not stamped out in the North. He walked into the interview room with the superior air of an ROK Foreign Minister and the fidgety apprehension of a person bound for the guillotine.

A short, round, bald man, he nonetheless held his head back far enough to look down his nose at me; I remembered the many times I observed South Korean officials entering a room, ramrod straight, exemplary Confucian disdain for everyone, underlings scurrying about to wipe off chairs and shoo away bystanders. Mr Ch'oe was all this, but he also sweated profusely in spite of the air conditioning, a nervous tic working the side of his face as he spoke.

I would ask him a question and he would give back a peroration, going on for the whole clip no matter how many times I drew my hand across my throat. He began by reciting a grade-school-level textbook account of how the South started the war, which he had discovered to be true after (and only after) he got to P'yôngyang. I asked him about his experience at P'anmunjôm, where he was an ROK representative, and he said how much he admired the uniforms and 'dignified manner' of the North Koreans, whereas he chafed under the bullying of American officers. He told us he came to P'yôngyang to visit his familial graves, nor could he resist the kind invitation of you-know-who:

> He is really great, much greater than many famous persons whom I have met
> . . . . I think he is a great politician, too. I can see that the Juche idea
> provides the basis for his successful politics. I was attracted by him, so I
> decided to settle in this utopia.

Mr Ch'oe was a performing seal who looked the part.

Li Wôn-gyun is a famous movie actor in movie-mad North Korea, handsome in a faintly Occidental way, and with only a hint of crepe under his square chin to indicate his age of sixty-three. I had enjoyed chatting with him before the interview, but only when we got the cameras going did I see that he had confused the medium. He had committed to memory a script about all of Seoul's people rushing forward to support the DPRK flag in June 1950, after hearing for decades about 'the fame of General Kim Il Sung.'

As he railed on his face punctuated the text now with humor, now with sadness, his long eyelashes fluttering here, cast downward there. Soon he got into the hortatory, emotion-choked throat that Korean actors love, and I had a fit of laughter that I could not hold back. That did not faze him, either, he just kept emoting. After the first clip Max asked me to translate the gist, and I said something like 'a dramatic rendering of the conquest of Seoul.' 'Well, should we do another clip?' 'No, that was quite enough.' 'Can't we get some more out of him, now Bruce?' 'No, Max, forget it.' All this was said *sotto voce* so Mr Yun wouldn't get upset. Fortunately Max took my advice.

We got a good, heartfelt interview out of Li Sun-im, a hefty nurse who served the frontlines during the war; all foreign correspondents, no matter on which side, remember the intrepid, devoted, and tender care administered by Korean nurses. She had the matriarchal air of authority and quiet satisfaction that motherhood and a life of self-sacrifice bequeath to Korean women, and I found her earthy and delightful. Pak Yông-ju, a former guerrilla from South Chôlla Province in the ROK, got so expressive during his interview that he sprayed both of us with spittle, while providing several dramatic clips that survived into the final film. Pak Chang-uk was quite amazing, a double-amputee who rose from his chair to a standing position by throwing his trunk forward and leveraging his wooden legs under his weight; he gave us a blow-by-blow description of the subduing of North Korean POWs in Camp 76 on Kôje Island in 1952, in a spiel so striking that we thought he was clearly ready to fight it all out again. After the war he sired three daughters and a son, the eldest daughter now being an architect and the son a railway engineer.

My favorite was Shin Gi-ôn, former long-time secretary to southern middle-road politician Kim Kyu-sik, and eighty years old when we interviewed him. His mind was acute and his wit sharp, and he said whatever he wanted to ('I'm too old for anyone to do anything to me because of what I say'). He told us some droll stories about General John Hodge, commander of the American Occupation in South Korea from 1945–48, not without respect and a trace of nostalgia for that period. He remarked that Acheson's famed Press Club speech, allegedly reading Korea out of the American defense line five months before the war, was 'deception, and our leaders knew that.' Our Korean counterparts, who dozed through several interviews, said they learned something from that one.

DARK NIGHTS OF THE SOUL IN P'YÔNGYANG

In spite of our success in getting back into the country, with filming and interviewing on the docket, the second trip was unsettling and somehow ominous to me, from the day we landed. Part of it was finding that Mr Yun was onboard again and realizing that I was going to have to do a lot of the translating, and that my brain doesn't travel well on quick around-the-globe trips.

More uneasiness descended when I thought about Max, who is a perfectionist for himself and expects the same of others, a bit of a stickler on anything important to the business at hand. He was the best director I met at Thames, a brilliant maker of documentaries, but also a good man to work with because he was always prepared, punctual, diligent, and efficient in getting the work out, and fairminded except for any hint of the sloppy or slothful, about which he was rightly intolerant. I would find him late in the evening in the hotel, dictating changes and appropriate edits for the rough cuts of programs four and five, while Eric, Ray, and I were draining another bottle of scotch and having a high old time. Max was as he should be, but he could also be a pain now and then, impatient if I wasn't on call and alert for anything Korean that he wanted translated – like every signboard in the rice paddies on our way to the DMZ (here's one: 'communism is nothing other than rice').

But the larger problem was the atrocious character of the war itself, and the heavy weight of its memory in present-day North Korea. This country probably took more casualties per capita than the Soviet Union or Poland in World War II, and thus from time to time one still senses the smell of death, and the nearness of evil. This sense was ever-present in October when we reviewed newsreel footage, but it may also issue forth merely from looking at the sad, careworn faces of the older generation.

It will surprise my detractors to learn that I have in my viscera a strong attachment to my own country, which I love for the vast and often untapped strengths of its diverse people, just as I regret its late-twentieth-century conformity and frivolity. North Korea has always made me uneasy, but not because it offends my residual patriotism.

When the North Koreans rail on about American imperialism, it doesn't make a dent because I read it every day in their central news reports; I only look for new variations in the tone. If they tell me how awful our policies are, I'm interested in what they say. None of it offends my remnant love-of-country, for the same reason that George Bush doesn't mind the USA being called 'The Great Satan.' What difference does it make? This small country has every reason to disparage us, and it isn't the sort of country that dignifies you by having it as your enemy. When you're with them, furthermore, they always maintain the distinction between the US regime (bad) and the people (good), so there are never moments of anger or rudeness (at least not rudeness on that score).

The problem for me is when they parade their record of our behavior in the war, with its inevitable combination of patent exaggeration and residual truth, or when I meet North Koreans and sooner or later find out how many of their loved ones they lost in the bombing holocaust.

I feel two sensations: the first, a sick feeling in the pit of my stomach because I am one of the few Americans in a position to know that they are right, they suffered one of the most appalling, unrestrained, genocidal bombing campaigns in our genocidal twentieth century; the second, an awareness that they are organically incapable of grasping the Nietzschean truth that the perpetrators, buzzing around in their F-85s and B-29s, were not evil men, just human-all-too-human; I might have done it myself at age twenty, just as one of my fraternity brothers did in the skies over North Vietnam, just as our 'kids' (Bush's usage) did over Iraq. More daunting is that The Great Satan doesn't know or care a thing about what was done in its name (actually in the name of the United Nations) back in the early 1950s. The Koreans are shouting themselves hoarse at a nation of amnesiacs, who aren't listening.

Let me give you two examples of this latter point. The first is John Glenn, astronaut with the 'right stuff,' Senator from Ohio, one-time Presidential candidate, and ace fighter pilot in the Korean War. We interviewed him on the snowiest day in Washington in recent years, in February 1987. We hung around while the Senator dealt politely with a constituent, and ruminated about whether he'd be able to pilot his own plane back to Ohio, what with the weather.

Glenn was eager for the interview. In the course of it, among other things, he said the pilots took a lot of ack-ack fire from 'Ping Pong' (otherwise known as P'yôngyang), so 'we'd detour around Ping Pong going up to Indian Country' along the Yalu.[304] Ping Pong had been pretty well destroyed, he related; elsewhere, 'we did a lot of napalm work . . . . You came in on what we called a nape scrape which is where you came in so low you were almost flying into the target that you er were going to put napalm on and er . . . .'

When I later screened the full documentary for some (South) Korean friends, one of them told me he found Glenn the most abominable person in the whole six hours, because he had no conception or self-consciousness about what he had done.

The second example materialized in the P'yôngyang Koryô Hotel, as the lead actor in an Italian spaghetti spy story being filmed when we were there. We first got a sniff of this new fruit of the DPRK's joint-venture law one day when we witnessed a four-door black Cadillac of mid-1970s vintage roaring through the streets, snow tires fixed to the front of this rear-drive vehicle, its top chopped off and inside a full Korean camera crew, filming in the streets and driven by a wild-eyed Korean who laughed, I imagine, the way it was said the guy did who crashed a truck loaded with explosives into the Marine camp in Beirut.

This surreal vision was topped by meeting the crew itself, one evening when they filmed a chase scene at our hotel. The Italian company had come to P'yôngyang because the yen had gone so high that Tokyo was prohibitive; they were going to say the film was done in Japan, anyway. The director was a seedy Englishman, and the female lead was a sultry brunette of indeterminate ethnicity; until I heard her speak Italian I thought she might be Portuguese-Chinese from Macao. She hung around the vast lobby of the hotel, usually leaning up against a pillar with a pouting, comely look on her face.

The male lead is our example, however, a well-muscled blond stallion from Hollywood whose career there, whatever it might have been, was unavailing, so he took his slightly overripe but still passably pretty face to Italy, and wound up in the twin-tower Koryô Hotel. He greeted me incongruously one day as if I were a long-lost friend, after someone told him I was a fellow American. The vapors leaving his lips rendered the larger miasma in the space between his ears; I realized that John Locke's postulation of a *tabula rasa* at birth was only half the story, it could last into one's late twenties. Within seconds he was railing on about how awful the Koreans were:

These people, okay, they really hate us, like, they say imperialist-this and atrocity-that, and ya know, they don't let even one newspaper into the country that you can read, like they just blab on in Korean on TV, Kim whassisname's face is everywhere, and they really hate us, I mean, they'd just like us to go take a flying leap, all of us, okay, the whole country, a big flying leap.

'Yeah,' I said, 'it's a bitch,' and changed the subject to what he might be doing in P'yôngyang. The amnesiac had spoken, the *tabula rasa* had something written on it after all.

A couple of days after we arrived back in P'yôngyang, I ate an enjoyable lunch, bantered with the friendly staff, and headed up to my room for a nap. I stood by myself as the elevator opened, and inside was a lone shriveled man with no face. He had been burned to a crisp at some point, and I thought I knew the point: a 'nape scrape.' If I never knew the full meaning of the verb 'to blanch,' I learned it as I stood there paralyzed, until the door began to close and I moved not forward but back, at a lurch. I went up to my room and vomited, appalled at the sight and even more at myself for adding one more gratuitous insult to this man's unfortunate life.

I have always found it difficult to look at badly burned people since I was four years old and, with my family, nearly died when an Indiana tornado plowed like a freight train through our home, leaving one wall standing and a big tree crashed next to my parents' double bed, under which we all survived (without a scratch). That was rather exhilarating to a four-year-old, to peer out from under a bed and see not walls but the woods behind the house, now mostly blown down. That evening we took shelter in a town hall, however, and I saw an old woman near death, with her face erased by fires that spread just after the tornado, and I took a sock to the solar plexus I never forgot.

I wondered if the burned man just happened to be in the hotel, or if he was one of the people lined up for us to interview. I guessed the latter, but it also occurred to me that he might be checking up on the people we were working with; what better person to guarantee loyalty? That night I woke at 4 a.m., an hour when I can believe the worst about myself or anything else, to the sound of explosions. I ran to the terrace, just in time to see the vast, shrouded P'yôngyang skyline lit by dancing bolts of lightning. Then came the cracking and rolling thunder, and I surveilled the sky imagining B-29s and F-85s howling over the city; it also occurred to me in that lonely darkness that I might get myself caught in a new war and a new bombing campaign.

Instead of bombs, however, the rains burst and I went back to bed. Rising under my closed eyes was the face of the man with no face. Rather than fight it I read some more *Faust*. An hour or so later I heard the rhythmic, hoarse chants of men in formation echoing through the streets and gave another start; but it was just a phalanx of young men, probably students, galloping through the streets, herded on by men with bullhorns. Terrible, totalitarian North Korea, the reader is thinking. I witnessed the same thing many times in Seoul.

It was not an auspicious night for a following day when we interviewed Kim Myong Ja, one of the only survivors of the Sinch'ôn massacre, at the site of the crime. Max thought it appropriate for me to ride down to Sinch'ôn with her, according to his standard-operating-procedure for getting interviewee familiar with interviewer, and with Thames method. I balked, saying the last thing this woman needed was to jounce along the road for several hours with an American, and I was thinking to myself that I didn't need it, either. But Max eyeballed me, and I jumped in back to meet Mrs Kim.

She was wearing a silk traditional dress, her hair nicely coiffed, and she struck me as the solid, reliable mother of four that she said she was, now working in the Revolutionary History Research Center. She had the polite, firm manner and the nurturing self-confidence so charming in middle-aged Korean women, and she was happy to answer my questions about her life and family, which I held to a minimum. She didn't send many in my direction, which was fine with me since I hoped she thought I was an Englishman.

Mrs Kim said she was nine years old at the time of the atrocity, and that her father had been an official in the local people's committee, imprisoned shortly after the area was occupied by American and South Korean forces. Her parents and most of her six brothers and sisters died in the war, and she attended one of the many schools set up for orphans, eventually graduating from college.

Sinch'ôn is a good bit south of P'yôngyang; the main road to Kaesông was being refurbished (probably in anticipation of the upcoming Olympics), so we went over to the coast at Namp'o and down through roads mostly made of hardpack dirt. The small cities we saw were not much to write home about – mostly collections of five-story apartment houses and state buildings in the utilitarian, functional, and ugly Stalinist style of the early post-Korean War period. They were not as homely as southern cities of the early 1970s, say, Iri or Chôngju, which at that time were rundown, smelly, dour, and depressing; but they likewise couldn't compare to the modernity of smaller southern cities of the late 1980s. The residents always tried to brighten the places up, though, by keeping things clean and by daubing colorful paint on storefronts. The roads, whether in town or out, were pretty terrible. We could see on apartment walls the ubiquitous portraits of Father and Son.

We stopped in a village to stretch our legs and try to get a bit of filming in, which was resisted and mostly blocked by our guests. Max was enterprising and adamant, however, in arguing out a little time for Frank and Eric to film; we even succeeded in filming a peasant tending his oxcart, which horrified the Koreans because they were sure we would use it to measure their backwardness: 'Why shoot that, and not our tractors?' The village was plain, bucolic, and little different from South Korean villages, except that there weren't many televisions. The homes had weathered tile roofs in various states of repair, electricity, and the usual barnyard animals running around. Mangy, skinny dogs scurried about, foraging what they could; if you approached them they ran like the curs they were, no doubt hoping to stay out of someone's soup pot.

Fetid streams in the villages suggested less than adequate sanitation. I was surprised by the large numbers of people standing around in mid-day, gaping at us as if we were Martians, and the continued, inefficient use of massed human labor for construction in a country with a shortage of skilled labor. There were many tractors in the fields, however. Signs urged 'self-reliance,' using the Maoist phrase *charyôk kaengsaeng*, which literally means something like regeneration through your own efforts. I hadn't seen these signs in the cities, and figured it was a way of saying, don't expect much investment from the center. There didn't seem to be much, either.

As in P'yôngyang, little old ladies got out with brooms to clean the public streets, instead of sleeping in them as bag ladies do in New York; private gardens were built to the edge of one's property. I was always astounded by the care people took to preserve what they had in North Korea, or just to provide a service.

The small towns had one or two restaurants, maybe one beer hall, now and then a movie theater in the bigger towns. I was surprised to stand in the rice fields and smell nothing; in the South nightsoil is still used, which gives off an overpowering stench on warm days. Nor did I see anywhere the 'honeypot man,' as Americans liked to call him, who scooped out the cesspools beneath the homes. North Korea both produces and drops on the soil a great deal of chemical fertilizer, and I suppose that made the difference.

We pulled into a Sinch'ôn whose small city center was getting a new road. There were only one or two machines, supplemented by lots of kids scooping the ground or carrying rocks, who looked like local fifth-and sixth-graders. I strolled around and then stopped to chat with the driver of our older Mercedes, who was sitting on his haunches, drawing patterns in the dirt. He was the same man who had argued mightily with our guides about his payment for taking us sightseeing back and forth to the vaunted Namp'o lock-gate, the newest of Kim Il Sung's erections. He was willing to make a scene and to squawk about his payment in front of the capitalist guests, which gives some indication of the bargaining that goes on between different bureaucratic lineages, and the concerns of cab drivers.

He started asking me a bunch of questions, as he leaned up against the fender of the car. 'How much do you make per month?' 'How much does it cost for your kid's education?' And then on down the line – housing, the car, the bank loan – until he did some quick calculations and concluded: 'Why, you don't have anything left at the end of the month.' 'Right you are. And welcome to academic life in the US of A.'

Then I asked him a bunch of questions, and we were having a fine time, but before we got to the end of it the cadres walked over, and we were off to the atrocity museum. When I tried to talk to this funny and uncomplex driver later in our visit, he said as little as possible, made an excuse, and walked away.

The site basically consists of two big tombs, like the moundbuilding Indians produced in southern Ohio only much larger, one for mothers and one for children, plus an empty concrete storehouse, and a tunnel. We observed a weathered picture of Mrs Kim as a schoolgirl, round face and hair tied neatly in two pigtails. The storehouse and the tunnel became the charnelhouses into which some 400 women and children were herded in November 1950, kept without food and water for days, while they were prevailed upon to reveal the location of their husbands and older sons. According to Mrs Kim, when they begged for water for the children, a big American threw buckets of shit on them. After a few days they were doused with gasoline and burned to death, save Kim Myong Ja and a couple of other kids, who found themselves at the top of the heap, near a ventilation hole, when it was all over.

I did the interview with her, a thousand thoughts rushing through my mind as this little woman stood in the middle of the charnelhouse in her fine silk dress, telling her story. At the climax tears filled her eyes and she fixed first me and then the camera, vowing her thousand-fold revenge against the Americans who did this.

It was a sickening experience, unmediated by my ability to chalk it up to another good propaganda routine. On the way back Mrs Kim told me she had not been to Sinch'ôn in years, and that the very sight of the town always ruined her for days. She held her face in her hands most of the way back to P'yôngyang.

We asked some of the locals at this museum who the perpetrators were, and they uniformly attributed it to an American officer named Harrison. When I asked his first name, they said 'Dumaiden,' or something that sounded like that in Korean rendering; none of them spoke English and the event occurred in the vast havoc and chaos of successive, back-and-forth military occupation of the area by all sides.

My research has never uncovered anything about Sinch'ôn in the National Archives. An awful atrocity occurred one day in Sinch'ôn, however, because we were later able to compare our visit against newsreel footage taken when the bodies were discovered and that could not have been faked. (Max painstakingly counted and measured the bricks in the charnelhouse wall to verify the footage.) We could verify nothing, however, about its authorship.

Journalist Eli Schmetzer of the *Chicago Tribune* would disagree. He also visited Sinch'ôn, misspelling it as Chichon, and titled his account 'North Korean Museum Stokes Loathing of U.S.'[305] He quoted an unnamed East European: 'Chichon stinks. It smells of fraud.' Schmetzer went on to say that 'each year 300,000 North Koreans are brainwashed at Chichon.' All this is part of the 'twisted version of history that North Korea has dished up,' warning people that unless they're loyal to Kim Il Sung, 'the bogeyman GIs will come back to rape, torture and burn everyone alive.'

I have this to say to Mr Schmetzer: it happened.

I did not see the burned man for the next few days, but toward the end of our visit our counterparts told us that they could not produce for us a victim of bacteriological warfare, as we had requested, but they would allow us to interview a victim of chemical warfare. And sure enough, this was Pak Jong Dae, whom I had seen in the elevator.

I went to Max and said I couldn't do it. He looked at me and said let's think about it. It occurred to me a few minutes later that whatever my problems with badly burned people, this man had lived with it for nearly four decades. So I went through it as if he were anybody else. Our Korean counterparts did the same, with fitting compassion – except for the interpreter, Mr Yun, who evaporated for most of the interview. When I reached to shake Mr Pak's hand, he presented to me a claw, the bent fingers of which were fused to pieces of kelloid skin. His nose and lips had been reconstructed in some thirty-six operations, but nothing could hide the fact that he somehow survived a direct napalm hit, indeed was the only one of some twenty people repairing a bridge who did so. His speech was a bit slurred, but he had a curiously proud sort of politeness and humility, and like Kafka's *Hunger Artist* he had probably learned long before that those untutored in the human capacity to tolerate suffering found such encounters more difficult than did the afflicted.

I was amazed to find that Mr Pak, born a poor peasant and cruelly disfigured, had later married a schoolteacher and sired three children (all now university graduates), and was now vice-manager of an electric factory – although I don't know why I was amazed. Perhaps because it didn't fit my expectations of North Korean society, or is it my own? Do our faceless veterans have three children and hold commanding positions in ordinary factories? Perhaps Bob Fall of CBS News would know the answer.

The man had but one functioning eye, the other clouded and blind. I found during the interview, under the hot lights, that I could conduct it by focusing on the pupil of his good eye, and through that aperture, like

Nietzsche's 'purifying eye,' I saw the person underneath the awful mask. 'Everybody has his youth which is precious and important,' he told us:

> My youth has gone with thirty-six operations. I had a lot of laughter and hopes for the future. I had two hands with which I could play the accordion. All these that bomb took away from me . . . . I do not think there should be any more victims like myself in this world. Never again. Never on this globe a victim like me.

I don't know what this experience was like for Mr Pak. But it was good for me. That afternoon I found Mr Pak in the elevator again, and had a nice chat with him. As the door opened a Korean from Japan entered, gawked at Mr Pak, circled around him slowly, and hissed out something like 'sheeeee . . . .'

Thames Television put Mr Pak's moving 'never again' statement at the end of the final hour of the documentary. WGBH dropped it, without explanation.

AT THE WAR MUSEUM AND THE D.M.Z.

There is no memorial to the Korean War in the US, although finally in 1989 a design for one came forth. In North Korea there are many, but none as elaborate as the Museum of the Victorious Fatherland Liberation War. As you enter the building you tread on a mammoth carpet with stunning, psychedelic-bright colors woven into it. Striding across the carpet to meet us was General Pak Yôn-ch'un, a hardy, stolid, and occasionally humorous man with small, rough hands, who gave us a tour of the exhibits and who later submitted to an interview. He had been in the first battle with American soldiers at Osan.

As he told us about his experience, he noted that some American soldiers died with their mouths open at Osan: 'so, not wanting them to be hungry, we put dirt in their mouths.' He illustrated the scene, laughing the while. All the South Korean peasants thought it was funny, too, he related. Eric later said this was sickening, as indeed it was; General Pak happily repeated the story on camera.

In the basement of the museum is a cavernous, warehouse-sized exhibit of captured American war booty, including F-85 Sabre jets, M-51 tanks, big guns of all sorts, jeeps, plus a MIG-15 said to have been blessed both by Kim and his son in 1952. Elsewhere we viewed a room-sized electric display of intrepid locomotive engineers and truck drivers ferrying supplies over and through mountains to the front, American planes buzzing them. As the room darkened a mountain came alive in relief, with search lights, flares, and the headlights of trucks. Jets appeared overhead, the trucks cut their lights, and anti-aircraft guns blasted the sky – this being simulated by snapping electrical sparks, somewhat like a child's July 4th sparkler. The narration says both Father and Son gave sage guidance to the truck drivers (even though Jong Il was about ten at the time).

We also found electric displays of the start of the war, which have little red arrows depicting a southern advance at three or four places, barely across the parallel, followed by big red swooshing envelopment of Seoul by the KPA. I was most interested in the wall-size exhibit depicting the summer 1949 border fighting at Ongjin and Kaesông, which was mostly accurate (except for denials that the North ever attacked first). Few of the great Korean military leaders who fought for years in China and then led the KPA charge in 1950 were in evidence, except for Kim Il Sung's buddies like Kim Ch'aek and Ch'oe Yông-gôn.

The next day we got our entourage together and motored south in the direction of the demilitarized zone. We passed through Sariwôn after dark, a small city that changed hands many times in the war and that was therefore utterly obliterated. It was still a dump full of tacky apartment buildings, each identical flat dimly lit, but not so dim as to miss the pictures of Father and Son on each wall.

Mr Shin sat in the front seat, mostly silent. But then, as if to read our thoughts, he turned around and said, 'we still don't live well,' attributing this to the war, and the unremitting pressure from outside (meaning from the US, mainly, but also the Russians). 'We need some more years yet, then it will be nice.'

As we neared Kaesông we could see a white statue high on a hill, shimmering in distant floodlights. It was so elevated as to appear to be in the sky and Christ-like, but as we drew nearer it was, of course, the iron-willed ever-victorious commander himself, on a spot in Kaesông high enough to be seen across the DMZ to the south.

I rose early at our hotel in Kaesông, for a long and unattended walk. An ancient commercial city long the home of absentee landlords, it still had a few vintage aristocratic residences, now turned into public buildings. Sôngak Mountain, on the north side of town just across the 38th parallel, still showed the marks of incessant artillery bombardment. Stores advertised fish, vegetables, children's clothes. I walked through labyrinthine back alleys, mostly clean and rarely smelling of garbage or offal. Little vegetable patches occupied every spare inch of land. Water was piped into homes, but it must have been unpotable; drinking water was supplied through a network of '*mulbang*s' or 'water rooms.' Occasional outhouses suggested some (many?) people were still without indoor plumbing.

That morning we went down to P'anmunjôm, entering a secured area several thousand yards north, and getting a briefing from a sharp young officer about what not to do. We went by the Potemkin village that no one apparently lives in, a showplace put there to offset the Potemkin village on the other side. Some people did farm inside the DMZ, however, including several well-tended crops of 'Kaesông red ginseng,' renowned for its tonic and restorative powers. We reconnoitered in the big building just above the quonset huts where military talks go on, bisected by the armistice demarcation line.

As our party moved out of the building and down to the line, an American soldier standing about six feet six, wearing elevator boots and what looked like a pilot's broad-shouldered flight jacket, began huffing and puffing in his best imitation of a tough guy. Quick strides up to the line, big scowl, now a few paces back, arms folded, another scowl-skulk-glare, turn on the heel with hunched-over shoulder, as if to flex the biceps, back front again, more skulking and scowling. I stood there looking at this man from 'enemy territory,' who resembled a cross between Slim Pickens and Rambo, wondering how my compatriots could have become so deluded as to think this sort of posturing was worthwhile, or convincing, and not simply demeaning.

Shortly the spell was broken when a blond-haired officer simply walked through a hut and across the line to shake our hands, he being a Swede on the Neutral Nations Supervisory Commission and the only human being who could do what he had just done without being shot dead. We did a couple of desultory interviews at this site, and then headed off to a sentinel post above the DMZ. In the distance we could hear the reverberation of artillery and machine-gun fire.[306]

We drove over hills and valleys to a People's Army observation point, a concrete revetment atop a small mountain that commanded rice valleys flowing off into South Korea. Loudspeakers barking propaganda from both sides mingled together in an incomprehensible but menacing din. Through binoculars we could see a big color billboard on the other side showing a pretty half-clad girl holding the door handle of a Hyundai sedan, both of which were offered to defecting soldiers. My simultaneous thought was that this was typical of the crass materialism of the South, and probably more tempting to the soldiers of the North than I liked to think.

But this pin-prick on a map was mostly dismal, the microcosm of more than a million Korean soldiers challenging each other to another fight like the last, which left them both spent, and with no real gain except to their great power antagonists. At this point we were joined by Kim Yong-ja, who was one of the peasant women Meray had observed, tilling fields under hails of machine-gun fire. She was a stout, compact woman with sun-bronzed skin and calloused hands attached to sturdy forearms. She greeted me with even less warmth than Rosa Kleb, if that is possible. I exchanged a few words with her, but she was not interested in small talk.

Max came along about this time, urging me into the back of her car for the ride to the interview site. 'Nothing doing, I spoke with her already, she has nothing more to say.' Max was not pleased and let me know it, but the woman scared me. We interviewed her standing in the ricefields as the pale November sun set, in an aurora of brown, red, and orange Hallowe'en glows. She gave us stock, word-for-word memorized replies, delivered with no less gusto for it being well rehearsed. As she railed on, my mind wandered to red graffiti on walls outside Columbia University in the late 1960s: 'Vietcong women carry guns.'

She was formidable, I had never met a Korean woman whom you wouldn't want to confront in a dark alley. I told her American pilots say they never shot at women in the fields, and she burst back that this was an absolute, filthy lie; the effect was stunning, but that clip survived only into the rough cuts.

That evening we drove back to P'yôngyang, our hosts trusting the night to hide the landscape and the tawdry towns. Mr Shin was in good form, regaling us with stories of filming in New York – entry gotten, I suppose, using credentials from their United Nations observer mission. He did a short piece on Americans and their dogs, showing the folks back home canine hospitals and grooming boutiques, the latest fashions for Fifth Avenue mutts, doggy psychiatrists, and culinary delights from Madison Avenue pet stores. Max wasn't too amused with this slap at Anglo-Saxon culture, but I found it uproariously funny, in part because I had wondered what the Koreans did besides sit in their penthouse at 225 East 86th Street.

THERE WILL ALWAYS BE A KOREA

One day after lunch we went for a walk along the banks of the Taedong with Mr Kim. At one point he stopped and pointed out to some ducks fluttering about on the water: 'Eat duck, it's good for you.' 'Why?', I said. Without answering, Mr Kim put both fists between his legs and then drew them out, his elbows stiff. He then added gratuitously, 'eat duck, your penis will grow big,' and continued sauntering down the walk with the matter-of-fact look of someone who had told us that milk builds strong bones. Mr Kim liked Max's story about traveling from Beijing through Manchuria to P'yôngyang for twenty-four hours in a train compartment with three Chinese, their feet reeking to the point of asphyxiation. 'Chinese are people who sometimes forget to take a bath,' he said knowingly.

One evening in the hotel we witnessed an entire Korean family, some with the brown faces of peasants from the countryside, get increasingly and more raucously drunk, with the older women in especially fine fettle. They were drinking P'yôngyang boilermakers, Korean beer washing down a ginseng whiskey chaser. One woman in her forties with a lined, weathered face was having a high old time; her typically Korean laughter, with a lot of wind forced through the jowls, was infectious. They had a plain-living, hard-working Confucian-residue politeness about them at the start of the evening, and a flushed-face, fully satiated look of void immobility by the end.

Another day in the lobby of the Koryô Hotel I observed a high-level cadre, probably in his seventies but looking much younger, waiting to meet a group of Japanese businessmen. He was perhaps five-five, but carried himself with a perfectly poised and authoritative dignity making him seem much taller. He had finely combed gray-white hair, a sculptured face that never betrayed a hint of his thoughts, and handsome eyes that seemed etched into his head at a forty-five-degree angle with a chisel. He wore an impeccably tailored gray Mao suit, but other than that, he could have been a high official in any Korean government going back to the first glimmerings of Confucian statecraft. I have seen people of such dignified carriage, men and women, many times in Japan, Korea, and China, in some ways they are the norm after a certain age, but I rarely see them in my own country.

One day Max and I ventured out for lunch at a Korean restaurant, which had a signboard saying only '*tan'gogi chônmun*,' meaning they specialized in 'tan-meat,' and I didn't know what that was, other than the literal meaning of 'sweetmeat.' Sometimes I am glacially slow on the uptake, plus I always flail myself for not knowing what something means, so I wanted to find out and dragged a trusting Max along with me. Although this was a restaurant allegedly available to foreigners, all the patrons were Korean and you couldn't order a glass of water in any language but Korean.

I asked the polite, warily expectant waitress for the menu, which was no help in divining the sweetmeat, since that's all it sold, in various dishes. We ordered two of them, plus some *kimch'i*. We got full plates, and dug in. The meat was flecked with red pepper, but otherwise had little taste. 'Pork,' I said. 'Something else,' Max responded. It wasn't bad, though, and we were hungry, so we cleaned our plates, all the while politely but persistently observed by nearly everyone else in the restaurant.

We returned to the hotel and asked Mr Kim what '*tan'gogi*' was. He exchanged glances with his comrades, then got up from his chair with fingers on either side of his head, and hopped along the carpet making a hooting noise. 'Rabbit,' I said, and he shook his head, laughing heartily. (Since pork and rabbit are the same words in North Korea as in the South, I couldn't think why they called it sweetmeat, anyway.) Finally Mr Kim began to gobble, and I yelled 'turkey!' Yes, they said, it was turkey. Max was still skeptical, since, as we learned in our germ warfare inquiries, there were supposed to be no turkeys in Korea (and so where did the germ-laden turkey feathers come from), but there the matter was dropped.

More than a year later I told this story to my old friend and Korea-hand Ed Baker, who, it turned out, had been to the same restaurant. 'It's dog meat, Cumings, why couldn't you figure that out?' Of course it was dog meat; I had blocked on it both because I can be remarkably dense, and because it's called something else in South Korea. But I was glad that my stupidity kept Max from learning that, and especially Frank, whose face clouded over at the mere thought of anyone eating canines; after all, it is said the Brits love their dogs even more than do the Poles.

Max and I kept thinking we might get an interview with Kim Il Sung, and our guides did not disabuse us of this fantasy. We kept looking here and there for signs of an impending interview with Il Duce. The day before we left, two of our guides asked us to accompany them to a remote floor of the hotel, where we sat in isolation gazing out a window at the city from the hallway. The guides averred that this spot was better than a hotel room, where we might be overheard.

'This is it,' Max and I agreed; 'they're going to take us to their leader.' The two guides, however, looked rather sheepish and distracted by the time we got to talking. After much hemming and hawing, accompanied by handwringing and wan smiles, it turned out that they merely wanted to take us for money – a bribe, a Westerner would call it; a return on service, a Korean might call it. Max and I talked it over and at length gave them nothing: whatever the substance of this request, we needed to hearken to the appearances. ('Whitby and Cumings bribed two North Korean officials . . . .')

Max and I had our obligatory concluding banquet with Mr Pok and his entourage, Pok now expansive and relaxed, looking like Marlon Brando when he first began to sample the onset of middle age. Plenty of meat and shrimp, P'yôngyang boilermakers, and lots of toasts to a great documentary. The next day we headed for the airport with our interviews and films under our arms, an Indian Summer sun still hanging over the mountains before the Siberian winter blew in.

That's the last we ever heard from them. They never sought to collect the rest of the money due them for their newsreels, never came to London to see the rough cuts, and after a few months we heard that Mr Pok and his entourage had all been fired from their jobs.

Today P'yôngyang seems to be coasting along on the path of 'building socialism,' no matter what may befall all the other socialists in the world. As North Korea's close friends, the East Germany of Honecker and the Romania of Ceausescu, crumbled to the ground, Kim Il Sung's scribes let loose one of their vintage programmatic documents, entitled 'Let Us Vigorously Advance Along the Road of Socialism, Repulsing the Challenge of the Imperialists.'[307]

Taking off after the Fukuyamas who proclaim 'the victory of the free world,' the authors instead project 'the inevitable doom' of capitalism and imperialism. 'History does not flow from socialism to capitalism but vice-versa,' they say, reversing the East European dictum that capitalism is the highest stage of communism.

'A person with money enjoys the freedom of buying everything, unlimited freedom of buying not only things, but also human conscience and dignity.' The imperialists are 'shameless' enough to ask us to open our market, they write – but a door 'flung open [will] allow the infiltration of corrupt imperialist ideology and culture.' Instead North Korea will hew to its well-trod path, in a society where

> There is nobody who is exceptionally better off, nobody who goes ill-clad and hungry . . . no jobless people, no people who go bankrupt and wander around begging, no drug addicts, alcoholics and fin-de-siecle faggots who seek abnormal desires.

CHAPTER EIGHT

THE POLITICS OF

'THE UNKNOWN WAR'

> The series, in present form, is not appropriate for an American
> audience. If shown without extensive editing or caveats or both,
> would be ill received by that audience and thus an embarrassment
> to sponsors and station [sic] . . . . It is simply not an objective
> portrayal of the war.
> GENERAL RICHARD STILWELL, *USA Ret.*

> [The television text is] a state of tension between forces of *closure*,
> which attempt to close down its potential meanings in favor of the
> preferred ones, and forces of *openness*, which enable its variety of
> viewers to negotiate an appropriate variety of meanings.
> JOHN FISKE

The proof of the political pudding American television has become is told
in what happened to our documentary as it coursed through the legitimator
of television's claim to independence and community service, non-
commercial Public Television. If the Korean War is 'forgotten,' it seems
hard to understand why public broadcasting would not simply screen a
British documentary with such scholarship, effort, and expense behind it.
Instead WGBH producers decided to revise it and effectively ended up
censoring it, and thereby *The Unknown War* entered a labyrinth of politics
that fully expressed the split verdicts, unresolved conflicts, and evasions
with which this war was named, buried, and forgotten, and that illustrated
the highly contingent nature of our liberal programming.

As the process of revision ensued over a two-year period at WGBH/
Boston, producers Peter McGhee and Austin Hoyt succeeded in (1)

eliminating Jon Halliday and me from the project (thus outdoing the South Korean regime); (2) turning to the 'intelligence community' for expert help, much like the networks during the Gulf War; (3) altering the documentary to accord with visceral American lore about the Korean War; and (4) doing all this in service to 'facts' and 'accuracy,' a sleight-of-hand in which they became the 'historians' and Halliday and I became the hucksters.

This is a true story, and not an idle one, because WGBH/Boston is the 'showcase' of PBS, run by a board that brings 'Boston's elite educational and cultural institutions' (including Harvard and MIT) together with representatives of major corporations, like New England Telephone and Telegraph.[308] If documentaries are the 'facts' of television fiction, WGBH is the flagship documentary producer of American television, the cultural pinnacle of the industry. The problems of American television, in other words, begin at the top, and the educator needs education.

THE BRITISH PRODUCT

The final documentary produced at Thames was a partial victory but still one worth all the effort. Like all television authorship, its voice was diffuse, mixed, incoherent, and ultimately, therefore, irresponsible.

This offended my sense of propriety since I am used to authoring texts by myself (and, in the sense understood by authors, for myself). The documentary was instead a committee effort: two fine hours by Max Whitby, two good hours by Phillip Whitehead, two hours by Mike Dormer that did not meet the same standard (for which Whitehead also bore responsibility, as executive producer). And no consistent voice. But *The Unknown War* was infinitely better than Max Hastings's BBC-produced potboiler and anything else ever done on the Korean War, and in that was no small victory.

The closer we were to the completion deadline in April 1988, the more political the process became: fights raged over how to winnow the 'rough cuts' and how to pitch the script, Channel 4 (which was to televise the film first) squawked about content, the picture book Jon and I did migrated from being the book of the series to the book with the series to no airtime acknowledgement at all, and Thames people sought to bury Jon and me in the anonymity of the whole: to submerge authorial identity, thereby to mitigate political flak, but still to keep the film within our hard-fought 'consensus' (which is where the victory happened).

As the deadline for delivery of the film drew near, dangling threads, incomplete sequences, unfilled gaps, and decisions on interpretation that Jon or others had insisted upon got squashed together in the rush to have the film assembled and ready. This is typical of any commercial documentary, and was not unexpected; I had been given a fair chance to have my say on the rough cuts and in the seminars where we evaluated the six segments, and so my original hopes to have an input and make a difference were satisfied (even if the film could have been a lot better).

Paradoxically I owed this to Jon Halliday, yet because of his far greater role in the film he could not be satisfied with the final product, for reasons that are imbedded in the nature of the medium: the author of television is the editor, not the writer. Jon became, in the rush to completion, the disappearing author of his own text. Orson Welles once remarked, 'For me, everything that's been called direction is one big bluff. Editing is the only time when you can be in complete control of a film.'[309] This was the rushed point at which the flow, the soundbites, the juxtaposed images, and ultimately the programs took on a life of their own . . . or at least a life given them by the editors.

By the time Jon got to 'write' his commentary, film and interviews had been assembled and edited such that they were the 'text' of the documentary, and Jon's role was to gloss the text and fill in the gaps. With Max Whitby there were fewer problems, because of the intelligence of his editing and his punctuality, which left Jon sufficient time to ponder the film and make his points; they fell out mainly over the germ warfare sequences.[310]

With Phillip we had wrestled through the assembly, so that programs one and six did not violate the consensual interpretations we had worked out. However, this left these two programs sometimes incoherent, and Jon had little time for his commentary. But they were still good hours; I was particularly proud of hour one on the origins of the war, which is skipped over in most books and films on the conflict, and to which Max Hastings and the BBC devoted about seven minutes, not one of them acceptable as history, in my view.

With Mike Dormer (programs two and three), who saw eye to eye with neither of us, was less than brilliant as an editor, and who by that time disliked Jon intensely, there was simply a wrestling match. It was almost literally so, on one afternoon during negotiations over the script when Mike threatened to have the security people bodily throw Jon out of the Thames building – perhaps the most extreme affront to Jon's insider-as-outsider position at Thames. Still, Jon's tenacity won several important little battles, like elucidating the Japanese Army background of the ROK Army brass.

While Jon struggled to maintain both the name and the reality of 'writer' of the series, my role was surreptitiously downgraded. In the rough cut credits my consultancy was bracketed with that of Farrar-Hockley, Gavan McCormack, and Robert Oliver. None of them had remotely the role I did in the documentary (as Gavan was the first to point out), but it was safer to place me there, hoping I wouldn't notice, than to give me my (contractual) due. I fought back on this, with very great help from Jon (who threatened to resign over the issue), and in the end was credited as 'principal historical consultant.'

The model for the picture book Jon and I did, in form if not content, was Stanley Karnow's for the PBS Vietnam series, the on-screen advertised book 'of' the series. Our book was, like our series, titled *Korea: The Unknown War*. By early 1988, however, it was clear that the documentary was not our series, but would have multiple authorship and no consistent voice. Furthermore we had to complete the text of the book before we could see the 'text' of the film. So in that sense, the text of our book now differed here and there from that of the film.

We gave the book to Phillip so that he could verify 'its likeness to the Thames series' (in the publisher's contractual wording), and have it plugged on-screen. Completed contracts with Viking/Penguin in London and Pantheon Books in New York assumed that this would be done. Phillip penned a memorandum to Roy English of Thames,[311] putting the problem rather differently: 'To some degree Jon and Bruce have gone their own way and we have gone ours'; he thought that in spite of revisions we did at his behest 'the book and the series are still divergent.' We all knew how the 'divergence' had come about. But he agreed that the book should be plugged on the air, as a book 'produced concurrently' by two people central to the making of the documentary. This agreement was duly drawn up, accepted by all, and then pressed upon the people at Channel 4 – who, according to Phillip, agreed to screen a blurb for the book.[312]

That 'agreement' lasted for three days, when a memo came back from Channel 4 saying that as a matter of policy they could only show the book 'of' the series, whereas this was merely a book 'with' the series.[313] With this Catch-22 argument the matter rested. The book never got any airtime.

Our film aired in London in the summer of 1988, running six successive weeks on Channel 4, as planned. This channel was brought onstream in England in 1980 as an outlet for alternative programming, and Thatcherites found the idea 'deeply disturbing.'[314] They needn't have worried. I hadn't had much to do with the Channel 4 people, who contributed little to the seminars. Indeed I never met some of the people they sent over. I merely noted one of them scowling furiously in my direction one day, after I had made some point in a seminar; he turned out to be Thomas Malinowski, freshly exiled from Poland after Solidarity was crushed in 1980, with no standing on the Korean War but all indulgences to his expertise on the behavior of communists. That Korea was not Poland, I am sure, made little difference to him.

The people at Channel 4 had marginal input on the film during its making, waiting until the end to bring in their advisors for objections that were mostly political, so far as I could tell. A scathing Channel 4 critique of our documentary, signed by Adrian Metcalfe, arrived on Phillip's desk in February 1988.[315] It went on about 'balance' and 'bias.' It accused us of being 'disingenuous' about North Korea, raised questions about the propriety of using our hard-won North Korean footage, and referred to our communist interviewees as 'well-coached'; meanwhile we had only 'mainly liberal' testimony from American interviewees.

Phillip's rebuttal pointed out that 'we all knew from the start that this would be a delicate project.' The two sides to the conflict 'have diametrically opposed views on everything.' He noted that one of the 'well-coached' communists mentioned by Metcalfe was Tibor Meray, who had fled Hungary and was deeply anti-communist; that many conservative Americans appeared on the program; that the complaints about North Koreans

were not matched by ones about South Koreans, also quite 'well-coached.'
As for bias,

> It would of course have been far simpler to have taken the 'filmic' route of an
> opinionated presenter striding over the hills of South Korea. When these
> opinions are delivered in the sonorous tones of the editor of the Daily
> Telegraph [Max Hastings], of course, no one worries about 'balance.'

Phillip also had a ringer for Channel 4, an ultimate trump card. Charlton
Heston had read four of Jon's scripts. He had 'marvelled at how dispassionate we had been,' according to Phillip; 'this is the same Charlton Heston
who narrated the "Accuracy in Media" rebuttal of WGBH's Vietnam
series.' (Heston read our scripts before consenting to be the 'voice of
MacArthur,' which he mimed with consummate skill.)

Rather than continue to quibble with us, Channel 4 accomplished a
kind of pocket veto: they simply stuck the film in a Saturday time slot in
mid-summer, widely known among TV moguls to be the worst pocket for
audience attention that can still be called 'prime time.' The predictable
result of that, and of Britain's lesser participation in or interest in this war,
was that our contentious and expensive documentary notched a record low
for Thames products, capturing a tiny fraction of the viewing audience (the
estimate was 669,000 viewers for the first program, which would barely
merit a 'one' on the American Nielson system, where each unit represents
930,000 some-odd viewers, and a ten is barely acceptable).

The last hour of the film was timed to coincide with the 1988 Olympics
in Seoul, and I expected PBS to screen it around that time. I heard rumors,
however, that the South Korean government had brought pressure to bear
to assure that it was not shown in the fall of 1988; when I asked Austin
Hoyt about this matter, he said there was nothing to the rumors; the delay
was occasioned by the requirement to make the film more 'American.'
This, however, had only taken six months in the case of the much longer
PBS Vietnam series.[316]

It was too bad that the film was not shown then, because the games went
off with only the North Koreans and Cubans boycotting, and for the first
time since 1976 the competition was splendid. The opening ceremony was

a magnificent homage to Korean culture, both the high if constricted one of the Confucians and the low but diverse and vital one of the masses; the organic choreography was worthy of a Kim Il Sung extravaganza (and often like it). Predictably the herd of foreign journalists who descended for a look at Korea didn't like what they saw (too noisy, too spicy, too proud, too nationalistic, too uninterested in us, these people), since Koreans were being themselves rather than doing a soft-shoe shuffle for the foreigners. Thus the commentary ranged from the stinking racism of P. J. O'Rourke in *Rolling Stone* to the veiled bigotry of Ian Buruma in the *New York Review of Books*.[317]

Meanwhile most of the London newspapers had had time to deliver themselves of opinions on our documentary, and most of them were very good—the reviews emphasized the depth of the research, the rare footage and interviews, and the balance of the documentary.[318] The *Sunday Telegraph* – associated with Max Hastings, who had done the BBC Korean War documentary – was a predictable but shameless exception. It outdid itself to slam Thames's competing film, with David Rees's silly diatribe, 'Truth is the Victim in this TV Distortion of the Korean War,' and another by Richard Last under the title 'Grown-up Fairy Tales.'[319] Worst of all, another *Daily Telegraph* staffer got a broadside into the *Times Literary Supplement*, to my mortification, since this is read like the Bible by American academics. He, too, wondered about the propriety of our North Korean interviews, and hinted darkly about the process by which we obtained them. Jon and I were given plenty of space to answer the attack, and although the *Supplement* gave him the opportunity of a response, there was none.[320]

THE HARVARD HIJACK

As weeks turned into months in 1988–89, with no PBS screening, *The Unknown War* became the little-known documentary, which nonetheless became an object of power grabs and shameless behavior that I never could have predicted.

Gregory Henderson, a good friend of mine who was a former Foreign Service officer in Korea and scholar on the country, was also all Harvard in undergraduate and graduate degrees, and with his venerable mother was a fixture at Harvard graduation ceremonies. Thames used his eloquent interview several times in the film. He had been given copies of the documentary by Whitehead and showed them at Harvard University, glamorized by an unwarranted enlargement of his role in the making of the film, and by a critique of my and Jon Halliday's work: which he promptly dispatched to WGBH/Boston (WGBH never bothered to inform me of this critique, described as a 'screed,' or get my reaction). There was nothing uncharacteristic or shameless in this, of course, but it set a train in motion. Then Gregory abruptly died, taking one of the truly interesting people in our little Korea field away, and so let me just say this: rest his large, irrepressible, and deeply missed soul.

Then one late fall day (November 14, 1988 to be exact), I happened to be in New York and saw our film advertised: it would be shown to the public at Columbia University. Neither I nor Jon had been contacted about the showing, and the film was supposed to be embargoed in the US until it appeared on Public Television. I asked a friend to attend the proceedings, since if I showed up it would skew the discussion (and the theater, if any).[321]

The theater began immediately, as none other than Ted Conant, the in-your-face hulking presence whom Phillip loathed, strode forward as master of ceremonies. Conant was also a relative of Henderson's (from whom he presumably got copies of our film). It was, as it happened, not our documentary but Ted Conant's that was to be on display.

Presenting himself as a key consultant to Thames, Ted used the collective 'we' to indicate that 'we' had been all over the world collecting materials and interviews, 'we' had even been to North Korea. 'We' had suffered the slings and arrows of the outraged Right (Conant, son of a Harvard President, has impeccable credentials in the genus *liberalis Americanus*) to make a 'controversial' film anchored by left-leaning social democrat Phillip Whitehead and 'even' including radicals Jon Halliday and Bruce Cumings.

This he validated by placing in full view copies of the *TLS* attack on our picture book. He allowed as how Max Hastings's book-of-his-documentary was 'simplistic,' but our book-(not)-of-our-documentary was also 'disturbing' because of the lack of footnotes. (Conant becomes the historian, I become 'disturbing.' Karnow had no footnotes. Our publisher didn't want footnotes.)

Phillip Whitehead, left-leaning social democrat, had objected to our book being linked to the screened documentary, according to Conant, because Thames researchers had been 'unable to verify some of our claims.' (This is contrary to my view of events. Phillip had supported the link with the book, and the Thames researchers never bothered even to ask for the manuscript of my second book, with its thousands of archival references.[322]) But in the world according to Conant, left-leaning social democrat Whitehead was courageously holding the tide against even further-left-leaning Cumings and Halliday.

Now there was a new threat on the horizon, Conant intoned. WGBH/Boston was thinking of chopping up the film and showing only two or three hours, because it's 'too controversial'; the reviews spread out before him were the partial cause of this consternation, he intimated. Rumor had it that the South Korean government had prevailed upon WGBH not to broadcast the documentary during the Olympics. So: to show or not to show our documentary, that was the question.

Good transparent weathervane of objectivity that he is, Conant said he would take a 'straw poll' after showing the first two hours of the film, to see if those in the audience thought it ought to be aired uncut and unexpurgated in America. The lights dimmed, the machine whirred, and in focus was hour one and then hour two – each halted just before the credits rolled, lest it be revealed that Ted was nowhere mentioned. Then came the 'straw poll,' which revealed that everyone thought the film should be shown, and most thought it good.

Many wondered why it should be controversial. One South Korean Army general in the audience (then studying at Columbia) didn't like it, but said that cutting it would be unwonted censorship. The one Columbia political scientist present at the screening averred that I was biased for talking about the North Korean land reform and not mentioning the South Korean land reform (of which there was none before the Korean War).

I dashed off a letter to Phillip, asking him what the hell was going on.

I find it hard to believe that Ted Conant knows something about PBS that I don't, but if he does, it is even harder to believe that PBS thinks it can somehow politically censor this film and get away with it.[323]

Phillip then wrote to Conant, and in so doing delivered himself (for the first time in my experience) of his real feelings about the documentary:

I feel intensely proud of the collective effort we all put into 'Korea – The Unknown War', ensuring that we could screen a work which all of us could endorse even if, as with all collective enterprises, we might have individually placed nuances of emphasis differently . . . . There isn't an ounce of 'bias' in the six programmes.[324]

Some days later the phone rang in my office, and it was none other than Conant, his Cambridge accent resonant. It seemed there had been a bit of a misunderstanding. I had been misinformed about the showing at Columbia, it wasn't really as I had told Phillip, he had merely wanted to get the film out and around. I told him my information was impeccable. 'How could you discuss our film and our book, and pass out critical reviews, and not ask us to be there?' He mumbled something, and then began rambling on, more or less repeating what he had said (and just denied that he had said) at the Columbia screening. Austin Hoyt had expressed reservations directly to Conant about the documentary being biased; Conant had indeed laid out reviews of our book; he railed on and on, like the loudspeakers blaring in the DMZ. Since I couldn't get a word in edgewise, I said I had to go and hung up.[325]

Austin wrote me that he had not said anything of the sort to Conant, and related that 'we have no plans to re-edit the programs. We might have to add for time, [as] the UK version is short . . . . But we who were part of the process of consensus are not about to destroy it.'[326]

Conant lumbered onward over the next several months, showing the film here and there, whenever he was asked, or even when he was not. And I did, too, determining that if WGBH did have an interest in censorship, better to let the interested public see the Thames unexpurgated version. At length an old friend of mine who teaches at New York University, Moss Roberts, set a trap. Conant was going to be the emcee at an NYU screening, put on by one of Conant's friends. I lent Moss my tapes, and when Conant marched in with his tapes to monopolize the proceedings,

Moss occupied the podium and had the film start up immediately. Conant harrumphed and whined, but was defeated and, thus, departed.

Another friend of Henderson and Conant is Phillip West, holding a Ph.D. from Harvard. He had not published on the Korean War or indicated any interest in it until 1989 when *The American Historical Review*, journal of record in my discipline, published his review essay where among other things my work is referred to as anti-American, and Jon Halliday's work is attacked. Nothing is ever what it seems where Korea is concerned. This article actually had its origin at a conference in Seoul held in December 1988, sponsored by the Council on US–ROK Security Studies based in Seattle. What is this council?

Some years ago an acquaintance of mine, a Korean political scientist, was denied tenure at Puget Sound University. After peddling fish in Tacoma for a while, he got the bright idea to organize a council of retired South Korean military officers and some Korean and American scholars, funded by the Seoul regime or its backers, and to make himself the salaried director of said council. He wanted the University of Washington to help sponsor it, and thoughtfully sent me a copy of the proposal. I demanded that the University have nothing to do with it, on the grounds that retired military officers from Seoul, coming from a military group that had devastated democracy and academic freedom for thirty years, were not the best interlocutors for intellectual debate. So my acquaintance got no backing from us, but he did find it elsewhere: from Gen. Richard Stilwell, who shortly became very active in the Council.[327]

Mr West presented a paper to the Seoul conference entitled 'Heroic and Inquiring Modes: A Draft Design for an Oral History of the Korean War.' Theme: the 'heroic' mode is done by people like me, the 'inquiring' mode by people like West. (Translation: I'm biased and he isn't.) But why an 'oral history?' Because Phillip Whitehead, his senses taking leave, had shipped off the transcripts of all 250 of our interviews to Mr West – if he would pay the postage, that is.[328]

I learned about all this only when I was employed to review some research grant proposals – which included Phillip West's, for doing oral interviews in China. In his proposal he described our Thames interviews as his 'valuable asset' now lodged at the Mansfield Center at the University of Montana, where he teaches. Thames had accomplished, he wrote, 'the largest oral history project carried out on the Korean War.' He also applied to the National Endowment for the Humanities for a grant to set up a 'documentation center' in Montana, according to a friend of mine who read the proposal, which also included references to our interviews.

I wrote to Professor West expressing my surprise at his sudden interest in the Korean War, and my dismay at his 'regrettable, and unethical' use of the Thames interviews. He wrote back denying any wrongdoing.[329] West was kind enough to inform me, however, that he also organized, with said 'Council,' a screening of our film in November 1988 at the University of Hawaii: 'in honor of Gregory Henderson' (who had passed away and was therefore not around to ask why he should be so honored). West wrote that the film was 'well received, including positive comments by General Paik himself.'

This would again be, of course, General Paek Sôn-yôp. Imagine: the imprimatur of General Paik! Why, if we had also gotten the imprimatur of General Kim (Il Sung), we'd have the two guys who eyeballed each other across the parallel on June 25, 1950. What more could a scholar want?

THE WGBH HIJACK

By now the reader may disbelieve me, but until the spring of 1989 I still had warm thoughts and fond regards for WGBH and our two colleagues there, Austin Hoyt and Peter McGhee. When my television is on it is mostly on PBS, in the morning so my son can watch *Sesame Street*, a multiracial, open-minded, educational, and endearing program that I could hardly think how to improve upon; this is followed by *Mr Rogers*, an island of sanity and love in the television sea of inanity. I believe in the pristine, unsullied visceral judgement of little kids, and both of mine, separated by an eighteen-year interval and who knows what trend, fad, or new star, decided around four months of age that Fred Rogers was okay, and watched him in rapt silence.

I watch PBS in the evening, *MacNeil/Lehrer* at least, and often its documentary programming (which often means watching WGBH), which varies from superb and compelling to weak and superficial. But without

PBS and a couple of cable networks (like CNN and Discovery), American television would be an unrelieved wasteland.

Austin Hoyt had been involved with some of the best programming at WGBH, and I had empathy if not sympathy for what I took to be his attempt to shade our documentary for an American audience, without changing its substance. I have seen a thousand Austin Hoyts in academic life, decent individuals who may take few stands on their own, but who will often support those who do, up to a point that often includes a tenured sinecure for life. I understood Austin's style because I had myself drawn on all my powers of ingratiation to find a way to get along with (and get around) the Stalinists who also populate the groves of academe, hell bent to deny positions to people who happen to disagree with them politically, regardless of their academic merits.

So Austin's desire to finesse people like Richard Stilwell struck me as politically necessary; these were not matters of substance. But in the spring of 1989 I concluded that the substance of the documentary was being altered, that truths were being finessed in deference to the Stilwells of the world, and that Austin had gone back on his word to me ('we who were part of the process of consensus are not about to destroy it').

In early 1989 Austin sent his 'wish list' to Phillip, interviews and films he would like to have in Boston for WGBH's editing process. The stated goal of this editing was merely to add five minutes to each program (Thames, being commercial, has a fifty-two-minute television hour, PBS does fifty-seven minutes). It was an ideal opportunity to retrieve some of the clips that had been taken out of the Thames rough cuts (which ran well over an hour). WGBH also wanted to edit the film for the American audience, meaning the substitution of narration in American accents rather than British. There was no suggestion that WGBH would edit the substance of the film, nor was there any justification for that, since the Thames group had through great effort achieved consensus on most points of interpretation, had produced the film, and Hoyt and McGhee had attended the seminars and viewed the film as it took shape. WGBH had already been given every opportunity for its own input.

Jon and I busily wrote up our own suggestions for the five-minute additions, quite naturally pushing for those things that Thames had dropped – for example, a clip from the I. F. Stone interview. I was perhaps impolitic in telling Austin what he no doubt did not wish to hear:

> The [Thames] documentary remains biased toward a Western and South Korean point of view to a much greater degree than the PBS series on Vietnam . . . [which] leaves an inaccurate picture of the [Korean] war . . . appropriate additions might help to rectify this.[330]

I also said that 'one-third of the documentary is fundamentally and at this point irremediably flawed,' that being the two hours done by Mike Dormer. Hour three, in particular, combined hero-worship of MacArthur with 'an inaccurate blaming of [him] for the decision to march North'; it had 'endless talking white faces, mostly American.' I proceeded to make many (surely too many – thirteen single-spaced pages' worth) of suggestions for changes and additions to the Thames film.

I ended by repeating something I had earlier written to Phillip, for Austin's consumption:

> I really can't fathom how liberals can have such very different perceptions about Korea than they have about Vietnam, Central America, Chile, Cuba – must be something opaque and impenetrable about the country, something that makes people think that processes that are well understood in other civil wars, Red–White conflicts [etc.], don't operate in Korea . . .

> Part of it is that Korea came at the height of the Cold War, and the Cold War has truly blighted the old virtue of verstehen, of trying to fathom the way the other half lives in spite of one's own distaste for the system, of being able to listen to someone saying it is not all a nightmare on the other side without thinking that person is a fellow-traveller . . . .

Jon's wish list[331] included a Japanese admiral commenting on the substantial Japanese participation in the Inch'ôn landing, a big secret until recent years; also some new and important information on the germ warfare controversy from a Japanese specialist; British Maj. Ellery Anderson's colorful description of the travails of sending southern agents (and going himself) behind the lines into the North; Kate Fleron on the devastation wrought by American bombing in the North. He also commented on Austin's suggestions for changes and additions.

As I read his remarks, not having seen Austin's suggestions, I realized that the 'additional five minutes' had turned into a justification for a process of revision that would shade, alter, perhaps misrepresent, or perhaps eliminate several crucial interpretations in the Thames film. Jon was particularly incensed about the POW and the germ warfare issues, and indeed his memo dwelt for six pages on them. In our division of labor these were in Jon's bailiwick; after fighting the issues out for weeks and months, he succeeded in getting WGBH to change two clear misrepresentations in the Thames segments on germ warfare.[332] Jon also rightly made a number of suggestions for changing the existing commentary, and asked for 'the right to write new commentary' for the additions. After all, he was still the writer of the series. Jon closed with this:

> I have heard from Phillip that there is concern [at WGBH] about a 'frontlash' from the US military (I trust I have this correct). We all expressed our commitment not to yield to pressure. Our job is to bring the truth to the screen, however unpleasant it may be to some people. If the going gets tough, remind yourself that our audience is not only retired US Marines and Farrar-Hockley, but also admirers of I.F. Stone – and millions of Koreans.

We found out by accident that the 'frontlashing' was coming from General Richard Stilwell (no relation to 'Vinegar Joe' – indeed, none whatever; Vinegar Joe would roll in his grave to see how his namesake rolled around in the same bed with Asian generals).

Jon and I had turned up in Washington in March 1989 for the annual get-together of the Association for Asian Studies, the principal professional organization in that field, to show and discuss the film; in predictable fashion the floor was hogged by an American who had done thirty years' worth of intelligence work in Korea and who nonetheless accused us of bias.

In the course of the discussion a man stood up in the audience and informed us that his office (the US Army Center for Military History) had received a request from Stilwell to vet our documentary for 'accuracy.' Yet much of what Stilwell wanted checked out was, according to this man, out of his bailiwick; he could tell you what happened on the battlefield but he could not make judgements about policies, the politics of the war, or the interpretations of historians.

I was flabbergasted by this information. I knew that Reed Irvine of 'Accuracy in Media' had prevailed upon Hoyt to interview Stilwell (with the implied or explicit threat that if he did not, AIM would deem our efforts 'biased'), but I never dreamed Hoyt would vet the film through Stilwell, employ him as a consultant, or even place the Thames version in his hands before it screened in the USA.

Furthermore, I knew Stilwell's background and thought any involvement by such a man would call into question the film's integrity and leave it open to questions about our intentions: exactly the response AIM would take to learning that we had vetted the film through the KGB's covert operations chief for East Asia circa 1950, now a virtual agent for North Korea and head of a group to set up a memorial to the Korean War in Moscow. Far-fetched you say? Well then learn about Mr Stilwell.

Richard Stilwell, who died on Christmas Day 1991, was an early member of the first covert operations department of the CIA, the Office of Policy Coordination (OPC), Frank Wisner's wholly owned and mostly uncontrolled covert operations subsidiary within the CIA, probably reporting to 'Wild Bill' Donovan on Wall Street more often than to Truman's befuddled CIA chief, Roscoe Hillenkoetter. When the Korean War began, Stilwell was its Far East division chief.[333] The OPC was very active in East Asia before the war, especially after it began to control Civil Air Transport (forerunner of Air America), run by General Claire Chennault and Whiting Willauer, both with close ties to Chiang Kai-shek. CIA funds flowed to Civil Air Transport by the summer of 1949 if not earlier, through a dummy corporation set up by Tommy 'The Cork' Corcoran, T.V. Soong's agent in Washington.[334]

In events that I cover in detail in the second volume of my *Origins of the Korean War*, Willauer returned to Washington, DC, from Taiwan in mid-June 1950, to meet with OPC/CIA officials. At the time, Willauer was close to Hans Tofte, who had arrived in Japan in May to direct OPC efforts in Japan, and to Richard Stilwell. I think, although I cannot prove, that Stilwell was involved in the American-sponsored coup against Chiang Kai-shek – perhaps to push it forward, or perhaps to block it. Anyway, it would appear that Mr Stilwell left a good bit out of his interview with Thames.

The good general had a long record of service in the Vietnam War. He was instrumental in the development of counterinsurgency forces and doctrines in the Kennedy administration – or what he called at the time 'Army Activities in Underdeveloped Areas Short of Declared War.'[335] As chief of operations for the US Military Assistance Command in 1963, he conducted last-minute negotiations with Ngo Dinh Diem's generals, trying unsuccessfully to get American-demanded reforms just before the coup in which Diem lost his life; when the coup came, Vietnamese general Tran Van Don bypassed the American commander, General Paul Harkins, to ask Stilwell 'to order all US military advisors to remain neutral and to inform Washington that the coup was under way,' which Stilwell dutifully did.[336]

Neil Sheehan knew him a year later as a person assiduously 'suppressing dissent' within the staff over his commander's roseate predictions of the impending defeat of the Vietcong, courtesy of the victorious progress of the Strategic Hamlet Program; Stilwell was penning long memoes then, too, in rebuttal of the critical reportage of Sheehan, Peter Arnett, and David Halberstam – the Three Musketeers of independent journalism in early 1960s Vietnam. Sheehan penned a rare portrait of this secretive man:

> He had an unwavering trust in authority that led him to place loyalty to superiors above other concerns. He aspired to gain the pinnacle of [Army] chief of staff, an aspiration he was to be denied. He had graduated near the top of his class at West Point . . . in mid-1964, Stilwell . . . became chief of staff to Westmoreland.[337]

Stilwell headed the 'United Nations Command,' that is, the American troop contingent, in Korea from 1973 to 1976 – the period of Park Chung Hee's worst repression when emergency decrees flew about like bats at dusk. When the rightwing 'rollback' current had its Indian Summer in the late 1970s and the early Reagan years, Stilwell was in the thick of it. He was a director of the Committee on the Present Danger, a regime-in-exile during the Carter administration; as President of the Association of Former Intelligence Officers, Stilwell fought against Congressional attempts to monitor covert operations.[338]

As a deputy under-secretary of defense (a position he held from 1981–85), he was 'a prime mover' behind the creation of 'an ultrasecret organization whose own members never knew everyone else in the unit,' called the Intelligence Support Activity (ISA), but known better under its cover name, Tactical Concept Activity (one of several cover names designed 'to mislead military officials with top-secret clearances').[339] Among other things, Stilwell helped to get the Contras organized along the Nicaraguan border, and played an instrumental role in Reagan's 1983 rollback of the 'leftist thugs' running Grenada – where Stilwell worked with none other than Oliver North.[340]

Stilwell was also an agent for various South Korean firms. According to press reports in 1986, for example, Stilwell was a 'business consultant' to Hanil Synthetic Fiber Company, the flagship firm of the Hanil conglomerate.[341] His compensation was not given, but I would guess it ran around $50,000 per year. When President Roh Tae Woo made a state visit to Washington in September 1988, he walked into the Korean Embassy party with Stilwell on one arm and John Singlaub (of Iran/Contra fame) on the other.[342]

Although repeated requests to WGBH to see Stilwell's commentary on our documentary went for naught, a source leaked a copy of his critique – at least, the critique dated January 25, 1989 (there may be others).[343] It explained to me why Austin had kept coming back to a handful of points with the regularity of a homing pigeon: they were all Stilwell's points.

Stilwell referred first to 'the accuracy checks, which you [Austin] particularly requested,' and then gave his 'overall conclusion':

> the series, in present form, is not appropriate for an American audience. If shown without extensive editing or caveats or both, would be ill received by that audience and thus an embarrassment to sponsors and station [sic] . . . . It is simply not an objective portrayal of the war.

He also urged that 'reputable' historians be utilized to put the film 'in perspective.' (Implication: Cumings and Halliday are disreputable historians.) Let's call a spade a spade: this is a stark call for censorship. Covert operator Stilwell determines what is 'appropriate for an American audience'; not only that, he decides what is 'objective.' Hard rock mayhem, Madonna's blasphemous softporn orgies, your neighbor's hemorrhoids, and Pat Robertson are fit for American TV, but our documentary is not.

Besides that mouthful, our friendly South Korean lobbyist thought the film represented a 'British view' that America 'bumbled about' in Korea, which might 'play well in London, but not in middle-America.' His first two examples of 'grossly inequitable (or unfair) treatment,' however, had nothing to do with American audiences or 'British' views:

> (1) Considerable coverage of senior retired NK officers (carefully outfitted for the occasion and obviously rehearsed), [with] no comparable commentary from the SK Officer Corps.
> (2) SK police depicted as cruel and inhuman; actions of NK Security Forces are not discussed.

These are complaints on behalf of a *South Korean* audience,[344] not an American viewing public which has never – not even once – heard a North Korean general speak; because of widespread TV coverage of demonstrations in Seoul, this same audience would show no surprise in learning of the brutality of the ROK police.

Is it beside the point also to mention Stilwell's inaccuracy? We interviewed several ROK Army officers, including three top generals, and not only 'discussed' but depicted in film atrocities by the North Korean 'Security Forces.' Is it equally beside the point to note that a person like Dean Rusk is also 'obviously rehearsed' – rehearsed by decades of knowing the real story and knowing by heart the rendering of that story for public consumption. Indeed, isn't this his real skill, his forte?

Stilwell said his objections had been concurred in by Clay Blair, 'Billy' Mossman (an official military historian), 'and by the experts at the US Army Center for Military History.' The only evidence on this comes from a source in that Center, who did not like Stilwell vetting political interpretations through his office. Stilwell concluded his general comments with a remark that he thought perhaps 'gratuitous and out of line':

> Sponsors deserve to be alerted to a probable rash of complaints. You have a difficult job. Good luck.

Well, the good General is not stupid. He knows the bottom line, he knows how to blow in the ear of a television weathervane.

Stilwell appended a list of twenty-two objections to the six programs, 'facts known to be inaccurate,' culled from consultations with 'Paul Nitze and a number of other key sources.' Two of these comments are not 'factual,' that is, there is no way to judge their accuracy. (Example: 'True or not, [this] should be edited out. American audience will be revolted and irate.')

Of the remaining twenty comments, as a historian of the Korean War I would judge one to be correct and nineteen to be false, inaccurate, badly judged, or simply wrong. For example: 'Fact is that the South Korean Army had not greatly expanded [in 1949].' Well, 'fact is,' it nearly doubled (from 50,000 to 98,000) in the summer of 1949, a strength level the North Koreans did not match until the spring of 1950. Stilwell said the ROK Army had not been supplied with American anti-tank mines; in fact it had. But perhaps the comment I liked best was this: 'Cummings [sic] has this all wrong according to [Paul] Nitze who has first hand knowledge.'

Stilwell must have blown a lot more wind in the direction of the WGBH weathervanes, because many of these objections (unattributed) were heard in the fall of 1988, well before his memo arrived, through the lips of Mr Conant and over the phone from Austin. Conant, in particular, harped on the question of whether the film was fit for an American audience. And they long outlasted the memo in question. (After the documentary aired, Hoyt told the press that he had accepted twelve of Stilwell's twenty-two suggested changes, but denied any unwonted rightwing influence: 'We spent a lot of time and money checking [accuracy]. I played researcher, personally.')[345]

A source at WGBH indicated in the spring of 1990 that Stilwell had scared off 'the original' sponsors from backing the program.[346] A friend also related to me that at a conference in Seoul (the conference where Phillip West had his debut as Korean War historian), participated in by many retired ROK military officers – including key Korean War principals like Paek Sôn-yôp and Chông Il-gwôn – Stilwell took credit for 'blocking' the documentary in the US, and also used the occasion to slander and Red-bait another retired American general who happened to disagree with Stilwell on Korea policy, calling him a 'card-carrying member of the KGB.'[347]

The first WGBH script revisions came my way in April 1989, and I was appalled. Hoyt had prefaced the revisions with a scrawled note to me that slandered Thames Television in general and Jon in particular: 'the [Thames] narration was less a rigorous argument by proof than by innuendo.'[348] Hoyt later told a journalist that he disliked 'having a narrator express a point of view,' and busied himself with sanitizing the 'anti-Western bias' of the Thames script.[349] Hoyt had metamorphosed into the historian seeking rigor through proof and the positivist weathervane with no point of view, whereas Thames Television and Jon Halliday (and presumably I) peddled insinuation, invective, gibe, perhaps untruth: the synonyms I derive from my dictionary entry for 'innuendo.' As for 'bias,' Thames Television's broadcast charter explicitly forbids biased programming, and such a charge could be the *prima facie* basis for legal action in England.

The changes were greater than I had been led to expect, and virtually all were political, in two senses: first, the revisions were gauged to weaken the thrust of the film, to make it less damaging to the accepted but unexamined American wisdom. Second, virtually every point Stilwell had raised was still neuralgic to Hoyt, indicating that his desire to please liberals still barely overshadowed his fear of the Right. Appeal to the facts carried little weight, if those facts were unpalatable to the American taste. (Perhaps this is what Adorno meant when he said, 'even if it was a fact, it wouldn't be true.'[350]) The film was again being 'balanced' politically, but in the far more constrained context of America in the Reagan/Bush era.

Here are excerpts of my response to Hoyt:[351]

I find myself in the position of looking at a fait accompli in which I had little role as a consultant, which is not to say that the revisions are not in many cases welcome . . . .

There are many suggestions that I made that you did not act upon . . . just one example: where is IF Stone? . . . so I'm not sure if I use my time wisely in once again offering my views . . . . But, I've decided to go the extra mile with some reactions . . . .

I imagine that [Jon] will find some of the revisions in the narration to be unfortunate, particularly the germ warfare segment. I also take strong exception to your remark in your April 3 note to me . . . I don't know which 'innuendoes' you refer to, and 'proof' depends on what evidence one accepts as valid, and you seem more content with evidence from Stilwell or Mossman than from me or Jon. The film is full of unproved innuendo about the other side, and to some extent the S. Korean side . . . .

I must say that it never occurred to me when I signed on with this project that a person like Stilwell would have any role in this documentary except as a possible subject of it. [He is] . . . under lifelong strictures to withhold precisely the evidence the historian needs to find out exactly what happened . . . . It is frankly embarrassing to me, and I should think to WGBH, that he has had a role in preparing the American version.

I proceeded to review the WGBH programs serially, suggesting numerous changes. Hoyt worried about Mossman's assertion that the ROK Army was a lightly armed Constabulary (it had been in 1948 but was doubled in 1949, as we have seen). Hoyt had the US Air Force 'largely in mothballs' in 1949, when in fact it was the designated carrier for our rapidly expanding atomic arsenal. He cavilled at Jon referring to terrors 'real or imagined' during the North Korean occupation of Seoul after the war began, asking if we would say the same about 'Kristallnacht' in Germany. I responded,

The responsible officials charged at the time with finding out what was happening . . . that is, the CIA etc., did not find a high level of terror . . . your comparisons to Kristallnacht reflect your own biases. North Koreans occupying the capital of their country are not Nazis in the holocaust.

(Hoyt later told Whitehead that when he sought out the CIA documents on which I based my judgements, he found Stilwell's name on some of them.)

Earlier Hoyt had questioned my figures on guerrillas in the South, since Mossman didn't seem to know about them; now he simply eliminated them. 'I see that you have just elided the figures on guerrillas killed,' I wrote; 'I have to demand that they be put back in; otherwise there is little or nothing to indicate the importance of guerrillas in the summer 1950 fighting.' (They weren't put back in.)

The second program's treatment of the Inch'ôn landing, by Mike Dormer, had accepted most of the MacArthur-as-hero mythology, which declassified documentation now showed to be false. The documents had little effect on Dormer, but Hoyt listened to me and made several good revisions, I think for two reasons: first, Clay Blair had come to similar conclusions in his book called *The Forgotten War*, and Hoyt didn't have to rely just on me; second, and more important, deep in the politically constructed received wisdom on the Korean War is the desire to fault MacArthur anywhere and everywhere, so these revisions could go forward because they would not disturb the liberal psyche, nor the liberal verdict on the war – MacArthur was simply and once again wrong. Thus was achieved the one significant WGBH improvement to the Thames film. (There were a number of minor improvements, and I would also give Austin plaudits for adding more interviews with American black soldiers, who vividly express their feelings about fighting in segregated units, on behalf of a segregated society.)

Stilwell had recommended to Hoyt that he take Paul Nitze's word rather than mine on the possible use of nuclear weapons in late 1950 after the Chinese came into the war. Not knowing that at the time, I said 'Nitze statement false – a high JCS committee in December 1950, and Ridgway in May 1951, urged that [atomic bombs] be used; Ridgway renewed Mac's request for 30 bombs. So Nitze has to come out if the narration doesn't refute him.' Stilwell had said none of the massive new 'Tarzon' 14,000-lb conventional bombs had been used in 1950,[352] but I pointed out to Hoyt that one was dropped on Kanggye, where Kim Il Sung was bunkered, in December 1950. (Nitze stayed, was not refuted, and the reference to Tarzons was deleted.)

Hoyt wanted to change the narration of Operation Hudson Harbor, where in the fall of 1951 the US dropped dummy atomic bombs on North Korea, trying to gauge what effects real ones might have. Jon said this 'dropped the ultimate hint,' but Stilwell had told Austin that atomic threat 'was not the purpose' of the exercise.[353] Thus Hoyt wanted proof from me that there were 'psychological warfare' or atomic blackmail elements in Hudson Harbor (perhaps they just wanted to get the technique straight). I asked him if he would say the same, were he to learn that Lyndon Johnson dropped dummy A-bombs on North Vietnam. 'I cannot believe anyone could think that such bombing runs, appearing on the radar like the B-29 over Hiroshima, would not intimidate the enemy, and be designed to do so.'

I wrote Austin again on April 10, when I learned that he had taken several things *out* of the documentary, which I had not noticed.[354] Austin had sprinkled Rusk and Nitze all over the place; they may take up half of the extra thirty minutes. But he had dropped the one Dean Rusk clip with an important admission, where he said that the US bombed 'everything that moved, every brick standing on top of another brick' in North Korea.

This, presumably, was cut in deference to the delicate American sensibility. Suddenly Rusk wasn't so credible, after all.

Jon weighed in a few days later, with his strong reaction to the script changes:

> Some [revisions] are acceptable, many are improvements – but some are subtractions from knowledge and truth and quite unacceptable. I am still astonished at the way double standards are employed on the Korean War in a way unthinkable on Vietnam.

Jon mustered the impassioned tone that the British deploy so well when feelings are bruised and fair play not observed: 'I cannot allow you to put out words under my own name which I have not cleared,' Jon wrote; he offered to fly over to Boston and noted that he had left a copy of his memo with his literary agent, 'who is empowered to protect my interests and my good name.' (He also requested that Hoyt give an on-screen credit to our picture book, which I thought courageous but about as likely as Hoyt asking me to join the WGBH board.) Jon made many, many suggestions for changes to the film and the written script.[355] I agreed with nearly all of them, and they represented an enormous investment of time and effort, but hardly any of his suggested changes were acted upon at WGBH.

Jon noted many changes in the script that had, in fact, been ones suggested by Stilwell. For example, Austin dropped from program three commentary to the effect that both sides (not just the North Koreans) killed prisoners in the field. I had documented this for both Americans and South Koreans. But Stilwell had objected to any suggestion that Americans committed atrocities like those of the Koreans. Around this time Jon also began referring to a 'My Lai' that he had discovered in Korea, which WGBH also paid no attention to.

Here is the paleosymbolic logic: My Lai happened in Vietnam. It happened once (because no one can deny that it happened). Any suggestion that similar atrocities happened elsewhere in Vietnam, or in Korea, is to be rejected (even when much eyewitness testimony is on the record). Ergo: My Lai was an aberration. Implication: the American fighting man has scruples higher than the Asian fighting man. Bottom line: PBS doesn't get indignant calls.

Austin had removed MacArthur's statement about American airpower creating 'a wasteland' in North Korea after the Chinese intervention, with no substitution that would indicate to the viewer the true horror of this scorched earth policy. Jon said this would be like 'not mentioning defoliation in the Vietnam War.' It all fell on ears deaf to well-documented facts.

These ears were attached to weathervanes calling us biased and sending pubescent 'fact-checkers' after our hard-earned discoveries; they were attuned to a different drummer, the drumbeat that Stilwell knew how to play so well – irate veterans, bad reviews, above all outraged sponsors. Amid that racket, nothing we said or wrote made a difference.

Shortly thereafter Austin called me, and finessed or fuzzed over many of the objections we had made to the WGBH revisions. I.F. Stone's interview was kept in London, he said, and so he had not used it. (London was presumably the other side of the moon and therefore Stone was irretrievable. In fact WGBH had sent Thames a 'wish list' of things it wanted to see, for possible addition to the film.) He hadn't relied on Stilwell as a historian, he said, but wanted to know 'where the brickbats would come from the Right.' He hoped I didn't write anything about all this, as I had suggested I might: 'a whole lot of dirty linen will come up.' I was busy then, in the middle of servicing about 175 students, tired of Austin's weak nerves, and so I mostly listened as he explained his way through the script. Later I heard that he had told Phillip that I had 'approved' it.

That was the last time I heard from Austin about the WGBH editing. Later I learned that several more revisions had ensued at WGBH, without our knowledge, consent, or concurrence. Jon reviewed some of the revisions done at WGBH in July 1989, and his long response made me understand that the worst was happening: Hoyt and his friends had placed many of our interpretations up for grabs and were changing things about.

As Jon pointed out, many of these revisions ensued not simply without our participation, but without a consideration of our evidence, with much reliance on prominent policymakers with much to hide, and without our longstanding conviction that 'a document from the time must take precedence' over fallible memory. Jon closed by saying the new script could not go out under his name. Jon also asked again that Hoyt give us a copy of Stilwell's critique – to no avail.[356]

Hoyt's flipping nystagmus[357] where Stilwell was concerned had led him to elide the fact that prior to the tank-led DPRK blitzkreig, South Korea had not placed its anti-tank mines. Stilwell had falsely claimed they had none; I had said they didn't place them because (1) they would get in the way of their own invasion, or (2) their absence would draw the North deeply into the South, the proper strategy to deal with a blitzkreig. Hoyt had taken Stilwell's falsehood rather than probe this lapse.

Most infuriating to me, however, was Hoyt's removal of the statement that virtually all of the top officer corps in the ROK Army had served in the Japanese Imperial Army; Austin deemed this 'a sidebar whose significance would be lost unless there was further elaboration.'[358] I realized that there was no further use in pretending that WGBH was paying attention to my views, and so I responded with a sledgehammer:[359]

> Many of [your new revisions] seem designed to cover your rear end politically in this country . . . you reportedly told Phillip that you and I had come to 'complete agreement' on the new script. That is false . . . . Anyway, there is now a newly-revised script, and I haven't seen it. . . .
>
> I think it unconscionable that Jon Halliday has not been involved except indirectly in revisions of a script for which he is the writer . . . I feel as if I have been 'handled' by an effective politician, but not consulted with seriousness. This was not my experience with Thames; whatever my disagreements with the final version, Phillip and Max heard me out and gave me my due as the principal consultant . . . if you encapsulate the documentary when it is aired with a panel of 'experts' to which Jon or I are not invited, I will hold a news conference to examine how such a thing could occur in re a documentary for which he is the writer and I the major consultant . . . .
>
> I will not allow you to remove the information on the Japanese Imperial Army background of the ROK General Staff. This is fully documented in the official South Korean history of the war for Chrissakes . . . and if you do not see why this is significant in the context, then you should have your head examined for editing a documentary on the Korean War . . . .
>
> Stilwell's buddies in 1950 like Paek Son-yop and Kim Paek-il were not simply in the Japanese army, but in the Kwantung Army in Manchuria,

notorious in the 1930s for provoking incidents as prelude to war . . . .
[How about doing] a docudrama on the American Revolutionary War, and
leaving out the distinction between patriots and tories; then let's do a
documentary on the Vichy regime while we're at it and fail to tell our
viewers of Petain's background . . . . The crowning achievement can be a
new documentary on Vietnam . . . [treating] Bao Dai as a true nationalist
and Ngo Dinh Diem as the father of his country (the oft-stated Nitze/Rusk/
Stilwell position in the 1940s and 1950s).

Phillip Whitehead explicitly requested that WGBH send me the new
scripts in October 1989, but they never showed up; by this time I thought
it beneath my dignity to ask for the scripts myself.[360] Needless to say I
never was asked to review the final films. (WGBH did, however, ask Sir
Anthony 'I was theah' Farrar-Hockley to review them.[361]) None of the
purported 'fact-checkers' ever contacted me or Jon about archival sources.
Jon asked Thames Program Director David Elstein to intervene with
WGBH and assure that Jon and I were involved in ensuring the accuracy of
their revisions; he got a response indicating that Thames was not going to
go to bat for us, or the agreed consensus.[362] Whitehead always expressed
himself willing to defend the film (and us), but few positive results came
from this; ultimately Thames' unwillingness to confront WGBH over the
changes rests with him, as the executive producer of the documentary and
as the person who dealt directly with WGBH.[363]

By the end of 1989 Peter McGhee had become the designated hitter for
WGBH Halliday–Cumings bashing, taking up Hoyt's cudgel with nasty
intent. He bludgeoned Jon and me for our insolence in suggesting that we
ought to be able to review the new scripts, insulted us, and declared us
'outsiders' to our own project. As McGhee put it to Jon,

> WGBH is reviewing the programs for its own reasons and out of its own
> sense of responsibility to history. In doing so, we have considered your
> various letters and vituperations, giving them the same weight we would to
> charges brought by any outsider. But we feel under no obligation to satisfy
> you or to submit our programs to you for approval nor do we to Bruce
> [sic].[364]

WGBH had contrived to do what the South Korean government had long
been trying to do by all means: to get Halliday and Cumings off the

project. If the philosophical meaning of film, according to Stanley Cavell, 'is to show us what the world might look like in our own absence,'[365] we now could savor the ironies of seeing our documentary as it might look like in our own absence.

Shortly I wrote to McGhee, saying the following:

Consultancy has never implied 'approval' of scripts, either at Thames or WGBH. But it certainly means that I am allowed to review and to comment upon the final version which is to go out under my name. If you do not allow me to view the tapes before airing, you must remove my name from the documentary.[366]

McGhee's last missive informed me that, indeed, I would not be allowed to view the final programs and would not be credited on screen for my work with WGBH, but only for Thames. McGhee also gave me the same contemptuous stuff he gave Jon: the WGBH editing process, he said, was intended 'to make the American version of the programs as close to the truth of history as we know how to get it.' Translation: McGhee and Hoyt are the historians pursuing truth, I am the pundit with an axe to grind. In fact neither offered evidence for the changes they made, and when we offered our evidence, they ignored it. McGhee closed by saying that my references in an earlier letter to Stilwell's role were 'reckless, malicious, and, most of all, wrong.'[367]

Moss Roberts, who as we saw above confounded Conant's shenanigans, got incensed about WGBH's behavior and sent a petition to McGhee, signed by various academics, expressing 'concern that the American audience may never have the opportunity' to see the documentary. McGhee wrote back intemperately to him, too, but floored me by referring to the film as 'Korea: The Forgotten War.'[368] Was it an innocent slip, a Freudian slip, a conscious slip, or no slip at all (maybe WGBH had even changed the title!)? It turned out to be Freudian, since WGBH kept the same title.

In August 1990 I learned indirectly that the film would finally be screened in the US, and asked Austin to show me the new tapes.[369] He refused, saying that only recognized journalists who might write about the film could have advance copies. So there you have it: the series historian can't see the series. I used my sources and had the new films in hand within two days, however, along with the publicity material WGBH made up. I found yet more changes, of course, but just two big ones merit mention: NSC 68, and the removal of MacArthur.

Scholar-consultants such as Laurence Freedman, Callum MacDonald, Rosemary Foot, and myself had told Thames its version was very deficient on the significance of NSC 68, which was the most important Cold War document of our time, promulgated in the spring of 1950, committing the US to an enormous military buildup, and inaugurating the military-industrial complex that still gobbles our tax dollars in fell swoops. Acheson got Truman to approve the new policy in April 1950, but didn't have the money for it until the Korean crisis 'came along and saved us,' as he subsequently put it.

Austin thought that section was bad in the Thames version, too. But instead of consulting the historians who know something about it, he turned instead to the author of NSC 68, Paul Nitze, for a bland and general comment that buried the fascinating history of this watershed change in the American position in the world, occasioned by war in Korea.

In the US the most controversial of all episodes in the Korean War is MacArthur's relief. Recently historians – especially Roger Dingman of the University of Southern California – have uncovered evidence that just at the time MacArthur was relieved in April 1951, Truman seemed about to trade the man for his policies, by hitting China with A-bombs. The first evidence of this came in a declassified top secret Joint Chiefs of Staff history: just in a little, unobtrusive footnote, but there it was. Truman actually issued an order to blast several Chinese cities (including Shanghai city center); for reasons that are unclear the order was not implemented, but just at that time MacArthur was sacked. Since there is still much we do not know about this episode, Thames presented what we do know. The script said that 'the real issues [in MacArthur's removal] were more complex,' and then used my interview where I begin, 'The sacking of MacArthur cannot be understood simply as a question of civilian supremacy,' and proceed to discuss Truman's release of atomic cores to the military.

WGBH, however, begins the sequence by saying, 'MacArthur wanted to widen the war to China with atomic bombs. Those were not the policies in Washington.' (Thames had said that MacArthur 'wanted to widen the war to China,' which was true, but said nothing about this not being the policy in Washington – since Rosemary Foot's book had amply documented how many times the Truman administration had considered extending the war to China.) Instead WGBH trots out Dean Rusk yet again: 'Washington did not want a general war with China . . . [there] was no taste for a larger war against China.' Now, Rusk is correct in his limited sense that Truman did not want a land war in China; but he sidesteps (as does WGBH) the issue of hitting Chinese installations with airpower.

WGBH then cuts to me, but cuts out what I say about MacArthur's sacking (then the rest of my clip is the same as in the Thames version). And then it brings on Rusk again, to say that 'the central idea' was to keep the prerogatives of the Presidency in Truman's hands: that is, it was only about civilian supremacy, after all – the lore of the 1950s as shaped by the Truman people. MacArthur, once again, is the raving warmonger wanting to send our boys into China, or hit the Chinese with A-bombs. Thus WGBH's episode becomes one of differing views on whether Truman might have used A-bombs against China, rather than the stunning Thames suggestion that Truman sacked MacArthur in part so that a reliable field commander would be in control should China be attacked from the air.

I would summarize the overall effect of WGBH's changes this way: WGBH improved the Thames version in regard to the Inch'ôn landing, marginally improved the failure of all American intelligence agencies (not just MacArthur's) to predict the Chinese entry into the war, extended Thames' coverage of American blacks in the armed services to very good effect, and made various minor alterations at a ratio of one good change for five or six bad ones. On the Korean side of things, every change WGBH made bolstered the South's version of history and detracted from the North's, relative to the Thames version. Yet all we know in the US is the South Korean side. Of course, neither Korean side honors the truth of the war (or both think they possess it exclusively), and so such 'balancing' merely substitutes one morality tale for another.

Max Whitby, the crew, and I fought hard to get the interviews with North Koreans, people rarely if ever seen in the West since the war ended. Not once did WGBH use the thirty minutes of additional time it had to bring in more of these interviews; instead they deleted the most meaningful one, where Mr Pak, the napalm victim, beseeches the world not to repeat such a holocaust ('never again, a victim like me'), and put in a couple of South Koreans who added nothing.

By rewriting Jon's script, where he had tried to compensate for Mike Dormer's assembly, WGBH seriously weakened the two weakest programs, hours two and three, which happen to be about those parts of the war most interesting to Americans: NSC 68, how the war started, the UN role, the march North, MacArthur's generalship, and the developing Truman–MacArthur controversy.

Viewing the credits, you'd think Jon Halliday originated and wrote the film, and I was the main historian. The only consultants to WGBH were Stilwell, Mossman, and a journalist; these were listed in the version I saw, but were mysteriously dropped when PBS aired the series. WGBH's yearning for the truth had not led it to even one of the several scholars who have recently published books on the Korean War. Austin was listed as 'executive producer' for WGBH, but was credited only with 'additional writing' on the series, rather an understatement.

WGBH's publicity material was artful: I was touted as 'series historian' and my book on the war was praised. The material included excerpts of my interview with Kissinger, too. I thought perhaps Austin was trying to butter me up, in hopes that I'd shut up and not air the 'dirty linen.' Jon Halliday was nowhere mentioned. The originator and writer, Hoyt was perhaps hoping, would be missed in the yawning and stretching that would greet the credits as the programs wound down. Finally, the film went out with no sponsor. No corporation, no foundation, just the support of 'PBS viewers like you.' Austin denied, however, that this was because of Stilwell's activity in trying to block sponsors.

Pantheon Books had brought out our picture book in 1988, if with next to no publicity. In August 1990 I asked them about the paperback version, thinking it would be published around the time that the documentary aired. Pantheon disappeared, however, in 1989 – at least the Pantheon run by André Schiffrin and long an outlet for iconoclastic books. This fine group had published several essays of mine, including my first, in 1974, and I had plans for more books with it at the time it folded. Schiffrin's Pantheon went by the boards with the speed of light, marked only by some unusually vociferous but ultimately ineffectual, soon forgotten protest. It was a classic Reagan/Bush era saga, effective censorship draped in inanity.

'Parent' corporation Random House claimed that Pantheon was losing money and thus had made the unforgivable capitalist mistake of ignoring the 'bottom line.' *Publishers Weekly* intoned that Pantheon 'published too many left-wing books, and why could these not be better balanced by some right-wing ones?' (Of course: because otherwise right-wingers will have no outlet.) Random House chairman and chief 'parent' Alberto Vitale found yet another cause for the 'revolution of '89' in Pantheon's lack of business sense: Just look at what happened to the countries that considered "bottom line" the most obscene expression in their vocabulary.'[370] With 'parents' like this, no wonder our schoolchildren can't find the American continent on a world map.

Before he quit Pantheon in protest, our editor Jim Peck assured me that a paperback would be published in 1990. Penguin published the British paperback in 1990. When I called Pantheon in August to tell them that the documentary was finally running, in prime time, and in every urban market in the US (a concern of Pantheon earlier on), a woman named Alti Karper said over and over, 'Isn't that too bad.'

I was told that the hardback was then being remaindered. 'Put a paperback out, then,' I suggested. 'No time for that,' she responded. Shortly I read in the *New York Times* that Pantheon was turning a hardback on Iraqi politics into a paperback in three weeks, start to finish. I wrote back to Fred Jordan, who now controlled Pantheon, saying there were two months left before the film aired. He wrote back an intemperate letter, referring to Pantheon's publication as 'your book,' and saying that WGBH had denied any connection with it.[371] So it goes.

With experiences like this, by the time the documentary aired in November 1990 I thought the claustrophobic political atmosphere in the US, where reaction seemed to be running rampant, would guarantee a bad reception for the film – even with WGBH's alterations. I was wrong. The *New York Times* ran three articles on it, all of them fair and complimentary. Two people whose writing and reporting on Korea I had admired, Susan Chira and Michael Shapiro, both wrote fair and interesting accounts of the film itself, and Chira dealt with the controversy over its revision and screening, under an excellent title – 'America's Battle Over How to Remember Its Forgotten War.'[372]

I had great trepidation about what Walter Goodman, the *Times*'s television critic, would write. Often his reviews of controversial television documentaries position himself in a putative 'middle,' from which point he berates right and left for political bias. His views are generally neo-conservative, a position which he may think occupies that same middle (perhaps it does). In the event he wrote a complimentary review of our program, for which I was most grateful. He began by zeroing in on the film's politics:[373]

> The series . . . has already been criticized for a revisionist tone . . . . To this congenitally suspicious reviewer, however, the documentary . . . is filled with sharp and memory-jogging details and does not seem to be pushing any extreme line at the expense of the record.

He ended on an enigmatic note:

> Viewers with a memory of television's treatment of the Vietnam War may find themselves wondering how matters might have turned out if Americans at home had been a nightly audience to scenes from the bitter battlefield of Korea.

Shapiro, too, focused on 'the war not fought in the living room,' saying that 'the parallels with Vietnam abound,' but television was not the centerpiece of the American home in 1950 and so the images did not come into the living room every night.

Whereas Shapiro clearly thinks Korea was the Vietnam before Vietnam, Goodman's comment is open to alternative readings. It might mean that Korea was much like Vietnam, in which case he is right; or it may mean he agrees with George Will's distrust of TV as inherently pacifist. Television's window makes it difficult to fight any war, the argument seems to be, regardless of whether it is a just or unjust war.

Goodman's judgement that the film was unbiased probably derived from what we might now call 'the Charlton Heston response.' Charlton, as we have seen, found our film much less biased than the PBS series on Vietnam. Goodman's bloodhound-like instincts for leftist cant also found nothing. A younger, leftwing colleague of mine collared me after seeing the film, and twitted me as to what was so 'controversial' about it. The review in the *Washington Post* was favorable, and the *Los Angeles Times* had a fine essay. Neither brought up issues of leftwing bias.[374] They were all viewing Korea through the television lenses of Vietnam.

Then there were those who viewed Vietnam through Korean lenses. I got on talk radio, and a Korean War veteran blasted me for doing six hours 'stuffed with leftwing propaganda.' And then there were those of no honest position whatsoever, just shameless fabrication and McCarthyite *ad hominem* attack: Reed Irvine got together with 'Accuracy in Media''s resident Korean War expert, Joseph Goulden, to say this in the Moonie-funded *Washington Times*, under the title 'Rehash of Old War Lies':[375]

> The taxpayer financed Public Broadcasting System set itself a new record for mendacity . . . the series repeats America-trashing lies even the communists have abandoned as nonsensical . . . [so on and so forth]:

Irvine and Goulden quoted Stilwell many times on how terrible the series was, bludgeoned PBS for 'twist[ing] history beyond recognition,' and launched one *ad hominem* assault after another against Jon and me. Jon was said to have been given access to 'politically reliable veterans' from Communist China, when in fact China would not let us film or interview in the country. This is a good sample of Irvine's standard operating procedure, which the television moguls still fear; it was the only purely negative criticism the film received in the national media, which I take to be a big fat compliment.

During this period Stilwell busied himself by circulating a packet of Jon's writings on Korea, during the Vietnam era, and slandered me by telling journalists that I was a 'pro-communist historian.'[376] While Stilwell continued his McCarthyite tactics, no doubt egged on by the South Korean Embassy, his own undeniable background in covert activities and agentry on behalf of South Korean firms remained unmentioned. The *Times* discussed Stilwell's charges, but did not mention his covert background; nor did the Associated Press in its accounts. Only two journalists did, Tim Weiner of the *Philadelphia Inquirer* and Doug Ireland of the *Village Voice*, both of whom wrote excellent accounts of the controversy with WGBH.[377] Perhaps it was Phillip Whitehead who wounded Stilwell where it really hurts, by telling a reporter that Stilwell and his allies were 'a bunch of fruitcakes.'[378]

Austin Hoyt sought to position himself politically: 'I think we'll catch flak from both the left and the right,' he told the Associated Press. Instead of saying that this was a Thames film, prepared with a shared consensus, he related that Halliday and Cumings had 'the revisionist view' – whereas Austin was the brave soul who sought to 'sanitize some of the anti-Western bias' in the Thames film.[379] Bias, that is, about which he never said a word to me or Jon – or, so far as we know, to Thames officials. After all, Hoyt was as much a part of the Thames consensus as anyone else.

In the midst of WGBH's hypocrisy I happened upon an account of its treatment of another British documentary, a decade earlier.[380] Not once in four years of work with Thames and WGBH had I heard of the lawsuit between WGBH and the filmmakers of *Blacks Britannica*, an indictment of British ruling class exploitation of blacks. The WGBH formula for discrediting the film and the filmmakers was identical; Hoyt was not involved in this case, but the course of events was the same:[381]

1. Fret about what the Middle American will say ('the guy in the wheatfields in Kansas. He'll call us communists.').

2. 'Frame' the film for the US audience with discussions and disclaimers, panels of experts, and the like.

3. Cancel or postpone the broadcast date, without explaining why.

4. Make solemn commitments never to tamper with the film, and follow that with surreptitious tampering.

5. Bring in someone to bash and Red-bait the filmmakers.[382]

6. Wait until the film runs and then insinuate to newspeople that the makers were leftists, with WGBH left in the 'middle'. (WGBH informed *Newsweek* that it was 'concerned with the film's endorsement of a Marxist viewpoint.')

WGBH cut very little from this film (no more than four minutes), but 'the film's *meaning* [sic] had been changed by the simple expedient of rearranging the sequence of shots. There are numerous instances of this.'[383]

A source inside WGBH told a reporter that its producers exhibit a 'consistent stubborn streak,' but he also described, in the reporter's words,

a schizophrenic 'corporate culture' which was a volatile blend of 'arrogance and hubris' on one hand and, on the other, extremely 'sensitive antennae' regarding outside criticism. Sometimes they 'do backflips and go crazy no matter how specious the criticism might be.'[384]

I suppose the response to our film that I found most gratifying came from Bill Stokes, columnist for the *Chicago Tribune*. The documentary got him musing about some letters sent home by a Marine in Korea in 1952. The letters overflowed with patriotic and heroic longings, written by 'a naive, uncertain boy, as obedient to authority as a circus dog.' The enemy was 'dehumanized into "gooks" and "chinks."' Stokes contrasted the 'mawkish absurdities' in the letters with the experience of Vietnam: 'hadn't the napalm in Korea burned as deeply? Hadn't our purpose been as confused, our tactics as heavy-handed, and our killer roles as mechanical?' The letters, he said, left him with 'a monumental sadness.' They were his letters.[385]

At the end, what is the history of our documentary about the history of the Korean War? For Thames, it was a political balancing act in which various claims to truth were represented, rather than a concern for getting at the truth itself in a consistent and coherent way. The result was four good hours and two weak ones, which, as I said, is still something to be proud of.

For WGBH, it was a matter of appearances, of simulation, of getting the sign straight, 'control of the code' – not getting 'the facts' straight, and certainly not a consistent logic of interpretation. Seeking the truth was as much a pose as Peter McGhee pretending to be the historian lecturing me about proper standards of inquiry. What was critical was that the documentary should *seem* to heed these principles. In the end WGBH wanted an appearance of probity, a semblance of objectivity, a package that would not offend, and a position in the 'middle' of television's fictive consensus. And thus: a rendering of 'the unknown war' as the well-known war. In the unraveling of this story we view not just the problems of television, but the problem of American liberalism itself.[386]

'The prevailing linguistic mode in advanced capitalist economies is the signal rather than the symbol,' Baudrillard suggests,[387] and that best explains Hoyt and McGhee: they always wanted to get their signals straight. Halliday as writer and Cumings as historian 'sent the wrong signal.' I.F. Stone, as opposed to Sir Anthony Farrar-Hockley, 'sent the wrong signal.' It is for Americans to contemplate the knowledge that having Richard Stilwell on board 'sent the right signal.'

John Fiske has written that there are two ways of organizing the television text: one is 'logic and cause and effect,' which is 'a strategy of closure.' It works according to consensually accepted Cartesian principles and thus is supposed to make 'common sense.' The second would be based on laws of association and would be 'open,' thus enabling its viewers 'to negotiate an appropriate variety of meanings.'[388] Our fights with the Thames and WGBH producers were won, if ever, only on the terrain of the first – empiricism, the historian's code, the deployment of facts and logic (mostly facts; we rarely got into logic).

WGBH, in particular, never accepted the open-ended journey of the second way, in which we might raise questions we can't answer, nibble at dangling inconsistencies, make a clear statement of the dilemmas inherent in the task, or plumb an interior logic resistant to 'the facts.' In the end WGBH was interested in docudrama, not history, if we define the latter as a narrative of closure, of finality, as if its conclusions were not open to argument, as if the factors that influenced it were not 'subject to intense disagreement.'[389]

This second way we might call a hermeneutic of suspicion: not the delusions of the paranoiac, but the educated guesses of a Columbo, the querulous integrity of an I.F. Stone. That would be the superior method for a documentary on this 'forgotten war,' but it barely got off the ground at Thames, and never flew at WGBH. This is also the way good historians do history: not as a narrative 'of what actually happened,' letting 'the facts speak for themselves,' but through debates about 'what exactly did happen, why it happened, and what would be an adequate account of its significance.'[390]

The historian should be a skeptic, a doubter, a detective, and an honest person. So should documentary makers who claim to do history.

EPILOGUE

Richard Stilwell had new prominence in 1990–91, as chairman of the Korean War Memorial Veterans' Advisory Board. Architects from Pennsylvania had won the competition to design a monument to the war, and produced a tasteful, somewhat enigmatic display that represented the mysteries and unresolved tensions of the Korean War, if not quite as well as Maya Lin's dark, brooding, and overwhelming Vietnam War Memorial.

Richard Stilwell didn't like it. He and his allies sought to revise the plan, to render the enigmatic figures more 'heroic' and to paste onto the design a mural telling the 'history' of the war. The architects stoutly resisted, saying their design was 'brutally changed,' acquiring a 'radically different character' that now 'glorified war.'[391] They launched a lawsuit against the revisionists.

Plans for this monument had begun some years ago, but picked up steam in 1988 after 'Dear Abby' used her column to alert Americans to the news that 'nobody ever heard of this war.' At a $1,000-a-plate gala at the Omni Shoreham Hotel in Washington, attended by Bob Hope, Rosemary Clooney, and South Korean Ambassador Tong Jin Park among others, Stilwell found his own explanation for the 'revolution of '89': The Korean War 'was the cornerstone for defense and foreign policy that provided the bulwark for what is happening in Eastern Europe today.' (It just took forty years, that's all.) And he discovered a great patriotic triumph: the Korean War 'was [our] last victory in stark geopolitical terms – we won and they lost.' So did Bob Hope: 'It was a tough war, a really tough war but they did a tough job and finally cleaned it up. They should all be decorated in my eyes [sic].'[392]

Go tell it to General MacArthur, 'Dear Abby' and tough guys Bob Hope and Richard Stilwell. With victories like that, we don't need any more losses.

By 1992 the Gulf War had faded into a distant memory, 'yesterday's news.' Yellow ribbons seemed quaint, prodigious flagwaving hadn't reversed American decline, and Norman Schwarzkopf's book-of-the-series appeared unlikely to earn back its $5 million (yes, you did not read it wrong, five million greenbacks) advance. In TV argot, 'it's history now.' Which is the ultimate proof of the name we gave it: our first television war.

Saddam may be licking his wounds in Baghdad, but the neo-conservatives have found a new bogieman, and this one prowls the halls of academe in the 1990s: the 'politically correct,' otherwise known as 'PCs.' Translation: sixties remnants who are wrecking academe. The media has pounced on this dangerous new tendency, with cover stories in *Newsweek* and discussions-cum-shouting matches on all the TV talk shows. The heat of the debates seems so strange, now that America has vanquished the evil-empire enemy. *MacNeil/Lehrer* ran a series on the death of communism in late 1991, selecting a broad, one might say all-inclusive, range of American opinion leaders: Betty Bao Lord, Daniel Moynihan, Robert Conquest, Midge Decter, and (for 'balance' . . . and perhaps for some rightwing gag?) Paul Robeson Jr. So, how can any American not see that all's for the best in the best of all possible worlds? Or as Midge Decter put it elsewhere:

> Virtually no one believes any more that there is a system preferable to ours: more benign, more equitable, more productive . . . [except for] certain enclaves of absurdity and irrelevance such as the universities and the Public Broadcasting System.[393]

If we've reached the American valhalla, why not just call it a loony bin?

Or perhaps we should let the PBS 'enclave of absurdity' speak for itself. When WGBH/Boston was basking in the glory of its Civil War documentary, its bigwigs opened their minds to the press.[394] Peter McGhee opined that 'you can't ignore this kind of success.' Former PBS president (and spawner of Karnow's Vietnam book) Lawrence Grossman argued that this documentary's lesson for producers was 'to take a chance . . . take the big risk and encourage an independent approach.' Take, for example, a less successful documentary: had the WGBH series on Korea been 'less conventional,' Grossman said in a reporter's paraphrase, 'it might have had more of an impact.' And now in Grossman's direct words,

> I think it is essential today to have a thesis and a reason for being other than a review of the past . . . . It should have an impact as opposed to being a worthy project for its own sake.

The title of this WGBH documentary, according to Grossman? 'Korea: The Forgotten War.'

NOTES

1. The symbiosis between the historian and this concept is cogently examined in Peter Novick, *That Noble Dream: The 'Objectivity Question' and the American Historical Profession*, New York 1988.

2. See in particular the passage on Adorno's understanding of totality, in Fredric Jameson, *Late Marxism: Adorno, or, The Persistence of the Dialectic*, London 1990, pp. 26–27.

3. The *locus classicus* here is M.M. Bakhtin and P.N. Medvedev, *The Formal Method in Literary Scholarship: A Critical Introduction to Sociological Poetics*, trans. Albert J. Wehrle, Cambridge 1985, pp. 7–15.

4. Allan Bloom, *The Closing of the American Mind*, New York 1987, p. 64.

5. Ibid., pp. 314, 332. Bloom writes that 'nothing positive' came to the universities in the 1960s; 'it was an unmitigated disaster for them' (p. 320). The defining event at Cornell was the takeover of a campus building by armed black students. For a very different view of Cornell at the time, see Alison Lurie's novel, *The War Between the Tates* (New York 1974) where a Bloom-like character appears as 'Professor Dibble.'

6. Harry Summers, *On Strategy: A Critical Analysis of the Vietnam War*, Novato, California 1982.

7. See chapters 21 and 22 in my *Origins of the Korean War, II: The Roaring of the Cataract*, Princeton 1990.

8. 'The Terrible Art of Designing a War Memorial,' *New York Times*, July 14, 1991.

9. 'Against positivism, which halts at phenomena – "There are only *facts*" – I would say: No, facts is precisely what there is not. We cannot establish any fact "in itself": perhaps it is folly to want to do such a thing.' Friedrich Nietzsche, *The Will to Power* trans. Walter Kaufmann and R.J. Hollingdale, New York 1968, p. 267.

10. Jean Baudrillard, *America*, trans. Chris Turner, London 1988, p. 85.

11. Lest you think this an exaggeration, D.J. Enright cites a 1986 *Winfrey* show in which rapists and child molesters faced an audience of women, many of whom had been victims of rape; the 'guests' proceeded to detail their predilections with the verisimilitude of a Scottish empiricist. Enright, *Fields of Vision: Literature, Language, Television*, New York 1990, p. 41.

12. Alasdair MacIntyre, *After Virtue*, South Bend 1981, pp. 18, 23, 40.

13. For further reading, the best discussion can be found in Fredric Jameson, *Postmodernism, or, The Cultural Logic of Late Capitalism*, Durham and London 1990, pp. ix–xi, 16–17, 363–67, and passim. His presentation of nominalism, totalization, television synchronicity, and the contemporary (postmodern) loss of self and memory (pp. 363–4) is unsurpassed in the literature.

14. *The Liberal Tradition in America*, Boston 1955.

15. Friedrich Nietzsche, *The Gay Science*, trans. Walter Kaufmann, New York 1974, p. 121.

16. Here I draw upon Adorno's idea that the Culture Industry demeans experience (or art) precisely by assuring us that it is taking place, and Jameson's equation of positivism and postmodernism. See Jameson's discussion in *Late Marxism*, pp. 147, 248–9.

17. Ibid. p. 249.

18. 'Equality before the enemy: the first presupposition of an *honest* duel. Where one feels contempt, one *cannot* wage war; where one commands, where one sees something beneath oneself, one has no business waging war.' Nietzsche, *Ecce Homo*, trans. Walter Kaufmann, New York 1969, p. 232.

19. Television also manages to profane this memory. These days I hear Little Richard singing 'Long, Tall Sally' on TV, but only in commercials featuring middle-aged, paunchy Midwesterners allowing themselves to look ridiculous (dancing 'the twist' or whatever) so that an album of fifties 'oldies' can be sold.

20. This term goes back to Plato in its notion of 'the identical copy for which no original ever existed' (Jameson, *Postmodernism*, p. 18), but it is central to the postmodern criticism of Jean Baudrillard, and to Guy Debord's insight that in postmodern society 'the image has become the final form of commodity reification.' See Debord's important book, *The Society of the Spectacle*, Detroit 1977.

21. *New York Times* bowl schedule, January 1, 1990. This is, of course, nothing new. When Milton Berle became the first certified TV star, it was on the *Texaco Comedy Hour*. Television merely followed radio, which had an important debate over the implications of commercial broadcasting in the 1930s. See Robert W. McChesney, 'Press–Radio Relations and the Emergence of Network Commercial Broadcasting in the United States, 1930–1935,' *Historical Journal of Film, Radio and Television*, vol. 11, no. 1, 1991, pp. 41–57. I am indebted to Professor McChesney for sending me this article.

22. Raymond Williams, *Raymond Williams on Television*, ed. Alan O'Connor, New York 1989, p. 5.

23. John Fiske, *Television Culture*, New York 1987, p. 21.

24. Robert C. Allen, 'Talking About Television,' in Allen, ed., *Channels of Discourse: Television and Contemporary Criticism*, Chapel Hill 1987, pp. 1–6.

25. Fiske, p.36.

26. Ibid.; Fiske rejects the Frankfurt School's notion that the mass media shape an inert mass in their image, in favor of the Gramscian idea that television is produced through 'a constant struggle against a multitude of resistances to ideological domination, and any balance of forces that it achieves is always precarious, always in need of re-achievement. Hegemony's "victories" are never final . . . .'(pp. 41–3). I

would like to think that Fiske is right, but I would also like to know where he finds 'a multitude of resistances' to mass television. For the contrary view and a brilliant defense of the Frankfurt School, see Jameson, *Late Marxism*, where he memorably argues that Adorno is precisely what we need in the 1990s (p. 251).

27. Baudrillard, *America*, p. 95.

28. Horkheimer and Adorno, 'The Culture Industry,' in *Dialectic of Enlightenment*, trans. John Cumming, London 1979, p. 167. This work was first published in 1944, and Horkheimer later repudiated it. I will therefore use Adorno as the author from hereon. I also think it important to remember Jameson's point, that 'the "Culture Industry" is not a theory of culture but the theory of an *industry* ... that makes money out of what used to be called culture.' *Late Marxism*, p. 144.

29. Williams, *Television: Technology and Cultural Form*, New York 1975, pp. 92, 105.

30. Ellen Seiter, 'Semiotics and Television,' in Allen, *Channels of Discourse*, p. 24.

31. Roland Barthes, *Image – Music – Text*, trans. Stephen Heath, New York 1977, p. 32.

32. Hal Himmelstein, 'Television News and the Television Documentary,' in Horace Newcomb, ed., *Television: The Critical View*, 4th edn, Oxford 1987, p. 267.

33. Todd Gitlin, *Inside Prime Time*, New York 1983, pp. 78–80.

34. Ibid., pp. 80–81.

35. *New York Times*, September 22, 1990.

36. Fiske, p. 73.

37. Jameson, *Late Marxism*, p. 16. Jameson then goes on to 'the counter-image,' and the presumed 'counter-boring' of postmodernism – the liberating 'ceaseless flow of the absolutely new.' This he rightly calls 'one of the great ethical fantasy-images of the postmodern' (p. 16).

38. Steven Connor, *Postmodernist Culture: An Introduction to Theories of the Contemporary*, New York 1989, p. 168.

39. Ibid., pp. 168–70; see also Jean Baudrillard, 'The Ecstasy of Communication,' in Hal Foster, ed., *Postmodern Culture*, London 1985, pp. 126–34.

40. Patricia Mellencamp, ed., *Logics of Television: Essays in Cultural Criticism*, Bloomington 1990.

41. The index in ibid. juxtaposes Walter Benjamin with Tony Bennett, Nancy and Ronald Reagan with Wolfgang Schivelbusch.

42. Bloom, pp. 68–81. See also his chapter on 'The Nietzscheanization of the Left or Vice Versa,' pp. 217–26, which is as poor a reading of both Nietzsche and the Left as I've come across.

43. There is no index entry for it in his book.

44. Walter Benjamin, 'The Work of Art in the Age of Mechanical Reproduction,' in *Illuminations*, ed. Hannah Arendt, New York 1968, pp. 217–51.

45. By way of contrast, Bruce Springsteen hired the fine, independent filmmaker John Sayles to make a video of 'Born in the USA,' in neo-realist style, intercutting unemployment lines and 'rustbowl landscapes' with the music; according to Pat Aufderheide it 'encountered difficulty in gaining time in [TV] rotation.' See her 'Music Videos: The Look of The Sound,' in Todd Gitlin, ed., *Watching Television*, New York 1986, p. 124.

46. See Robert D. McFadden's account in *New York Times*, October 20, 1990. Many other 'stars' did patriotic war-fever videos; I saw Cher in one, draped in flags and yellow ribbons.

46. Jameson, *Postmodernism*, p. 16.

48. *New York Times*, January 24, 1990.

49. *New York Times*, letters column, February 6, 1990.

50. Fiske pp. 104–105.

51. Adorno, 'Culture Industry,' p. 123.

52. His 1991 autobiography gives graphic details of his affairs with various well-known women.

53. Daniel C. Hallin, *The 'Uncensored War': The Media and Vietnam*, Berkeley 1989, p. 125.

54. Neal Gabler, *An Empire of Their Own: How the Jews Invented Hollywood*, New York 1988, pp. 1–7.

55. This is the Ted Koppel-approved way to say Beijing. As in jada-jada jing-jing, but with a softer j, between jing and shing. Even some China experts pronounce it this way to go along and get along, though it is as hard a j as you can get in Chinese; that their pronunciation sometimes betrayed no knowledge of Chinese whatsoever makes no difference to their representation as expert.

56. Arif Dirlik, Joseph Esherick, Germaine Hosten, Richard Kraus, Robert Marks, Maurice Meisner, Elizabeth Perry, Carl Riskin, Moss Roberts, Franz Schurmann, Benjamin Schwartz, Mark Selden, Marilyn Young, to name a few. (I did see Germaine Hosten on a minor talk show – the exception proving the rule.)

57. Benjamin puts the point a little differently: 'Every morning brings us the news of the globe, and yet we are poor in noteworthy stories. This is because no event comes to us without already being shot through with explanation. In other words, by now almost nothing that happens benefits storytelling; almost everything benefits information.' He means that good storytelling keeps the explanation until the end, or allows the reader to supply it, such that 'the psychological connection of the events is not forced on the reader.' Walter Benjamin, 'The Storyteller,' *Illuminations*, p. 89.

58. MacIntyre, p. 30. He ends the book by saying, 'We are waiting not for a Godot, but for another – doubtless very different – St Benedict.'

59. *New York Times*, December 14, 1989.

60. *New York Times*, April 19, 1990.

61. Paul Virilio, *War and Cinema: The Logistics of Perception*, trans. Patrick Camiller, London 1989, pp. 44–5.

62. 'Media's New King and Queen,' *M Inc: The Civilized Man*, June 1991, pp. 52–57.

63. Williams, *Williams on Television*, p. xii.

64. 'All the Usual Suspects: MacNeil/Lehrer and Nightline,' FAIR, New York, NY, May 1990. FAIR director Jeff Cohen noted that AIM had endorsed *MacNeil/Lehrer* for its 'balance.' *New York Times*, letter column, June 17, 1990.

65. Gitlin, *Prime Time*, pp. 203, 216–18. Sometimes things do not work that way, of course. The idea of a sitcom set during the Korean War, according to NBC executive Perry Lafferty, would've seemed a 'bad concept' – 'terrible.' Why a series about a

forgotten war? But *M*A*S*H* made it on the screen anyway because the movie caught the public's imagination, generating a parallax view of the ongoing Vietnam War by displacing it to Korea.

66. Douglas Kellner, 'TV, Ideology, and Emancipatory Popular Culture,' in Allen, *Channels*, pp. 471–503.

67. Habermas quoted in Kellner, ibid., p. 501. Kellner also attributes this idea to Alvin Gouldner, and says that neither Habermas nor Gouldner give a source for their claim that the paleoimagic concept derives from Freud; but it did, according to Kellner, and is consistent with Freud's use of archaeological metaphors for the topological structures of the mind (in Freud's *Civilization and its Discontents*). What he does not say is that Freud and all the rest of them get the archaeological metaphors from Friedrich Nietzsche.

68. Pierre Bourdieu, *Photography: A Middle-Brow Art*, trans. Shaun Whiteside, Stanford 1990, p. 5. Neither Habermas' *paleosymbolic* nor Bourdieu's *habitus* necessarily contradict the totalizing hypotheses of Adorno and, following him, Jameson; I make no judgement here on where such dispositions come from, but only assert that they exist.

69. Interview in Rosenthal, *The Documentary Conscience: A Casebook in Film Making*, Berkeley, ca. 1980, pp. 91, 99–101. Of course, there are simple cases where TV people find out what is balanced and what is biased: WNET, a public station in the New York area, showed the documentary *Hungry for Profit* on the activities of multinational corporations in the Third World. The chief of Gulf + Western (presumably a well-known expert on television documentaries) declared it 'virulently anti-business if not anti-American,' and canceled Gulf + Western's funding for WNET. Edward S. Herman and Noam Chomsky, *Manufacturing Consent: The Political Economy of the Mass Media*, New York 1988, pp. 17, 25.

70. Donald Watt, 'History on the Public Screen, I,' in Alan Rosenthal, ed., *New Challenges for Documentary*, Berkeley 1988, pp. 433–5.

71. Stuart Hall, 'Media Power,' in Rosenthal, ibid., p. 360.

72. Interview in Rosenthal, *Documentary Conscience*, p. 211.

73. Quoted in Barbara Zheutlin, 'The Politics of Documentary: A Symposium,' in Rosenthal, *New Challenges*, p. 230.

74. Am I right to think that humanity might have hit a depth where good old ethnic hatred turns to never-to-be-fathomed-or-repeated insanity, or is Max Von Sydow right in *Hannah and Her Sisters* when he says the wonder is that it doesn't happen more often?

75. Dae-sook Suh, *Kim Il Sung: A Biography*, Honolulu 1988, p. 115. For the full picture see Cumings, *Origins*, vol. 2. Dr Suh told me the publisher was responsible for this inadvertent elision.

76. Eric van Ree, *Socialism in One Zone: Stalin's Policy in Korea 1945–1947*, Oxford and New York 1989. Dr van Ree wrote to me asking if he could use several pictures from the picture book that Jon Halliday and I did (see below, note 87), which is presumably where he saw the 1948 photo.

77. Virilio, p. 13

78. *The German Ideology*, p. 14.

79. Bourdieu, pp. 6–8.
80. *New York Times*, February 19, 1990.
81. Sir Anthony was also the commander of Army suppression forces sent into Northern Ireland in the early 1970s, engaging in fierce battles with the Irish Republican Army. In September 1990 the IRA tried to blow him up in a terrorist attack.
82. Ulric Neisser, described by Associated Press as 'the father of cognitive psychology,' wished to test the accuracy of 'flashbulb memories' by recording exactly where Emory University students were when seven astronauts went up in flames with the *Challenger* shuttle in 1986. A short two years later he asked them to recap where they were when they heard the news, who told them, and how they felt: one-quarter were dead wrong, and only seven of the forty-four responded with essential accuracy. (*Chicago Tribune*, January 30, 1990.)
83. Roland Barthes makes similar points in *Camera Lucida: Reflections on Photography*, trans. Richard Howard, New York 1981, pp. 87–9.
84. Carlo Rim, 'On the Snapshot,' in Christopher Phillips, ed., *Photography in the Modern Era: European Documents and Critical Writings, 1913–1940*, New York 1989, p. 38.
85. Novick, pp. 26–31. Ranke's desire to 'empty himself,' which suggested to Leonard Krieger an erotic attachment to his *Werke*, was taken to mean a desire to turn himself into a Lockean 'blank slate' by American historians. Compare Nietzsche on 'emptying': 'A living thing seeks above all to *discharge* its strength – life itself is *will to power*.' Nietzsche, *Beyond Good and Evil*, trans. Walter Kaufmann, New York 1966, p. 21.
86. Walter Benjamin, 'Theses on the Philosophy of History,' in *Illuminations*, p. 255. See also Hayden White's critique of Ranke in *Tropics of Discourse: Essays in Cultural Criticism*, Baltimore 1978, pp. 51–3. Nietzsche was far better than Ranke, with his conception of 'the pure, purifying eye'; he urged us all to find 'a teacher of pure seeing.' See *Daybreak: Thoughts on the Prejudices of Morality*, trans. R.J. Hollingdale, New York 1982, p. 500.
87. See Jon Halliday and Bruce Cumings, *Korea: The Unknown War*, London and New York 1988.
88. Barthes, *Image – Music – Text*, pp. 17–20.
89. Ibid., p. 27.
90. Harry Truman Library, Dean Acheson Papers, Acheson Seminars, February 13–14, 1954.
91. *Image – Music – Text*, pp. 65–7.
92. Martin Heidegger, *What is Called Thinking?*, trans. J. Glenn Gray, New York 1968, p. 103.
93. Quoted in Bourdieu, p. 75.
94. Chris Marker, *Coréenes*, Paris 1958. Marker, an American living in Paris, also did a wonderful film called *San Soleil*, contrasting Guinea-Bisseau with Japan to reveal the polar opposites of how people live in our world.
95. Fredric Jameson, 'Reading Without Interpretation: Postmodernism and the Video-Text,' in Derek Attridge, et al., eds, *The Linguistics of Writing: Arguments Between*

Language and Literature, Manchester 1987, pp. 198–223. See also Connor, *Postmodernist Culture*, pp. 163–7. I am indebted to Harry Harootunian for these references.

96. Benjamin, 'Work of Art in the Age of Mechanical Reproduction,' pp. 235–6.

97. Duhamel quoted in Virilio, p. 30; see also pp. 8–9.

98. Ibid., p. 16.

99. Halliday and Cumings, p. 70.

100. Ronald Reagan, Letter to the Tower Commission, February 20, 1987, quoted in *New York Times*, February 15, 1990.

101. On trial for the murder of Harvey Milk, a gay city official in San Francisco, the accused pleaded guilty by reason of insanity – his brain having been sodden with Hostess 'Twinkies,' which consist of a lump of whipped cream ensconced in a hyper-sugared, gooey pastry.

102. *The Sorrow and the Pity: A Film by Marcel Ophuls*, introduction by Stanley Hoffman, trans. Mirelle Johnson, New York 1975, pp. 160–65.

103. Ibid., p. 25.

104. Ibid., pp. 84, 149.

105. The method is nicely elucidated by Raul Hilberg, the great historian of the holocaust: 'In all of my work I have never begun by asking the big questions, because I was always afraid that I would come up with small answers; and I have preferred to address these things which are minutiae or details ... to put together in a gestalt a picture which, if not an explanation, is at least a description, a more full description, of what transpired.' Claude Lanzmann, *Shoah: An Oral History of the Holocaust*, preface by Simone de Beauvoir, New York 1985, p. 70. (All page references in the text are to this version.)

106. *Shoah*, pp. 138–52.

107. Bloom, p. 55.

108. *The New Yorker*, January 8, 1990.

109. 'The antiquarian sense of a man, a community, a whole people, always possesses an extremely restricted field of vision; most of what exists it does not perceive at all, and the little it does it sees much too close up and isolated; it cannot relate what it sees to anything else and it therefore accords everything it sees equal importance and therefore to each individual thing too great importance.' Friedrich Nietzsche, 'On the Uses and Disadvantages of History for Life,' in *Untimely Meditations*, trans. R.J. Hollingdale, New York 1983, p. 74.

110. *New York Times*, September 23, 1990.

111. Brendan Gill finally disclosed that this emperor had no clothes in a brilliant dissection of Campbell's elitist views and mediocre mind in *The New Yorker*, but it read like an ancient text, a Dead Sea scroll from antiquity: that is, it was pre-television.

112. William Boddy's excellent discussion of this case would suggest that most of the contestants willingly and silently went along with pre-program coaching by the *Twenty-One* producers. See 'The Seven Dwarfs and the Money Grubbers,' in Mellencamp, *Logics of Television*, pp. 101–107.

113. 'Zuckerman Unbound,' in *Zuckerman Bound*, New York 1979, p. 213.

114. *New York Times*, August 20, 1989.

115. *New York Times*, November 2, 1989.

116. Interview in Rosenthal, *Documentary Conscience*, p. 211.

117. Jay Ruby, 'The Ethics of Imagemaking,' in Rosenthal, *New Challenges*, p. 317.

118. *Beyond Good and Evil*, p. 127.

119. Ibid.

120. Nietzsche, *Will to Power*, p. 47.

121. Brian Winston, 'Documentary: I Think We Are in Trouble,' in Rosenthal, *New Challenges*, pp. 23–5.

122. Hayden White, 'Historiography and Historiophoty,' *American Historical Review* 93:5, December 1988, pp. 1195–6. See also the discussion in the 'Introduction' to Robert Sklar and Charles Musser, eds, *Resisting Images: Essays on Cinema and History*, Philadelphia 1990, pp. 3–5.

123. *Beyond Good and Evil*, p. 80.

124. *Chicago Tribune*, February 28, 1991.

125. Hallin, pp. 118–29, 136–7, 148. This is an excellent account of the 'television war' in Vietnam, which readers should consult for fuller treatment of the issues in this chapter.

126. Quoted in ibid., p. 3.

127. Quoted in Mark Crispin Miller, 'How TV Covers War,' in Rosenthal, *New Challenges*, p. 366.

128. Marshall McLuhan, *War and Peace in the Global Village*, New York 1968, p. 134.

129. Walzer's usually impeccable logic falls down at a key point in his presentation. In justifying the American invasion of North Korea, the US Ambassador to the UN called the 38th parallel 'an imaginary line.' Walzer comments: 'I will leave aside the *odd notion* that the 38th parallel was an imaginary line (how then did we recognize the initial aggression?) [emphasis added].' Walzer leaves this mouthful without further thought, yet it is basic to his argument that the US response to North Korean aggression was just ('it was the crime of the aggressor to challenge individual and communal rights'). Michael Walzer, *Just and Unjust Wars: A Moral Argument with Historical Illustrations*, New York 1977, pp. 117–23.

130. Hallin, pp. 31, 48.

131. See David E. James, 'Documenting the Vietnam War,' in Linda Dittmar and Gene Michaud, eds., *From Hanoi to Hollywood: The Vietnam War in American Film*, New Brunswick 1990, p. 245. *Why Vietnam?* was shown to all troops departing for Vietnam, and screened throughout the US.

132. Virilio, p. 9.

133. J. Fred MacDonald, *Don't Touch that Dial: Radio Programming in American Life, 1920–1960*, Chicago 1979, cited in Rick Berg, 'Losing Vietnam: Covering War in an Age of Technology,' in Dittmar and Michaud, *From Hanoi to Hollywood*, p. 44.

134. Rick Berg rightly notes that one of the better '*vérité*' documentaries on Vietnam, *A Face of War*, 'unwittingly documents nothing less than a documentary's inability to see the war in Vietnam.' (Berg, ibid., p. 49.)

135. Hallin, pp. 142–5.

136. Ibid., pp. 136–7.

137. Ibid., p. 135.

138. Quoted in ibid., pp. 138, 140.

139. Quoted in ibid., pp. 156–7.

140. Ibid., pp. 6, 15, 132.

141. On the ubiquity of this assumption in TV journalism, see James, p. 241.

142. From my diary, March 12, 1967.

143. Hallin, p. 170.

144. Acheson emphasized the latter, as can be seen in his memos in Acheson Papers, Yale University.

145. Quoted in Todd Gitlin, *The Whole World is Watching: Mass Media in the Making and Unmaking of the New Left*, Berkeley 1982, p. 205.

146. Hallin, pp. x–xi, 6.

147. Ibid., p. 123.

148. Martha Gellhorn, *The Face of War*, New York 1988, pp. 274–5; Berg, p. 44. Berg notes that journalists wrote a number of stories in the period 1973–5 about the 'forgotten war' in Vietnam.

149. For a straightforward account of the background and development of the film see Lawrence W. Lichty. ' "Vietnam: A Television History": Media Research and Some Comments,' in Rosenthal, *New Challenges*, pp. 495–505. McGhee's role is highlighted therein (p. 496).

150. Ibid., p. 501.

151. Ibid., p. 503.

152. Stanley Karnow, *Vietnam: A History*, New York 1983.

153. Ibid., pp. 172–3. After Bao Dai discoursed on the vast and sundry fields of knowledge he had made his own, Perelman asked if this included going to the movies every afternoon. 'If he did,' Bao Dai acknowledged, 'it was only in an effort to improve his English. . . . At this juncture, a bone-cracking yawn contorted the regal lineaments, clearly signifying that the audience was over.'

154. Ibid., pp. ix, 11, 395.

155. Ibid., p. 437. On 'high-tech' war in Vietnam see also Harry Summers, 'Man or Machine – Which Will Fight War Tomorrow?', *Defense & Diplomacy*, March–April 1991, pp. 18–19.

156. Karnow, *Vietnam*, p. 11.

157. Marilyn Young, *The Vietnam Wars: 1945–1990*, New York 1991, p. x.

158. Alan Rosenthal, 'Introduction to Part V,' in Rosenthal, *New Challenges*, p. 432.

159. David E. James has an excellent account of this film, which I follow here. ('Documenting the Vietnam War,' pp. 251–2.)

160. Gary Crowdus and Dan Georgakas. 'History is the Theme of All My Films: An Interview with Emile de Antonio,' in Rosenthal, *New Challenges*, p. 165.

161. Ibid., p. 167.

162. Ibid., pp. 168–9. De Antonio screened and discussed the film on May 1, 1969, at Columbia.

163. Linda Dittmar and Gene Michaud make similar points in their excellent essay, 'America's Vietnam War Films: Marching Toward Denial,' in Dittmar and Michaud, *From Hanoi to Hollywood*, pp. 2–3.

164. Coppola said he made the film to help Americans in 'putting the Vietnam experience

behind them.' See Frank P. Tomasulo, 'The Politics of Ambivalence: Apocalypse Now as Prowar and Antiwar Film,' in ibid., p. 146.

165. The commercial was made for Home Box Office; it is cited in Harry W. Haines. '"They Were Called and They Went": The Political Rehabilitation of the Vietnam Veteran,' in ibid., p. 81. Chrysler, of course, in 1987 became the only American manufacturer of 'Jeep' automobiles.

166. Michael Klein, 'Historical Memory, Film, and the Vietnam Era,' in ibid., p. 23.

167. Although it is also true that they supplied a fictive balm and attempted overcoming of 'the frustrations and desires of a white, male, blue-collar audience,' many of whom were also Vietnam veterans. On this see Dittmar and Michaud, 'America's Vietnam War Films,' p. 8.

168. Stuart Hood, On Television, London 1987, pp. 123–6.

169. Virilio, p. 7.

170. This is not a judgement limited to the 'left' side of the political spectrum. Just before the ground war began, Sen. John McCain, Patrick Buchanan, and Michael Kinsley – that is, the political spectrum from A to B – all thought Bush 'could, and probably should' accept the Iraqi withdrawal offer. See Christopher Hitchens, 'Minority Report,' The Nation, March 25, 1991. 'The McLaughlin Group' also screened a panel just before the ground war began, the consensus of which was that there was no need for a ground war. Chicago Tribune, February 25, 1991.

171. Accurate casualty figures are unavailable at this writing, and the Pentagon refused to give out 'body counts' (another reaction to Vietnam). Rashid Khalidi, a friend and colleague at the University of Chicago who provided unstinting and sterling commentary on the Gulf War, if mostly on local radio shows, estimated Iraqi dead at 85,000 to 175,000 ('Gulf War, In These Times, March 20–6, 1991). Military analyst Trevor N. Dupuy estimated 100,000 to 150,000 Iraqi military casualties, including 25,000 to 50,000 deaths (cited in The New Republic, March 25, 1991), and Saudi sources thought total casualties were between 80,000 and 100,000 (Christopher Hitchens, 'Minority Report,' The Nation, March 25, 1991). American deaths totaled over 300, of which about ⅔ were combat deaths. Most of these deaths (American and Iraqi) came during the ground war phase.

172. New York Times, March 2, 1991.

173. The Iraqi offer to withdraw was made through the Soviets on February 21. Randall Richard of the Providence Journal wrote on February 26 that 'Air strikes against Iraqi troops retreating from Kuwait were being launched so feverishly from [the carrier USS Ranger] today that pilots said they took whatever bombs happened to be closest to the flight deck.' Pilots described the traffic on the roads out of Kuwait as 'just bumper to bumper,' and called the fighting 'a turkey shoot.' Quoted in Christopher Hitchens, 'Minority Report,' The Nation, March 25, 1991. On the political economy of the shift from Desert Shield to Desert Storm, see Thomas Ferguson. 'The Economic Incentives for War,' The Nation, January 28, 1991, pp. 73, 76–7.

174. New York Times, February 23, 1991.

175. Michael T. Klare, 'One, Two, Many Iraqs,' The Progressive, April 1991, pp. 20–3.

176. Milton Viorst, 'The House of Hashem,' New Yorker, January 7, 1991. Viorst noted that the case for US and Kuwaiti 'collusion' against Iraq was 'circumstantial,' and

smacked of 'conspiracy theory.' Nonetheless he went on to argue the case in a tentative and provisional way, emphasizing Kuwaiti rather than American agency, and citing Jordanian advisors to King Hussein among his sources. In my reading this was the only article raising these issues in the mainstream American press.

177.   Molly Ivins, 'Small Favors,' *The Progressive*, April 1991, p. 46.

178.   On Brzezinski and Schlesinger's cold warrior role in the Carter period see my 'Chinatown: Foreign Policy and Elite Realignment,' in Thomas Ferguson and Joel Rogers, eds., *The Hidden Election*, New York 1982.

179.   A useful if churlish account of these views and the places they were made known is in Jacob Weinberg. 'Gulfballs,' *The New Republic*, March 25, 1991.

180.   *MacNeill/Lehrer*, May 15, 1991.

181.   FAIR reported in early 1991 that 'none of the foreign policy experts associated with the peace movement – such as Edward Said [and] Noam Chomsky . . . appeared on any nightly network news program.' Cited in Margaret Spillane. 'M*U*S*H,' *The Nation*, February 25, 1991.

182.   Jon Katz points out that, like many blue-collar workers, the TV experts find themselves employed only part-time, since the networks have ruthlessly pared down their own expert staffs to save money. See 'Collateral Damage to Network News,' *Columbia Journalism Review*, March/April 1991, p. 29.

183.   David Halberstam, *New York Times* Op-Ed, February 21, 1991.

184.   David Segal, 'Shrink Rap,' *The New Republic*, March 25, 1991. Segal is also quick to label Kipper 'anti-Israel.'

185.   *New York Times*, February 25, 1991; he used 'rampaging beast' again as late as September 25, 1991 (CBS morning program), when Saddam was merely trying to keep UN officials from running off with his nuclear weapons plans.

186.   *Wall Street Journal*, March 1, 1991; *New York Times*, February 28, 1991.

187.   'No Comment,' *The Progressive*, April 1991, p. 11.

188.   Andrew Kopkind, 'Imposing the New Order at Home,' *The Nation*, April 8, 1991, pp. 432, 446–8; *New York Times*, February 28, 1991.

189.   Safire's column, *New York Times*, February 28, 1991.

190.   'War Reporting Trends and Fads', *The Progressive*, April 1991; *Larry King Live*, CNN, February 12, 1991.

191.   Walter Goodman, *New York Times*, February 27, 1991.

192.   *Newsweek*, March 4, 1991.

193.   *New York Times*, February 8, 1991.

194.   *New York Times*, February 16, 1991. Goodman acknowledged, however, that Arnett was doing his job, 'a necessary job.'

195.   Quoted in *USA Today*, February 21, 1991. Summers said also that he thought the pool restrictions on reporters were 'dumb.'

196.   *Newsweek*, Periscope column, March 4, 1991; *New York Times*, March 11, 1991. The Republican National Committee sent out 500,000 appeals, asking recipients to sign preprinted letters and stuff them in envelopes preaddressed to their local newspapers. See also William Prochnau, 'If There's A War, He's There,' *New York Times Magazine*, March 3, 1991. On the bomb, see Michael T. Klare. 'High-Death Weapons of the Gulf War,' *The Nation*, June 3, 1991, pp. 721, 738–42. Arnett later

pointed out that some years ago, Senator Simpson had berated him for being too critical of Saddam Hussein. See Walter Goodman, 'Arnett,' *Columbia Journalism Review*, May/June 1991, p. 29.

197. Malcolm W. Browne, 'The Military vs. the Press,' *New York Times Magazine*, March 3, 1991; *USA Today*, February 21, 1991.

198. *Soldier of Fortune* editor Robert Brown, quoted in *Newsweek*, March 4, 1991.

199. *New York Times*, May 5, 1991.

200. Ibid.

201. *New York Times*, February 17, 1991.

202. Browne.

203. Margaret Spillane mentions both of these items in 'M*U*S*H.'

204. Adorno, pp. 144–5.

205. 'War Reporting Trends and Fads,' *The Progressive*, April 1991, p. 17.

206. *New York Times*, May 2, 1991. 'When they first heard of these guidelines, they should have raised an incredible obscene howl,' historian Paul Fussell said. 'Instead, they grumbled about the First Amendment but really acted as if they were honored to be in Saudi Arabia.' Quoted in William Boot, 'Covering the Gulf War,' *Columbia Journalism Review*, March/April 1991, p. 23.

207. 'Darts and Laurels,' *Columbia Journalism Review*, March/April 1991, p. 19.

208. On one program Walters cut off the Iraqi Ambassador and stormed at him about hostages: 'Why aren't these people released?' (Quoted in Arthur E. Rowse, 'The Guns of August.' *Columbia Journalism Review*, March/April 1991, p. 26.)

209. Assistant Secretary of Defense for Public Affairs Peter Williams (a frequent Gulf War briefer) told Senate hearings that 'the plan for combat coverage was not drawn up in a vacuum. We worked closely with the military and with the news media to develop a plan that would meet the needs of both'; the action on the battlefield would be chaotic, intense and violent (presumably unlike warfare in the past), so the Pentagon can't let reporters 'ride around in jeeps' or 'hop helicopters.' See excerpts of Williams' testimony, *USA Today*, February 21, 1991. Long after the war ended, the *New York Times* finally did a long investigative study of Pentagon planning for censorship of war news (May 5–6, 1991).

210. The plaintiffs were: *Harper's*, *The Nation*, *The Progressive*, *Mother Jones*, *In These Times*, *The Texas Observer*, *L.A. Weekly*, the *Guardian*, the *Village Voice*, Pacific News Service, Pacifica Radio News, and individuals Scott Armstrong, E.L. Doctorow, Michael Klare, Sydney Schanberg and William Styron. See one account in *The Progressive*, April 1991, p. 4. The Pentagon immediately decreed that none of its spokesmen could appear on TV with any of the plaintiffs. *New York Times*, May 6, 1991.

211. 'Darts and Laurels,' p. 19.

212. 'Trained Seals and Sitting Ducks,' *Harper's*, May 1991.

213. 'The Lonely Superpower,' *New Republic*, July 29, 1991. Krauthammer correctly notes that Korea was the classic case of 'pseudo-multilaterialism.'

214. Quoted in *Newsweek*, April 22, 1991.

215. *New Republic*, April 22, 1991.

216. I learned this in the course of several forums on Korean security held at The Carnegie Endowment, Washington DC, May–September 1991.

217. Judith Miller 'of the *New York Times*' and Laurie Mylroie 'of Harvard University,' as the cover put it, compiled *Saddam Hussein and the Crisis in the Gulf*, New York 1990, in record time. (Mylroie is merely a visiting fellow at Harvard.) Stephen R. Shalom pointed out in *The Nation* (February 25, 1991) that co-author Mylroie had been a booster of Iraq as late as 1988, even arguing that Saddam's centralized control served American interests because it made Iraq's diplomacy predictable.

218. Research by Sut Jhally, Justin Lewis, and Michael Morgan, cited in Alexander Cockburn, 'Beat the Devil,' *The Nation*, March 18, 1991.

219. *New York Times*, May 2, 1991.

220. *New York Times*, February 25, 1991.

221. James Warren, *Chicago Tribune*, February 25, 1991.

222. Ann McFeatters, White House correspondent for the Scripps Howard News Service, *Chicago Tribune*, February 28, 1991.

223. *Wall Street Journal*, March 1, 1991. Wattenberg is a pundit with the American Enterprise Institute.

224. Bundy adduced the lessons of Korea on the fortieth anniversary of the outbreak of the war, June 25, 1990.

225. Edward Said, *Covering Islam: How the Media and the Experts Determine How We See the Rest of the World*, New York 1981, pp. xi–xii, xx–xxi, 40, 101.

226. Ibid., pp. xi, 89–91.

227. Cumings, 'Chinatown.'

228. Said, *Covering Islam*, pp. 65–71.

229. Nietzsche, *Beyond Good and Evil*, p. 65.

230. Quoted in Spillane, pp. 237–9. Ms Spillane notes that this colloquy proceeded on January 21, Martin Luther King Day.

231. The phrase is David Gergen's, a former Reagan aide known for his deft use of images. *New York Times*, May 6, 1991.

232. Carter's National Security advisor, Brzezinski, wanted the Iranian military to stage a coup against the Ayatollahs, but was overruled by his boss and our Ambassador to Iran; Reagan had many advisors who wanted to invade Nicaragua and oust the Sandinistas, but moderates like George Shultz and Defense Department people like Casper Weinberger and several high generals blocked this option. The stalemated outcome was the 'Contras,' strong enough to pressure Nicaragua but not strong enough to topple the Sandinistas.

233. Nietszche, *Will to Power*, p. 17. Elsewhere he writes: 'ultimately [the utilitarians] all want *English* morality to be proved right – because this serves humanity best, or "the general utility," or "the happiness of the greatest number" – no, the happiness of England.' *Beyond Good and Evil*, p. 157.

234. See Foucault's discussion in *Discipline and Punish*, trans. A.M. Sheridan-Smith, London 1977, pp. 192–206; also the excellent discussion in Peter Dews, *Logics of Disintegration: Post-Structuralist Thought and the Claims of Critical Theory*, London 1987, pp. 148–56. I am indebted to Harry Harootunian for suggesting this book to me.

235. Dews, p. 149.

236. Mike Davis writes that Los Angeles' new King center 'plagiarizes brazenly' from Bentham's Panopticon, with closed-circuit TV, motion sensors, infra-red beams, and other devices connected to 'the "unobtrusive/panopticon observatory."' *City of Quartz*, London 1990, p. 243.

237. Edward Said, 'Orientalism Reconsidered,' in Francis Barker et al., eds, *Literature, Politics and Theory*, London 1986, p. 215.

238. Benedict Anderson, *Imagined Communities: Reflections on the Origin and Spread of Nationalism*, London 1983, p. 135.

239. 'Minority Report,' *The Nation*, April 8, 1991, p. 438.

240. 'War Reporting Trends and Fads,' p. 17. For a straightforward discussion of many of the weapons systems, see Alan P. Capps, 'Smart Weapons for a Desert War,' *Defense and Diplomacy*, March/April 1991, pp. 8–11.

241. *Chicago Tribune*, April 23, 1991. Former Defense Department specialist William Perry told Congress flatly that the Patriot 'is not effective' against battlefield missiles like the Scud. Ibid.

242. Figures quoted in Tom Wicker's column, *New York Times*, March 20, 1991.

243. Klare, 'High-Death Weapons of the Gulf War,' pp. 721, 738–42. On the firepower used against the air-raid shelter, see also Laurie Garrett's excellent eyewitness account, 'The Dead,' *Columbia Journalism Review*, May/June 1991, p. 32. ('Nearly all the bodies were charred into blackness; in some cases the heat had been so great that entire limbs were burned off.')

244. Quoted in Klare, 'High-Death Weapons of the Gulf War'.

245. 'The New Face of Techno-War,' *The Nation*, May 6, 1991, pp. 583–86. She remarked that 'very few people I've spoken to since I came back want to hear the good news that Baghdad wasn't razed.'

246. Virilio, p. 2.

247. Dziga Vertov, an early Soviet filmmaker, quoted in ibid., p. 20.

248. *Signatures of the Visible*, pp. 189–91.

249. I wasn't there, and rely on the account in *The Nation*, July 1, 1991, cover.

250. *New York Times*, June 3, 1991.

251. Rosenthal, *Documentary Conscience*, p. 212.

252. Adorno, p. 129.

253. *Korea: The 38th Parallel*, David Wolper Productions, 1965, written and directed by Irwin Rosten.

254. Rosenthal, *Documentary Conscience*.

255. Ibid., p. 49.

256. Ibid., pp. 113–16, 121–3.

257. The agreement between Thames TV, Channel 4 and WGBH also included ABC (Australia) as co-producers.

258. Researchers were chosen by Whitehead without consulting Jon.

259. Phillip had done several of the *World at War* programs and had worked with David on *This Week*, beginning with a famous and controversial exposé of political gerrymandering in Northern Ireland.

260. 'Schopenhauer as Educator,' in *Untimely Meditations*, trans. R.J. Hollingdale, New York 1983, pp. 127–28.

261. Trotsky goes on to talk about 'Asiatic' leaders as cunning and brutal, presiding over static societies with a huge peasant base. Leon Trotsky, *Stalin*, trans. C. Malmruth, 2nd edn, New York 1967, pp. 1–2, 358. See also Stephen Cohen, *Bukharin and the Bolshevik Revolution*, New York 1979, p. 291, for Bukharin's depiction of Stalin as 'a Genghis Khan'; also Isaac Deutscher, *Stalin: A Political Biography*, London 1949, p. 472: Stalin was 'primitive, oriental, but unfailingly shrewd.'

262. As Raye Farr (a film researcher for *The World At War*) put it, 'one of our biases was to say to people, "Look at the bias. Look at ours. Look at the Russians'. Look at the Germans". Look at it and then decide for yourself.' (Rosenthal, *Documentary Conscience*, p. 85.)

263. Since published as *Origins*, vol. 2.

264. Rosenthal, *Documentary Conscience*, p. 36.

265. *Among Friends: Personal Letters of Dean Acheson*, New York 1980, pp. 99, 103–4.

266. In February 1987 I found myself in an academic meeting with McGeorge Bundy, not a common experience. Historian Charles Maier introduced me and my work, whereupon Bundy said, 'what do you think about the march North?' Before I could answer, he remarked that it was a combination of absent-mindedness in Washington and MacArthur's 'craziness.'

267. In fact, as his biographer Roland Penrose has pointed out, French communists urged Picasso to make the identity of the aggressor clear; he refused, desiring that the mural condemn war in general.

268. Virilio, p. 25.

269. Reginald Thompson, *Cry Korea*, London 1952, pp. 39, 44, 84, 114.

270. *New York Times*, September 30, 1950.

271. Keyes Beech, *Newark Star-Ledger*, July 23, 1950.

272. I.F. Stone, *The Hidden History of the Korean War*, New York 1952, p. 258.

273. Macherey cited in Klein, p. 36.

274. The films are essentially of two types: battle sagas like *The Bridges at Toko-ri* (1954), *Men of the Fighting Lady* (1954), *Battle Taxi* (1955), or *Battle Hymn* (1956); and prisoner-of-war stories of varying sophistication – from Commie brainwashing to struggles to readjust back home – like *Prisoner of War* (1954), *The Bamboo Prison* (1954), *The Rack* (1956), and *Battle Shock* (1956). Fuller's *Battle Helmet* differs, perhaps, because it was shot in the first months of the war, when it was just Americans against Koreans.

275. Nietzsche *The Genealogy of Morals*, trans. Walter Kaufmann and R.J. Hollingdale, New York 1969, pp. 57–8.

276. Martin Heidegger, *What Is Called Thinking?*, trans. J. Glenn Gray, New York 1968, pp. 103, 138–41, 151–2. I am indebted to Gayle Turner for calling this book to my attention.

277. Fredric Jameson, *Sartre: The Origin of a Style*, p. 13.

278. The transcripts themselves were not always accurate, which yields yet another set of problems. Since they are now lodged at the British War Museum, researchers who use them should keep this in mind.

279. Jerome Kuehl, a Thames Associate Producer on *The World At War* with an academic background in history, made similar observations: 'I didn't learn a great deal working on the films. I knew what I thought about these events before I ever started to work on the series . . . .' (Rosenthal, *Documentary Conscience*, p. 52.)

280. Halliday to Cumings, February 12, 1990.

281. Information given to me by one of the Americans employed to investigate the scandal, September 1990.

282. His latest title, according to a conference program sponsored by the National Defense University in Washington, which invited Kim to give a Plenary Address on March 1, 1990; some colleague at my university anonymously sent me the program and I was happy to see that it also included McGeorge Bundy.

283. The Thames transcript has Kim saying, 'I think *you* [sic] are representing North Korea,' but my notes have it as in the text.

284. Whitehead seemed to stop trying to get North Korean participation in the seminars after Kim's outburst, and after his own visit to the ROK Embassy in London, to which Jon was also invited.

285. The Thames transcript from the fifth seminar is very bad and hard to follow, so I have combined Meray's comments there with his Thames interview, where he reiterated many of his points at the seminar.

286. The attacks on the dams came just after the laborious, backbreaking work of rice-transplantation had been done. The Air Force was proud of the destruction created: 'The subsequent flash flood scooped clean 27 miles of valley below, and the plunging flood waters wiped out [supply routes, etc.]. The Westerner can little conceive the awesome meaning which the loss of [rice] has for the Asian – starvation and slow death.' Many villages were inundated, 'washed downstream,' and even P'yôngyang, some twenty-seven miles south of one dam, was badly flooded. Untold numbers of peasants died, but they were assumed to be 'loyal' to the enemy, providing 'direct support to the Communist armed forces.' (That is, they were feeding the northern population.) The 'lessons' adduced from this experience 'gave the enemy a sample of the totality of war . . . embracing the whole of a nation's economy and people.' This was Korea, 'the limited war.' See 'The Attack on the Irrigation Dams in North Korea,' *Air University Quarterly*, 6/4 Winter 1953–4, pp. 40–51. For an excellent account of the air war and the breaking of the dams, see Callum MacDonald, *Korea: The War Before Vietnam*, London 1988, pp. 241–2; for more documentation, see Cumings. *Origins*, vol. 2, ch. 21.

287. In the Donovan Papers, Carlisle Military Barracks Archives, Carlisle, Pennsylvania.

288. Rosenthal, *Documentary Conscience*, pp. 72–73.

289. Stilwell was head of CIA covert operations in Asia, Paek was on the border near Kaesông, his brother was over on the Ongjin Peninsula where the war began and Hausman, then a military advisor, has been the official source for what happened on Ongjin. As for Paek's current status, he is active in the International Security Council, a Moonie-connected rightwing internationale supported by Japanese rightwing money. On the International Security Council, see General Paek's name listed on one of their full-page ads in the *New York Times* (May 4, 1986), along with Edward Luttwak, A. James Gregor of the University of California (who was working

on a book on the political thought of Ferdinand Marcos until the dictator was overthrown), various Japanese rightwingers, and Joseph Churba, a fellow Columbia University alumnus who founded the Council, and who acknowledged that its 'parent organization' was CAUSA International, a group funded by Moon's Unification Church (*Korea Herald*, May 25, 1985).

290. That is, done for the Operations Research Office of Johns Hopkins University, financed by the Department of the Army, and classified until about a decade ago. Henry was right, though; there isn't much to it.

291. A detailed account, based on eyewitness testimony, of just one of these massacres appeared in two South Korean publications in June 1990 (*Mal* and *Hankyoreh Sinmun*). In this one 370 alleged leftists were murdered by Rhee's forces.

292. Little, Brown brought the book out again in November 1988; I have seen but one review of it.

293. This business is covered at length in my *Origins*, vol. 2.

294. It surfaced again in an article on North Korea in the journal *Foreign Policy*, fall 1990.

295. Here is what Dr Wada said: 'Kim Il Sung began his activities at the age of 19 and did not return to Korea until 1945 when he was 33. He was still very young but had been involved in some of the fiercest fighting against the Japanese in Manchuria . . .

His name often appeared in Korean newspapers as Kim Il Sung, leader of the Korean guerrillas in Manchuria, so he was extremely well-known in Korea itself . . . . His deeds were exaggerated beyond reality and his fame spread. He became a sort of symbol of Korean nationalist resistance against the Japanese.'

296. *CBS Nightly News*, July 24, 1989; and *CBS This Morning*, July 25, 1989, Bob Fall reporting.

297. This is a common theme in Western reportage. Uli Schmetzer visited at the same time as Bob Fall, and remarked upon P'yôngyang's 'baffling absence of old and disabled people.' (*Chicago Tribune*, August 31, 1989.)

298. Bourdieu, pp. 7–8.

299. *New York Times*, July 22, 1980.

300. Baudrillard, *America*, p. 77. The Joint Commander of the anti-Iraq coalition forces, Saudi Prince Khaled bin Sultan bin Abdulaziz, said he 'decompressed' during the war by watching American TV programs: his favorites were *The Cosby Show*, *Murphy Brown*, and *Family Feud*. (*New York Times*, May 5, 1991.)

301. Perhaps this juxtaposition of modern Singapore and bucolic Alma Ata is the point. What we witness in North Korea is less the building of socialism, than an older transition, that with which we identify the modern world: from the country to the city, from the peasant to the farmer, from the landlord to the entrepreneur, from feudalism to capitalism. On this point see Jameson's excellent discussion in *Signatures of the Visible*, pp. 226–7.

302. Roland Barthes, *Mythologies*, trans. Annette Lavers, Frogmore, St Albans 1972, p. 149.

303. The title was *Chosôn ûi Mijae chônjaeng t'obal, charyo-jip* [War provocations of the American imperialists in Korea, documents], vol 2.

304. The Thames transcript of the Glenn interview differs slightly from my rendering,

showing no reference to 'Indian Country,' but that's what I heard and noted down at the time.

305. *Chicago Tribune*, August 21, 1989.

306. I later found accounts in both North and South Korean newspapers of a firefight that occurred that day; both blamed it on the other side, but I wondered if one side had wished to greet the arrival of our crew with some authentic pyrotechnics.

307. *Nodong sinmun* [Worker's news], December 22, 1989, as translated by Korean Central News Agency, dispatch 7711 of the same date.

308. Peter Biskind, '*Blacks Britannica*: A Clear Case of Censorship,' in Rosenthal, *New Challenges*, p. 406.

309. Quoted in Virilio, p. 65.

310. On bacteriological warfare (BW) there is as yet no 'smoking gun,' and the issue is so controversial that TV empiricism demands hard proof rather than the tantalizing but still circumstantial evidence suggesting that the US used some limited forms of BW. In the seminars a consensus emerged that we should at least call attention to the similarities between Japanese BW experiments in Manchuria in World War II and the Chinese allegations brought against the US – which had protected the ringleader of the Japanese program, Gen. Ishii, from prosecution. But this background never made it into the film. Jon also thought that Max handled the POW sequences badly, but I think they stand up reasonably well.

311. Phillip Whitehead to Roy English, February 15, 1988.

312. Phillip Whitehead to Susanna Yager (Channel 4), March 1, 1988.

313. Susanna Yager to Roy English, March 4, 1988.

314. Hood, p. 122.

315. I never saw the Metcalfe memo, but Phillip refers to it in Whitehead to David Elstein, February 8, 1988.

316 Channel 4 ran twelve episodes of *Vietnam: A Television History*, beginning April 11, 1983; PBS then redid the British narration and minor aspects of the film that had been prepared for the British audience, and screened the first hour on October 4, 1983. (Lichty, p. 504.)

317. O'Rourke did a sort of racist potpourri/travelogue in *Rolling Stone* (October 1988), dwelling on Korean facial features that he found outlandish. Buruma, with more subtlety but no less malice, compared the 1988 games to those Hitler sponsored in 1936. After visiting Korea's Independence Hall he asked if his 'revulsion' was 'a sign of decadence,' or is there something 'to the idea of the rise and fall of national, even racial vigor?' He was right on the first point, if not the second. See Ian Buruma, 'Jingo Olympics,' *New York Review of Books*, November 10, 1988.

318. See the *Guardian*, June 18, 1988; *Time Out*, June 23–30, 1988 ('meticulously researched'); *City Limits*, June 23–30, 1988 ('Jon Halliday's exemplary documentary . . . reconstructs the pattern of events with remarkable balance and clarity').

319. *Sunday Telegraph*, June 27, 1988; *Daily Telegraph*, July 3, 1988. Phillip wrote an effective response to Rees, which the *Telegraph* printed on July 10 – although he offered no defense of Jon Halliday, who was Rees's prime target. Jon, however, threatened a lawsuit against Rees and the *Sunday Telegraph*, which as a result

subsequently (August 28, 1988) printed an apology to him and paid all his legal costs.

320. Robert Fox, 'Review of *Korea: The Unknown War*,' *Times Literary Supplement*, July 22–8, 1988; Jon Halliday and Bruce Cumings, letters, July 29–August 4, 1988.

321. I cite from notes made immediately after my friend returned from the screening, and from Bruce Cumings to Phillip Whitehead, November 19, 1988.

322. Phillip later signed a public disclaimer dated January 7, 1989, disavowing what he termed 'false allegations' by people in Thames Television about our book.

323. Bruce Cumings to Phillip Whitehead, November 19, 1988.

324. Phillip Whitehead to Ted Conant, November 28, 1988

325. Notes taken on Conant phone call, December 8, 1988.

326. Austin Hoyt to Bruce Cumings, November 28, 1988.

327. The Council holds conferences to which it always invites high South Korean officials, like the Minister of Defense or the Minister for Political Affairs. Its Board of Directors includes Richard Stilwell, Gen. Paek Sôn-yôp, and former US Ambassador to Korea Richard L. Walker. Mr West sits on its American 'Advisory Committee,' along with several retired US Army generals and some American academics. A participant in one of the Council conferences provided me with these lists, but asked me not to reveal his name.

328. Jill Service to Phillip West, September 9, 1988.

329. Bruce Cumings to Phillip West, December 20, 1988; Phillip West to Bruce Cumings, December 30, 1988.

330. Bruce Cumings to Austin Hoyt, January 30, 1989.

331. Jon Halliday to Austin Hoyt, February 10, 1989.

332. The misrepresentations are very involved, and I still do not understand one of them. As for the second, WGBH at first dwelt even longer than Thames on the flawed testimony of Dr Arie Zuckerman, who had protested about the way his interview had been used in the Thames version (including one instance of clear misstatement), and who had asked that his interview be removed from future screenings. Jon at last convinced WGBH to take the misstatement out, although WGBH's treatment still remained misleading and scientifically unsound. (Halliday to Cumings, July 11, 1991.)

333. Stilwell told me he held this position; see also Joseph Burkholder Smith, *Portrait of a Cold Warrior*, New York 1976, p. 66, and Thomas Powers, *The Man Who Kept the Secrets: Richard Helms and the CIA*, New York 1979, p. 415. For an excellent account of the OPC and its ties to George Kennan and the Dulles brothers, see Christopher Simpson, *Blowback: America's Recruitment of Nazis and Its Effects on the Cold War*, New York 1988, pp. 90–96.

334. Cumings, *Origins*, vol, 2. chs 16, 17.

335. Andrew F. Krepinevich Jr, *The Army and Vietnam*, Baltimore 1986, pp. 43–4. In October 1961 Stilwell recommended the upgrading of the Special Warfare Division, but not just that: he wanted 'the Army as a whole to accept counterinsurgency as its mission rather than as a contingency limited to the Special Forces' (p. 44).

336. Patrick Lloyd Hatcher, *The Suicide of an Elite: American Internationalists and Vietnam*, Stanford 1990, p. 144; George McT. Kahin, *Intervention: How America Became*

Involved in Vietnam, New York 1986, p. 179. (Kahin refers to him as Gen. Joseph G. Stilwell Jr, and indeed there was another general by this name in Vietnam at the time, but I believe the reference must be to Richard Stilwell, who was Harkin's chief of staff.)

337. Neil Sheehan, *A Bright Shining Lie: John Paul Vann and America in Vietnam*, New York 1988, pp. 17, 338, 346. On Arnett's role in this period as a Saigon AP reporter, and the abuse he took, see Prochnau.

338. Ray Cline, *The CIA Under Reagan Bush & Casey*, Washington 1981, p. 300.

339. Steven Emerson, *Secret Warriors: Inside the Covert Military Operations in the Reagan Era*, New York 1988, pp. 50–51.

340. Ibid., pp. 145–6.

341. *Korea Herald*, November 18, 1986.

342. Singlaub was highly decorated for his work behind the lines with the OSS in France and China during World War II; he was also a CIA operative before and during the Korean War; like Stilwell he also had a big comeback in the 1980s, organizing the American branch of the World Anti-Communist League, working closely with Moonie-front organization CAUSA International, and doing his best to keep the Contras in the field. This League, of course, had South Korea and Taiwan as its founding countries, and along the way accumulated an appalling assortment of East European émigré war criminals, superannuated prewar fascists, anti-Semites, and Latin American death squad aficionados. See the extensive information in Scott Anderson and Jon Lee Anderson, *Inside the League*, New York 1986, pp. 55, 120, 150–51, 238.

343. 'Memorandum, General R.G. Stilwell, USA Ret., to Mr Austin Hoyt, WGBH, Subj: Comments on Thames' Korean War Series,' January 25, 1989.

344. What Stilwell thought inappropriate for an American audience was very nearly screened in South Korea. One of the major networks, MBC, submitted the Thames version to a state-managed Commission, which nixed showing the film by only a five to four margin; furthermore MBC union people protested this as an attempt at 'suppression.' Halliday to Cumings, November 17, 1989; Jon had just returned from a visit to Seoul and had spoken with high officials at MBC.

345. The Hoyt quote is from Kurt Jacobsen, 'WGBH Makes History,' May 1991. (Mr Jacobsen wrote the best account of WGBH's censorship, but could only get an excerpt of his essay published in the London *Guardian*.) Hoyt also told Whitehead, in a letter dated March 7, 1990, that he 'found Stilwell's big picture comments unhelpful,' but that doesn't explain why he accepted twelve of Stilwell's changes – as he admitted to the *Philadelphia Inquirer*, November 10, 1990.

346. I am not at liberty to reveal this source, nor do I know the 'original sponsors.'

347. Communication from Washington source, May 11, 1990; communication from a person who attended the conference but wishes to remain anonymous, April 7, 1990. The conference was held in Seoul in November 1989, by the same group that indulged Phillip West's shenanigans (see above). The retired general whom Stilwell slandered was Gene LaRocque of the Center for Defense Information in Washington, who has been an island of sanity in the sea of Pentagon inanity for many years. In 1976 the KCIA targeted LaRocque's institute for 'coopting,' given that it

was involved with 'anti-ROK factions.' See US House, International Relations Committee, Subcommittee on International Organizations, Investigation of Korean–American Relations (Washington, DC, October 31, 1978), p. 285.

348. Austin Hoyt to Bruce Cumings, April 3, 1989.

349. Jacobsen.

350. Quoted in Jameson, *Postmodernism*, p. 370.

351. Bruce Cumings to Austin Hoyt, April 8, 1989.

352. Austin Hoyt to Phillip Whitehead, March 7, 1989.

353. Ibid.

354. Bruce Cumings to Austin Hoyt, April 10, 1989.

355. Jon Halliday to Austin Hoyt, April 14, 1989. Jon ended his missive by saying this: 'I appreciate much of what you have done. I also appreciate that many of the problems do lie in the original assemblages . . . . But I am frankly appalled at some of the things you have done. You and some others have spent a lot of time challenging my information. . . . I have also been willing, unlike some others, to state my principles: all the most important information, from both (or all) sides, presented in a balanced way. . . . The time has come when you, as a filmmaker, have the responsibility to document every one of your unsubstantiated assertions in the revised version . . . the germ warfare sequence is a travesty of a travesty . . . I am extremely disappointed . . . I understand that I have the backing of Thames in attempting to honor our original commitment to the truth, the whole truth and nothing but the truth.'

356. Halliday to Hoyt, August 23, 1989, 'Changes to WGBH Scripts.'

357. In what follows I refer only to Halliday's August 23 commentary, since I never saw the new scripts.

358. Hoyt to Whitehead, July 13, 1989. Here is what James Hausman said about this matter in his Thames interview: 'I knew that [in the pre-1945 period] there was great opposition between Japanese and Russians, so it was more or less fair for me to assume that anybody with, trained with the Japanese army and certainly the Japanese Imperial military academy would be good candidates for South Korean forces, so a lot of those were picked because of their backgrounds and er anti-communist position.'

359. Cumings to Hoyt, September 21, 1989.

360. I also thought that my request would have been no more successful than Phillip's.

361. Halliday to Cumings, December 22, 1989; Halliday to McGhee, November 30, 1989. The information about Farrar-Hockley came from Whitehead.

362. Elstein responded rather cryptically, saying that 'amendments' to the Thames version 'continue to be made' at WGBH and that Thames would 'abide by the factual and legal checks now being carried out on the material at issue by WGBH,' and then suggested that Jon could always remove his name from the script if he liked, although Elstein regarded that as 'counter-productive.' Elstein to Halliday, November 3, 1989.

363. Phillip apparently said that he never saw or approved the final WGBH version, nor did he ever see Stilwell's memo. Nonetheless Phillip did not challenge WGBH's

version, and he seemed unconcerned with most of the changes. Max Whitby expressed one reason – perhaps the most important one – for Thames' unwillingness to go to the mat with WGBH: in a telephone conversation with me in November 1990 he said that all this was nothing new, he was used to having every series he had made messed up when it got to the US, by WGBH and others. Nothing could be done about it, he seemed to imply.

364. McGhee FAX to Halliday, December 5, 1989. Jon responded (FAX to McGhee, December 11, 1989) that 'it is my legal right as the author of the commentary' to see the final version of the documentary; he went on, 'You refer to my "letters and vituperations." I have never stooped to the arrogant tone of your fax. . . . If I have shown exasperation, it is because I am dealing with people who seem incapable of evaluating evidence and ... refuse the basic spirit of co-operation.'

365. Jameson's paraphrase of Cavell's insight, in *Postmodernism*, p. 248.

366. Cumings to McGhee, January 13, 1990. Historian Donald Watt is a bit of an idealist, in writing that 'the historian rash enough to take on the post of historical advisor must insist on the right to vet the finished article . . . . He must vet scripts before the film is dubbed. . . . It is his job to be the conscience of the unit. . . . ' (Watt, p. 441.) But then, why hire historical consultants, if television is not interested in their being 'the conscience of the unit'? For purposes of semblance and propriety, little more.

367. McGhee to Cumings, February 24, 1990.

368. Roberts to McGhee, May 15, 1990; McGhee to Roberts, May 19, 1990.

369. I also sent him a questionnaire relating to many of the points I make in this chapter, to get his side of the story; he never answered me, but Peter McGhee wrote that neither he nor Austin would respond to the questions. I wrote him back again on August 24, 1990, saying 'I have no desire to include in my book a one-sided account of WGBH's editing process,' but got in return only a nasty letter blaming all problems on me and Jon – a letter for the record and the file, it seemed to me. (Hoyt to Cumings, September 5, 1990.)

370. *New York Times*, March 6, 1990; *Publisher's Weekly*, editorial, March 9, 1990.

371. Jordan to Cumings, September 12, 1990.

372. *New York Times*, November 11, 18, 1990.

373. *New York Times*, November 12, 1990.

374. Ray Loynd of the *Los Angeles Times* called the film 'historically shattering and politically revealing' – although my favorite hour, the first, he deemed 'scholarly and rather stodgy.' (November 12, 1990.) George Wilson of the *Washington Post* liked it as well, but thought it less gripping than the PBS *Civil War* series. (November 12, 1990.)

375. *Washington Times*, November 21, 1990. The attack prompted a good letter to the editor from a Korean War veteran named Blaine Friedlander, who found the series enjoyable and fascinating, and who urged the *Washington Times* to respect freedom of speech and 'to understand the Korean War from all sides.'

376. He said this first to Associated Press reporter Jay Sharbutt, who related the comment to Halliday; Stilwell's office later denied that he had done so; but then Stilwell's secretary said the same thing to Tim Weiner.

377. *Philadelphia Inquirer*, November 10, 1990; *Village Voice*, December 4, 1990.

378. Jacobsen.

379. Hoyt also claimed that Jon and I had 'a lot of battles at Thames' with the 'official British military historians'; he neglected to mention that there was only one, Farrar-Hockley, and he like the rest of us was part of the consensus hammered out at Thames. Hoyt inadvertently reveals, I think, that he trusts official historians, who work under classification restrictions and require approval of their work by superiors, more than independent ones. Jay Sharbutt article, Associated Press, carried in *Wisconsin State Journal*, November 12, 1990, and in a longer version in *Albuquerque Journal*, November 13, 1990; see also *Philadelphia Inquirer*, November 10, 1990.

380. Biskind, pp. 401–7. For still another example of WGBH manhandling a British documentary, see Karl Sabbagh, 'Stealing the Show,' *Broadcast*, April 12, 1991.

381. Biskind, p. 405.

382. McGhee 'charged that [the filmmaker] had handed the film over to a small group of people who shared the same ideology.' What ideology was that, he was asked. 'It's clear from the moment when somebody mentions the word "Engels," replied McGhee.' (Ibid.)

383. Ibid.

384. Jacobsen.

385. *Chicago Tribune*, December 6, 1990.

386. An unnamed source, apparently at WGBH, told one writer that WGBH was 'caught in the classic liberal dilemma. Sure, they want to engage social issues . . . but only within the usual on-the-one-hand, on-the-other-hand format. Programs with strong points of view, with passion or anger, are either just not shown, or they are censored, or they are buried in disclaimers, rebuttals, or roundtable discussion.' Quoted in Biskind, p. 407.

387. Jean Baudrillard, *Simulations*, trans. Paul Foss, Paul Patten and Philip Beitchman, New York 1983.

388. Fiske, p. 98.

389. This is a characteristic of 'docudrama,' according to Robert Brent Toplin in 'The Filmmaker as Historian,' *American Historical Review*, 93:5, December 1988, p. 1221.

390. Ian Jarvie, quoted in Robert A. Rosenstone, 'History in Images/History in Words: Reflections on the Possibility of Really Putting History onto Film,' *American Historical Review*, 93:5, December 1988, p. 1176.

391. Tim Weiner, *Philadelphia Inquirer*, October 24, 1990.

392. *Washington Post*, May 3, 1990. I am indebted to Max Holland for sending me this clipping.

393. Quoted in *New York Times*, December 23, 1990.

394. *Boston Globe*, December 7, 1990.

INDEX

THE HAYMARKET SERIES

Editors: Mike Davis and Michael Sprinker

The Haymarket Series offers original studies in politics, history and culture, with a focus on North America. Representing views across the American left on a wide range of subjects, the series will be of interest to socialists both in the USA and throughout the world. A century after the first May Day, the American left remains in the shadow of those martyrs whom the Haymarket Series honours and commemorates. These studies testify to the living legacy of political activism and commitment for which they gave their lives.

Already Published

BLACK MACHO AND THE MYTH OF THE SUPERWOMAN *by Michele Wallace*

INVISIBILITY BLUES: From Pop to Theory *by Michele Wallace*

PROFESSORS, POLITICS AND POP: *by Jon Wiener*

THE LEFT AND THE DEMOCRATS *The Year Left 1*

TOWARDS A RAINBOW SOCIALISM *The Year Left 2*

RESHAPING THE US LEFT: Popular Struggles in the 1980s *The Year Left 3*

FIRE IN THE HEARTH: The Radical Politics of Place in America *The Year Left 4*

Forthcoming

THE INVENTION OF THE WHITE RACE *by Theodore Allen*

THE ARCHITECTURE OF COMPANY TOWNS *by Margaret Cameron*

SHADES OF NOIR *Edited by Mike Davis and Joan Copjec*

THE MERCURY THEATER: Orson Welles and the Popular Front *by Michael Denning*

NO CRYSTAL STAIR: African Americans and the City of Angels *by Lynell George*

THE POLITICS OF SOLIDARITY: Central America and the US Left *by Van Gosse*

BLACK RADICAL TRADITIONS *by Cynthia Hamilton*

RACE, POLITICS AND ECONOMIC DEVELOPMENT *Edited by James Jennings*

BLACK AMERICAN POLITICS: From the Washington Marches to Jesse Jackson (Second Edition) *by Manning Marable*

WHITE GUYS *by Fred Pfeil*

AMERICAN DOCUMENTARY FILM *by Paula Rabinowitz*

THE GROUNDING OF INTELLECTUALS *by Bruce Robbins*

FEMINISM IN THE AMERICAS *The Year Left 5*